Technical Building Blocks

A Technology Reference for Real-world Product Development

Gaurav Sagar
Vitalii Syrovatskyi

Apress®

Technical Building Blocks: A Technology Reference for Real-world Product Development

Gaurav Sagar
Bellevue, WA, USA

Vitalii Syrovatskyi
Issaquah, WA, USA

ISBN-13 (pbk): 978-1-4842-8657-9
https://doi.org/10.1007/978-1-4842-8658-6

ISBN-13 (electronic): 978-1-4842-8658-6

Managing Director, Apress Media LLC: Welmoed Spahr
Acquisitions Editor: Shivangi Ramachandran
Development Editor: Laura Berendson
Coordinating Editor: Mark Powers

Cover designed by eStudioCalamar

Cover image by Vasilis Chatzopoulos on Unsplash (www.unsplash.com)

Distributed to the book trade worldwide by Apress Media, LLC, 1 New York Plaza, New York, NY 10004, U.S.A. Phone 1-800-SPRINGER, fax (201) 348-4505, e-mail orders-ny@springer-sbm.com, or visit www.springeronline.com. Apress Media, LLC is a California LLC and the sole member (owner) is Springer Science + Business Media Finance Inc (SSBM Finance Inc). SSBM Finance Inc is a **Delaware** corporation.

For information on translations, please e-mail booktranslations@springernature.com; for reprint, paperback, or audio rights, please e-mail bookpermissions@springernature.com.

Apress titles may be purchased in bulk for academic, corporate, or promotional use. eBook versions and licenses are also available for most titles. For more information, reference our Print and eBook Bulk Sales web page at http://www.apress.com/bulk-sales.

Any source code or other supplementary material referenced by the author in this book is available to readers on GitHub (https://github.com/Apress). For more detailed information, please visit http://www.apress.com/source-code.

Printed on acid-free paper

To our families for their infinite patience and support.

Table of Contents

About the Authors

Gaurav Sagar is a director of product management at Salesforce, Inc. and has done product management at Indeed, Amazon Web Services, and Amazon payments. He has over 11 years of experience in building both consumer and enterprise products and has deep industry knowledge of cloud computing, online advertising, ecommerce, and fintech. He has multiple patents and speaks at conferences. He is also an avid programmer and was a data scientist prior to his transition in product management. He holds an M.S. in Business Analytics and a B.S. in Computer Science. In his off hours, he loves to hike and go on short road trips, besides programming for his hobby projects. Visit `www.linkedin.com/in/gauravsagar/` to learn more about him.

Vitalii Syrovatskyi is an engineering manager at Google. Previously, he was the software development manager at Amazon where he led the development of products and features for Amazon Web Services (AWS) and Amazon payment products. He has over 15 years of experience in developing technical products, managing, and building engineering teams in multiple industries, namely, search advertising, cloud computing, capital management, online payments, and computer networking. He is founder of a tech company and has firsthand experience in leading cross-functional teams and managing all end-to-end aspects of the business. Vitalii has an M.S. and a B.S. in Mathematics, and an M.S. and a B.S. in Economics. Outside of work, he enjoys exploring the beautiful Pacific Northwest. Learn more about him at `www.linkedin.com/in/vitalii-syrovatskyi/`.

About the Technical Reviewer

Jiang Wu is a seasoned software technologist with more than 25 years of experience in the area of distributed information management systems. He graduated from UC Berkeley with a B.S. degree in Electrical Engineering and Computer Science and earned an M.S. in Computer Science from Stanford University. Jiang has worked in companies of various stages, from startups, midsized, to large enterprises, developing B2C and B2B software that run in public or private cloud. He has architected, implemented, and operated a variety of software systems such as distributed network management, semantic search, unstructured data processing, big data, machine learning, ecommerce, data analytics, and application performance management. Jiang has over 15 granted software patents. Most recently, he has been leading the engineering architecture on building a cloud-based collaboration and project management SaaS tool suitable for businesses of all sizes and industries. Visit `www.linkedin.com/in/jiangwu2` for more information about him.

About the Technical Reviewer

Introduction

Software products are all around us, and some are so widely successful that we even use their names as verbs, like Google for searching on the Internet, Uber for getting a taxi, and Venmo for transferring money. Software as a Service (SaaS) and cloud computing have completely revolutionized how quickly products and new features in them can be brought to market. Due to the widespread success of so many software products, there is a huge demand not only for software engineers but also for professionals in these product development teams who act as a liaison between the stakeholders, the various cross-functional teams, the customers, and the leadership teams. These professionals are usually in the roles of product manager, program manager, or project manager and require some technical knowledge to be effective at various aspects of their jobs such as defining the customer needs for a technical product, ideating a feature to solve a customer pain point, evaluating the technical feasibility of their proposal, reviewing the long-term and short-term risks from using a particular technology for product development, providing updates to the stakeholders and leadership teams on technical blockers, etc.

Being technical is quickly becoming a critical trait for people in these roles, and companies are adding in technical interviews to filter out candidates who don't have these skills. However, technology evolves fast and can seem overwhelming to people looking to explore these roles. One needs to learn so many things starting with the tools and techniques used to develop software, different experimental design techniques, technologies to instrument and measure success, artificial intelligence algorithms to build features like personalized recommendations, etc., and the list goes on. Some try to self-learn by first trying to learn a programming language and then reading upon system design across various articles on the Internet or buying books on various technical subjects but achieve limited success. The problem is that the Internet is full of inaccurate and shallow information and the books picked on individual topics are meant to develop subject matter expertise and are too detailed, each coming up with its own prerequisites and time commitments.

How does one get technical enough for these roles then?

If you relate to this, then this book is for you. This book is an explanation of the various technologies and techniques used to build software products with just the right technical depth. You will learn everything ranging from software development methodology like agile, system design, and all the way to artificial intelligence, blockchains, and NFTs. There is a big focus on visualizations over just plain theory in this book to help you grasp complex concepts better and faster. By the end of this book, you will

- Learn the foundational technology building blocks of software products.

- Be able to understand the engineering design choices behind features and products.

- Identify better any associated risks with the use of a technology and the potential impact on the product/feature.

- Become better at communicating with engineering teams and synthesize technical information to the leadership and stakeholders.

- Be able to come up with novel technical feature ideas for solving customer pain points.

About You

This book is designed for professionals who are working as product manager, program manager, project manager, business analysts, etc., in product development teams and feel that having more technical understanding will help them be more effective at work and grow faster in their careers. It is also useful for people looking to transition to one of these roles and want to gain the required technical knowledge to pass those dreaded technical interview rounds.

Structure of This Book

There are seven chapters in this book that explain the various technologies and tools used by the various teams to develop products. While each chapter is self-contained and you can start with any of them, we feel going through the chapters in order will help you absorb the book material more effectively.

There is some code listed in a few chapters, and you can do without running it; however, read it at least as plain English. The goal is to just get you accustomed to what you might hear and see from your engineering teams. We don't expect you to know any programming language, nor will we teach you one as it's not required to become technical in these roles.

To aid you, the code is present in IPython notebooks, which you can download from the book's source code repository located at `github.com/apress/technical-building-blocks` and upload them to Google Colab at `https://colab.research.google.com/notebooks/`. From there, simply execute the code blocks right from your browser for free. We recommend this approach as it will save you from having to set up the environment on your local machine and not have to worry about dependencies. Since we build these code examples on Google Colab, they will work there without any issue.

Note   All views expressed in the book are solely of the authors.

## CHAPTER 1

Product Development: A Synergy of Teams and Techniques

Product development is a very involved process, and before we get into the technical blocks of any software product, it's helpful to get a general understanding into what a product is and by whom and how a product is developed and released into the market.

Product

Anything that is built to satisfy the need of a customer is called a product. Products are created through a process by resources, mostly people and machines, and offered in the market. Products are generally made to serve a sizeable customer base; however, some products are highly customized and made for only a few or even one customer, such as the space suits used by Apollo 11 astronauts called A7L. Products can be hardware such as a pen, software such as the Google Chrome browser, or a combination of both such as Oculus Rift – a virtual reality headset – or even more common, a smart phone. In this book, we will focus on the software products.

Products can be a composition of various subproducts, e.g., Facebook is a product that has multiple subproducts in it, such as Events, Marketplace, Groups, Ads, etc. This is an important consideration as each of the subproduct will have specific customer need(s) it is solving for and a dedicated product team to develop and improve the value proposition. These subproducts could have lived as independent products, but due to strong synergies between them, they provide more value to the customers when put together. This brings the concept of shared functionality, which are features (or capabilities) that span across products, e.g., "comments" are available for all the

© Gaurav Sagar, Vitalii Syrovatskyi 2022
G. Sagar and V. Syrovatskyi, *Technical Building Blocks*, https://doi.org/10.1007/978-1-4842-8658-6_1

Facebook products mentioned earlier. Besides lowering the cost of development through reuse of common capabilities, cross functionalities also help with product adoption as they bring familiarity to the end user when interacting with new products.

Product Categories

Software products can be categorized based on the kinds of tasks the product is used for, how close the end user is with the system hardware, if the product is freely available or with restrictions and licenses, and, finally, the delivery medium of the product. Let's explore each of them.

Based on Product User

Software products can be categorized into three categories based on how close they are to the hardware and who is using the software product, another software or an end user (human). These three categories are explained in the following.

Application Software

These are end-user software products used by humans for completing specific tasks, such as designing graphics, keeping accounting logs, etc., and constitute for most of the software products a person interacts with. When asked to name a software product category, most of us will categorize products based on the end-user need they meet, such as photo-editing products, e.g., Adobe Photoshop, music streaming products, e.g., Spotify, etc., as that's how it is shown in application marketplaces we commonly use like Google Play or the App Store from Apple. Application software products can be further classified into general-purpose products such as spreadsheet software or special-purpose products such as accounting software. We will focus on application product development in this book.

Middle Tier Platform Software

This is the type of software the application software uses for various of its functionalities and is packed either as a part of or along with the application software. The most common form of this type of software you may know of is a database, formally called database management system (DBMS), which is a software to organize, store, and access data. There are more software products of this type such as API gateways, event brokers, and messaging queues, which we will learn in detail in Chapter 3.

System Software

System software provides a platform for other application software products to run and enable interaction of end users with the hardware. In simple words, this software product is used to manage the hardware. The most popular system software is the operating system, e.g., Windows, iOS, Android, etc. Apart from the operating system, there are other software of this type that are less commonly known, examples being device drivers, which allow the control of the hardware device attached to a computer, e.g., a mouse, and language compilers and interpreters, which convert the high-level programming instructions written by a software developer into low-level (binary) machine code, etc. Figure 1-1 illustrates this relationship.

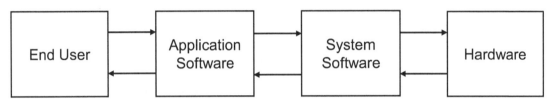

Figure 1-1. *Relationship between application software and system software products*

Based on Platform

In true sense the platform of a software used to be where the software runs, however, these days the platform is more of a medium where the end user interacts with the software product. The products often have components that are present in the cloud, and the platform just acts as an experience layer (interaction medium) for the end user. There are three main categories of software products based on the platform used for user interaction, namely, desktop applications, web applications, and mobile applications. Let's learn more about them.

Desktop Applications

These are stand-alone applications (software products) that are installed on a desktop computer such as a Windows PC or MacBook. They utilize the computational power of the machine (computer) they are installed on and are limited by it. These types of software products have been around the longest, and a lot of them come preinstalled with the operating system. Examples are Microsoft Office applications (Word, Excel, etc.), VLC media player, Adobe Photoshop, etc. Desktop applications require manual install.

3

When it comes to updates to the product, back in the days these updates (called patches) were delivered to the users in CD-ROM over mails, later these patches were made available on the Internet, and the user could download them over the Internet and self-install them. Nowadays, most desktop applications track updates themselves (if connected to the Internet) and notify the user if an update is available for download or automatically update themselves. While desktop applications in the area of productivity applications are losing popularity, video games, photo and video editing software, or any product where the amount of data over the network (usually internet) is prohibitively expensive or the network latency is too high, desktop applications continue to be popular.

Web Applications

These are software products where the user interacts with the product via a web browser such as Chrome, Safari, Edge, etc. The user sends a request through the web browser to the web application server which hosts the software application, which in turn returns a response back in the form of data that is rendered inside the browser as HTML to the user. Not all requests are sent to the web application server; some requests are handled by the browser itself through the JavaScript code running in it. The key distinction between static web pages and web applications is unlike the static websites, the user interacts with the web application, i.e., creates, reads, updates, and deletes data or content.

Initially, web applications were designed to run on desktop web browsers; however, with the increased Internet traffic on mobile phones, web applications are developed to provide optimal customer experience on mobile devices too through an approach called "responsive web design" that enables web applications to render well on a variety of screen sizes. Some examples of web applications are Gmail, Facebook (website), Google (search), etc.

Mobile Applications

These are the software products that are installed on a mobile device and run on the operating system of a mobile device such as phone, tablet, or watch. These should not be confused with web applications that run on mobile web browsers. Mobile applications are commonly called "Apps," and some are preinstalled with the mobile OS (Android, iOS, etc.) such as email client, calendar, calculator, etc. Apps are also available through distribution platforms specific to the OS platforms and are called App Stores, e.g., Google Play, App Store, Amazon Appstore, etc.

Due to their direct interaction with the mobile OS, these can access special services of the mobile device such as location services, biometric sensors, and motion sensors – accelerometer, gyroscope, and magnetometer. This enables these applications to provide features that aren't available for desktop or web applications and takes an edge over them. Mobile applications may not need the Internet; however, most mobile apps use the Internet to off-load all the heavy computation on an application server. Some popular mobile applications are Google Maps app, Uber app, Spotify app, etc.

Note   The same product may be available on all three platforms, e.g., Spotify – an audio (music) streaming product which is available as a desktop application, as a web application, and as a mobile application as well.

Product Team

Software products are developed with careful thought and process by a group of people who each specialize in an area. Let's understand what each of these areas is and the role and responsibilities for team members specialized in these areas. This will make you realize that software products aren't just made by software engineers and give you an appreciation of the specialists from multiple domains that work together to build the amazing software products you use. Figure 1-2 gives a high-level view of the different teams that work together to build software products.

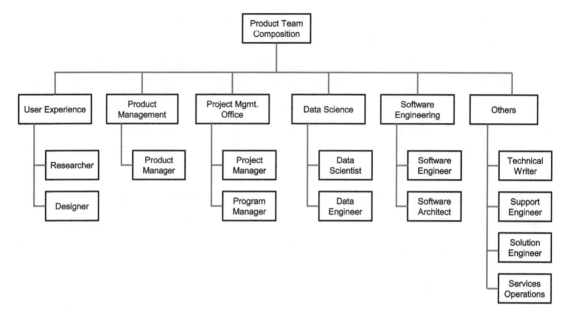

Figure 1-2. *Composition of a product team*

User Experience

User experience (UX) is how users (real humans like you and me) interact with a product and what they experience during and after the interaction. The experience maybe positive or negative and is driven by the utility of the product, ease of use, and the efficiency gained. UX design is the practice of researching, designing, and improving user experience across various platforms, such as desktop, web, and mobile, through which the end user interacts with the product while keeping in mind the interests of the stakeholders as marketing, branding, etc. UX design is hence a broad field which encompasses elements from both science and art.

UX Researcher

There is research which focuses on understanding the end users and their pain points and identifies gaps in the current product offering. This is where hypothesis/ assumptions about user needs and goals and product prototypes that solve those needs are tested with the users. This involves both quantitative and qualitative methods to accomplish its goals, the popular ones being:

1. Persona creation, which is the creation of fictional characters who are the target users of a product

2. Focus groups, which is a group interview among users with similar trails (behavioral, socioeconomic, demographic, etc.) to get their opinion on product features and their reactions to specific questions on the product needs

3. Surveys

4. A/B testing, which is usually done with the help of data science team to determine which version of a product or feature is statistically liked more by the users (or leads to a desired business outcome)

UX Designer

Then there is design. Visual design focuses on the visual perception of the user interface (UI) through elements like color, icons/symbols, layout, and images of the product. There is interaction design (IxD) that focuses more on the efficiency of the interactions between user and the product to enable users achieve their goals. Interaction design looks not only at the UI components but also motion graphics design and animation. One of the key deliverables from a UX designer are wireframes. A wireframe is a 2D skeletal outline of a website or a mobile application. It helps with ideation among team members initially and later serves as the blueprint for front-end developers to use while coding the website/app design.

The UX team also develops the information architecture, which focuses on logical structuring and organizing of the information in the product to help with information discovery and usability. Visual sitemaps (called screen tree for mobile apps) are a hierarchical diagram that are used to show the information architecture of a website. It gives you a visual representation of the site's organization and how different sections are linked together. Figure 1-3 shows a low fidelity wireframe and a wireframe. These are some types of assets the UX designer will develop.

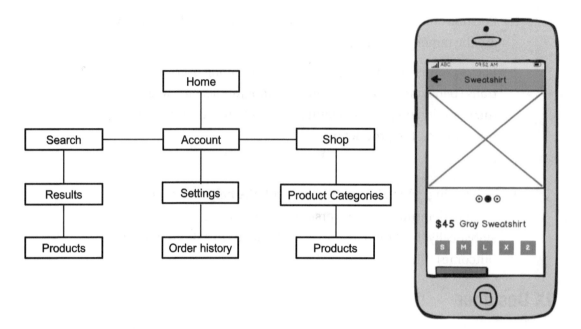

Figure 1-3.   Sitemap of an ecommerce store and wireframe of the Products page/ Wireframe Source: Balsamiq.com

Product Management

Product management is both a strategic and tactical function. It ties along every step of the product development life cycle: identifying customer need(s), developing a strategy, defining the feature(s), developing the go-to-market plan, etc. along with cross-functional teams like sales, marketing, finance, engineering, data science, UX, service operations, support, customer success, etc. The product managers are accountable for the success of the product and usually have goals defined in terms of business metrics for their products to achieve which tie with the uber organization or company goals.

The product manager sits at the intersection of UX, engineering, and business teams. A big function of product management is prioritization of feature requests. Product managers maintain a backlog of features requested for the product either by the customer, by stakeholders, or ideas from the team. These features requests are usually documented as "User Stories" if the product team is following agile; otherwise there are other ways as a feature specification and software requirement document (SRS) from the earlier popular way of developing software by following the software development lifecycle (SDLC) model. A user story is an informal explanation of a software feature written from the end user's perspective. It describes who needs what and why. The general user story format is "As a <persona>, I <want to>, <so that>." We will get into a bit more detail when we get into the subsequent section of agile development process.

Product manager owns the product roadmap which is a visual tool to communicate the product strategy by showcasing what are the major themes of work and what features constitute those themes along with their expected launch timeframe. Figure 1-4 shows a theme-based product roadmap.

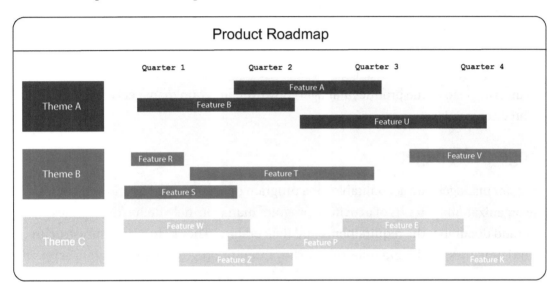

Figure 1-4. *A theme-based roadmap template*

A crucial responsibility of product manager is to prioritize feature requests and bring only those features onto the product roadmap that will help achieve the goals for the product and solve the biggest customer pain points. This requires shielding the development team (UX designers, engineers, data scientists, etc.) from stakeholder requests on updates, new asks, etc., so that the development team can be laser focused on building the product as per the product roadmap and not get randomized or distracted with anything else. Product managers also need to balance technology complexities and architecture concerns with time to market needs to ensure long-term success of the product.

Program Management

As defined by the Project Management Institute (PMI), a program is a group of related projects managed in a coordinated manner to obtain benefits not available from managing them individually. Program management is the application of knowledge, skills, tools, and techniques to meet program requirements. Big enterprises usually have a dedicated department that ropes in both program management and project management called project management office (PMO) which acts as a central place for all coordination and management of projects and programs to meet the uber company goals and objectives. Smaller companies, and most startups, may have very few or no program/project managers, and these activities may be done by the technical engineering lead or the product manager; however, program managers are a must-have in large companies.

Program Manager

Program managers are accountable for a program or set of programs and work across the organization. In terms of activities, program managers help define the business case and document the requirements and deliverables. They help set up infrastructure, (fluid) timelines, goals, and milestones. They monitor progress of the program across the various teams and share updates to stakeholders. They do risk management, i.e., raise awareness on what part (deliverable, milestone, team) of the program needs attention and of what help is required to bring the program back to green. Common program-level risks are missing deadline, change in requirements, and discovery of new stakeholders for a program in execution. They also help reset delivery timelines and milestones if unexpected blockers/hurdles show up during program execution.

Program managers that work on programs required for the development of technical products are called "technical program managers." They are not only well versed in the traditional product management skill sets but also have a high degree of understanding into the design and architecture of the product and ensure that the product in development meets the business needs. Generally, program managers are senior to project managers, and project managers may report into program managers.

Project Manager

Each project in a program is managed discretely by a project manager. A lot of times program managers are confused to be project managers and vice versa; however, there are clear distinctions in responsibilities. Project managers are responsible for defining the scope of the project and the breakdown of work within that scope into tasks which are then assigned to the stakeholder teams. They identify the project timeline and break it into phases along with identifying the critical tasks and any possible constraints. Tracking is commonly done using Gantt charts, which are an effective way to get a holistic view of the work breakdown structure (WBS) into activities (tasks), the timelines for each, and how the project is tracking against the timelines. Figure 1-5 shows how activities of a work are represented in a Gantt chart.

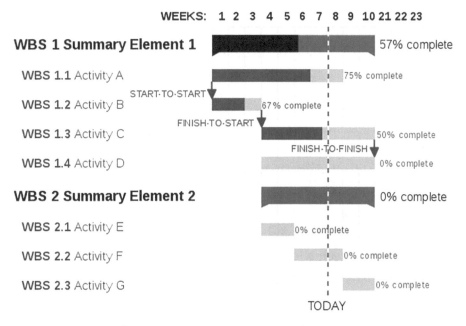

Figure 1-5. *Gantt chart[1] showing the breakdown of work across various activities (tasks) tracked over a timeline*

Project managers also anticipate risks and bring it up to the stakeholders for remediation to minimize impact on project delivery goals and hence need to work on tight deadlines in a fast-paced agile environment.

---

[1] https://upload.wikimedia.org/wikipedia/commons/thumb/5/57/GanttChartAnatomy.svg/640px-GanttChartAnatomy.svg.png

Data Science

Until the early 2000s, data was stored in traditional relational databases and was mostly used as a back end for web applications. There were databases saved historical aggregated data, and the analysts would pull data from these databases and generate reports and insights by analyzing this data through simple tools like spreadsheet software and in some special cases with products like SAS and MicroStrategy.

Hadoop – an open source technology – came as a break and revolutionized the way organizations analyzed data. It supported analysis of both structured (in rows and columns) data and unstructured data (text files) with sizes as high as petabytes. This led to the democratization of analytics to organizations of all sizes. These developments in data processing and analytics led to the formation of a new technical field called data science, which in simple words is the analysis of data both structured and unstructured, to uncover patterns and draw actionable insights for more informed decision-making. There are two roles that play a key role in data science teams.

Data Engineer

Data engineers build systems called pipelines that collect, manage, and transform raw, unstructured data into formats that can be used by data scientist and other teams for analysis. This process is called extract-transform-load (ETL). They create and maintain the infrastructure required for analysis such as databases, data warehouses, data lakes, data processing systems, data pipeline orchestrating systems, etc.

They are very technical, and apart from using tools specific to data engineering, they also use a lot of tools and technologies that are used by software engineers and in some organizations even a part of the engineering team and not the data science team. You will learn more of data engineering in Chapter 4.

Data Scientist

Called as the sexist job of the twenty-first century, data scientists analyze, process, and model data to draw actionable insights and conclusions to complex business questions. They have skill sets across computer science, statistics, and business domain. Data scientist isn't a net new field but rather an evolution of traditional roles like statistician, economist, business analyst, business intelligence engineer, quantitative analyst, etc.

Generally, data scientists query, analyze, and visualize data within a business domain as a part of product analytics to help business understand things like the key factor that led to the drop in new customers in a particular week or design experiments to test hypothesis to enable key business decisions. They usually use statistical techniques and ML algorithms to unblock business from making data-driven decisions fast. However, if most of their work requires techniques like deep learning, natural language processing, etc. and they are expected to write production ready code, they aren't called data scientists – Meta (Facebook's parent) calls them machine learning engineers and Amazon calls them applied scientists. You will learn more of data science in Chapter 5.

Software Engineering

Application of engineering principles to software development is called software engineering. Software engineering teams have the biggest team size and are primarily composed of software engineers. There are two key roles in the team explained in the following.

Software Engineer

They form the bulk of the software engineering team. They design, develop, test, deploy, and maintain software products. They are sometimes called programmers and sometimes developers. They are called web developers if they develop web application or application developers if they develop computer applications like games. If they work only on the back-end components of a product such as databases, systems APIs, etc., they are called back-end engineer, if they work only on the front end (technologies such as React and Angular JS) of an application, they are called front-end engineers, and if they work on the development of both front end and back end, they are called full-stack engineers.

Software Architect

Microsoft gives a very apt description of software architecture. It goes as follows:

> *Software application architecture is the process of defining a structured solution that meets all of the technical and operational requirements, while optimizing common quality attributes such as performance, security, and manageability. It involves a series of decisions based on a wide range of factors and each of these decisions can have considerable impact on the quality, performance, maintainability, and overall success of the application.*

> —Microsoft MSDN

Software architects are very experienced software engineers and experts at system design – the process of determining and designing how the various components of a product should be architected to achieve the requirements of the product/features in the short term as well as designing the software structure to be extensible for the long term. They create technical requirements and design documents which act as blueprints that the software engineers use to develop the software.

Other Teams

There are other teams as well which assist directly or indirectly in the development of a software product, but we wouldn't go deep into their roles and responsibilities as they aren't involved in day-to-day product development activities. Some of them are as follows:

1. **Technical writer** – They develop artifacts to aid product users use the product effectively (or a specific target audience). Some of their deliverables are instruction manuals, product documentation, API reference documentation, journal articles, and how-to guides. Their goal is to transform complex technical knowledge into concise and easy to understand documentation.

2. **Support engineer** – They support customers of a product with diagnosing, troubleshooting, and remediating any technical issue they may be facing. They are an important source to learn of the customer pain points and developing features to address them in the product.

3. **Solution engineer** – They are engineers that work alongside a salesperson to discover and understand the challenge(s) a customer is facing and create and demo a solution using the software product they want to sell that solves for the challenge(s). They maintain a professional relationship with the customer and keep them posted on new product updates and answer any technical questions the customer may have.

4. **Service operations team** – In the world of "Software as a Service," where products are hosted in the cloud and the end user connects to them over the Internet, the product team also has service operations team. This team would have infrastructure engineers – who design,

deploy, and maintain the IT infrastructure such as server hardware. It may have the data security and compliance team under it which ensures the data generated and processed by the product managed and stored in accordance with the data security and privacy regulations set by the organization and the governments.

Development Methodology

We have learned what a technical product is and who builds it, and, in this section, we will learn how it is built. Software products are built using a set of techniques to attain optimal effectiveness of development team and deliver a high-quality product. There is an established process consisting of a series of activities to develop and make changes to a software product – it is called software development life cycle (SDLC). In SDLC the first activity is to gather requirements on what needs to build in the product or feature and then comes the activity of designing the user experience and the system architecture of the product. The activity of product development and testing comes next, followed by the activity of product deployment to make it available to the end user. Last is the activity of product maintenance, where any bug (issue with the functioning of the product) is fixed.

There are many forms of SDLC that have been introduced at different points in time; however, the most popular ones and the ones used even today are *waterfall* and *agile*. Let's dive into them one by one.

Waterfall

This methodology breaks down the product development into a set of linear sequential phases, wherein each phase takes in inputs from the previous phase. The phases are

1. **Define** – Define the functional and nonfunctional requirements of the product to be built in a document called software requirement specification (SRS).

2. **Design** – Design the system architecture, i.e., breakdown of the product into its multiple systems and subsystems to meet the functional and nonfunctional requirements in a document called software design document (SDD).

3. **Develop** – Implement/code the functionalities of the product.

4. **Test** – Define scenarios called test cases, to test the software against to ensure the functional and nonfunctional requirements are met.

5. **Deploy** – Make product ready for use. Activities involve packaging (developing installers), developing configuration settings, etc.

6. **Maintain** – Fix bugs (issues) in the delivered product and add features to improve performance.

Waterfall methodology may be called the traditional way of software product development by some as it was widely practiced until a decade ago, but it is still used in the industry. The main benefit of waterfall is that it provides predictability in planning and is often requested even in the Agile world by upper management, sales, and marketing. Having a plan also promotes long-term thinking and avoids ad hoc engineering practices.

One of the key issues with this methodology was the lack of flexibility to go back to a phase. Let's say the stakeholders want to add a functionality or the engineers want to use a different architecture; the waterfall doesn't allow any change once a phase is complete. This meant that the product/features would take at least a couple of months from start to being delivered and there are no changes to the functionality that can be added during that timeframe. The other issue is that the future unknowns can make the efforts spent in planning stages of the waterfall go in vain.

Agile

This methodology is an incremental and adaptable form of product development. Agile is like waterfall in terms of phases, but Agile breaks down the project into smaller iterations, allowing for a continuous delivery of product features to the customer instead of waiting till the completion of all features. It allows feedback from the customer and ability to change/add functionality to the product after any iteration. This is influenced by the core values listed in the Agile manifesto:

1. Individuals and interactions over process and tools

2. Working software over comprehensive documentation

3. Customer collaboration over contract negotiation

4. Responding to change over following a plan

16

While waterfall has a lot of emphasis on process, documentation, and contracts, agile is just the opposite; however, in no way it should be perceived that agile is asking to ignore all of those. While agile has gained more popularity over waterfall to develop technical products due to the flexibility it provides and the smaller release cycles, agile has some shortcomings too, that come from short iterations and local decisions.

For example, agile is well suited for quick iteration to evaluate user experience changes. The risk of a wrong user experience is small as it can be reverted or fixed in the next iteration. However, the server-side development work cannot be purely agile. A short-term design for back-end services that power the features of the product can lead to long-term scalability and security issues. Fixing these back-end issues is very expensive from an effort perspective and may also require migrating a large amount of customer data, making it very complex and challenging for a live product. We recommend that for server-side work, a combination of long-term thinking and agile development should be used. Figure 1-6 shows a side-by-side comparison of waterfall and agile methodologies.

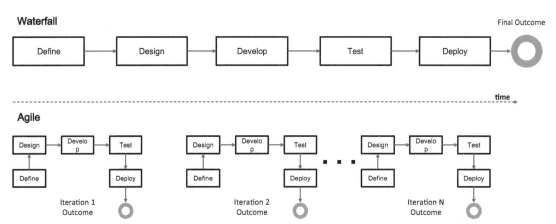

Figure 1-6. *Agile methodology delivers outcome in smaller increments over time that sums up to the final outcome from waterfall methodology*

There are two popular forms of agile development methodology, namely, Scrum and Kanban[2]. If you're working in the technology, you may already be using one or the other and may know of it. If not, let's have a quick overview.

---

[2] www.atlassian.com/agile/kanban/kanban-vs-scrum

Scrum

The development team here defines a fixed length time interval called sprint which is usually of two weeks, and there are ceremonies (activities) put on these sprints to aid the development and launch of a set of capabilities. A few user stories are chosen from the top of the product backlog based on the capacity of the development team and moved to the sprint backlog in a sprint planning meeting. The user stories in the product backlog are already kept in a prioritized order by the product owner. The team then starts the development process, and every day, each team member provides updates to everyone else on what they did and if they are blocked on something on which they need help in the "daily scrum" meeting.

At the end of the sprint, a product increment (software update) for all the completed user stories from the sprint backlog is released to the customer. The team reviews the functionality delivered to the customer (also called demo) in the sprint review meeting, which isn't a gate to releasing the product increment (value) to the customer to understand on if they need to adapt and update something in the product backlog to provide the most value to the customer. The last ceremony is called "retrospective" and where the team discusses what went well during the scrum and what problems were encountered and come up with improvements to make sprints more effective.[3] Figure 1-7 shows the various scrum ceremonies.

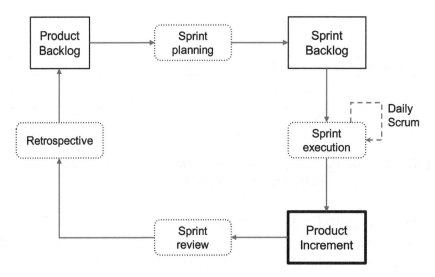

Figure 1-7. *The different ceremonies performed in a sprint*

---

[3] https://scrumguides.org/scrum-guide.html#sprint-retrospective

A key metric used by the scrum team is called "velocity." Each user story is assigned a proxy of effort by the team called story points. When the team starts the sprint, the sum of story points of the user stories in the sprint backlog is called "estimated velocity," and when the team ends a sprint, the sum of story points of all completed user stories is called "actual velocity." The closeness between estimated and actual velocity is a measure of how good the team is with estimation and if they need improvement there. Also looking at velocity values across multiple over time can show if the team is improving or if a change has impacted the team positively or negatively.

Kanban

Kanban (Japanese for signboards or billboards) is a simple continuous workflow management methodology and is great for teams that have a lot of incoming feature requests that vary in priority and scope. To follow this methodology, the development team puts four columns (can be more if the team wants, such as one for QA) as shown in Figure 1-8. The "To-do" column is what the team wants to complete in the near term and is picked from the product backlog, "In-progress" shows the features that are currently in development, and "Done" lists the features that are complete.

There are no roles and ceremonies in Kanban, and if bottleneck happens during the development, the team should work together to remove them and take the learnings to further adjust the process to prevent any future bottlenecks. Kanban has the following three principles:

1. **Visualize the workflow** – The Kanban board should be visible to every team member, and it should be reflective of the current work. It should be able to provide the project status as well.

2. **Limit the work in progress** – There should be a limit on the number of work items (features, user stories, tasks, etc.) that can be put in the in-progress column to prevent the team from losing efficiency from multitasking or reprioritization. Two work items per person working in the in-progress column is a general thumb rule here.

3. **Improve continuously** – The board should aid in spotting the problems. This will help in coming up with changes to fix the issues quickly. Also, the changes brought in should prevent any similar issues in the future; therefore, the methodology promotes continuous improvement.

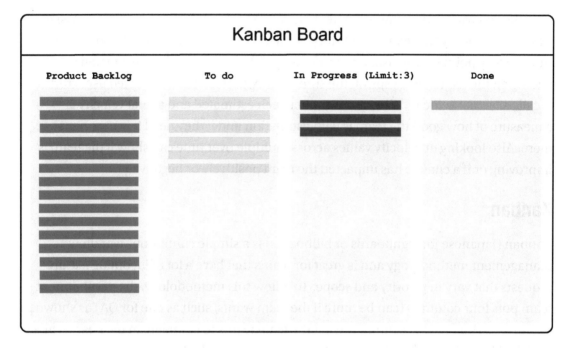

Figure 1-8. *Kanban board in its most basic form. This board has an in-progress limit of three work items. Each strip in the column is a work item*

There are two metrics that are of interest to the users of Kanban. The first metric is "lead time," which is the time it takes for a work item (feature request) to appear on the board to when it got done. This gives a measure of how long the customer must wait to get value delivered. The second metric is "cycle time," which is the time it takes for the work item to go from in-progress to done, essentially the development time. The development team strives to reduce the gap between the lead time and cycle time.

Product Development Tools and Practices

Software products are written by development team in the form of code, also called source code. Source code contains the instructions for the machine to follow and get desired results. The Linux information project defines source code as the version of software as it is originally written by a human in plain text[4]. Source code is usually held in

---

[4] The Linux Information Project. "Source Code Definition" Archived 3 October 2017 at the Wayback Machine. (https://web.archive.org/web/20171003223931/http://www.linfo.org/source_code.html)

multiple text files, which may not be in the same programming language. This program that has its source code in multiple programing language is called a "polyglot" and has become very common as different programming languages are best fit for different use cases. The collection of source code used to build a software product, or its component, is called a code base and is saved in a special folder/directory called code repository or simply repository. Code bases can be huge; famously, Google's code base has 1 billion files, 9 million source code files, 2 billion lines of source code, and 86 TB total size as of January 2015.[5]

Since multiple engineers work on the same source code to add/delete/update functionality, they need some standard way of collaborating so that they don't create conflicts by creating overlapping modifications to the source code while at the same time also being able to create backups of their changes along with being able to track changes made by others to the source code. All this is accomplished by a using a special software called version control system (VCS), also sometimes called source control. Git, Mercurial, and Subversion are popular version control systems. Let's understand its usage and design in more detail with Git being the VSC we will dive deep into.

Version Control System

Believe it or not, we all have used some form of version control. Recollect when you created a resume with the file name "<YourName>_Resume.docx" for your first job, and then when it was time to look out again, you took the same old resume, updated it with more skills and work experience, and did a "Save As" to save the file as "<YourName>_Resume_2018.docx," or if you were more savvy, you made a copy of the file as "<YourName>_Resume_v1.docx" – that is version control. However, this style wouldn't work where many developers are working on the same file (source code) and would need a well-formed VCS. The following are some key features of a good VCS:

- **Track changes** – Each version of the file(s) has information on what was added, deleted, and updated.

- **Roll back** – Enable the user to restore the file(s) to any previous version of the file. This is useful if the current version has bugs.

---

[5] https://cacm.acm.org/magazines/2016/7/204032-why-google-stores-billions-of-lines-of-code-in-a-single-repository/fulltext

- **Track ownership** – Each change made to the file(s) is saved along with the information of the user who made change.

- **Synchronization** – Users can stay in sync with the latest version of the file(s).

- **Sandboxing** – Users can make changes to a file in a temporary/ isolated area and test it out before saving the changes to the code base.

Based on if the code base is present on a single repository on a server vs. the repository being available or present on local machines of many developers, the version control systems can be categorized into two types, namely, the centralized VCS and the distributed VCS.[6] In recent times, distributed VCS has gained more popularity with Git and Mercurial being examples of it. Figure 1-9 shows an illustration of the two forms of VCS. A very simple explanation of the two along with their differences is provided in the following.

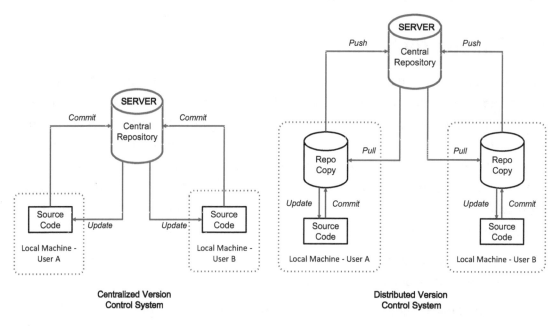

Centralized Version Control System

Distributed Version Control System

Figure 1-9. *A sample representation of a centralized VCS and a distributed VCS*

---

[6]www.geeksforgeeks.org/centralized-vs-distributed-version-control-which-one-should-we-choose/

Centralized VCS	Distributed VCS
1. In this system, the central code repository is present on a server. The developer periodically pulls the code from this repository onto his/her local machine. This step is called getting an "update" from the repository. Once the developer has made the changes to the source code on his local machine, she/he merges the local machine code with that in the central repository on the server. This step is called "commit."	1. In this system, every developer starts by cloning a copy of the central repository on their local machine. The developer periodically "pulls" in the changes from the central repository onto his/her local repository and then makes changes to the source code on his/her local source code copy and "commits" the changes in the local repository. Then the developer "pushes" the changes in the local repository back to the central repository.
2. Generally, actions are slower than in a distributed VCS as everything happens on the central repository and an active Internet connection is required.	2. Everything other than pushing and pulling changes is very fast as it is done on local repository and doesn't require internet connection.
3. Projects with a lot of change sets (group of commits) are easy to handle as the whole repository of historical changes isn't downloaded onto a local machine.	3. Projects with a lot of change sets such as 50,000 or more will take an impractical time to download the repository onto the local machine.
4. There isn't any issue with having large binary files in the repository as all the file versions reside on the central repository only.	4. Project can take a lot of hard disk space on the local machine if the repository contains many large binary files that can't be compressed easily as all the versions of these files will need to be stored.
5. If the central server goes down, no version control action can be performed.	5. If the central server goes down, all actions but pushing and pulling can still be done.

Git and GitHub

Git is the most popular version control system and a distributed form of version control system. It is a command-line tool (CLI); however, there are graphical user interfaces that can be used. You may have also heard of GitHub, a subsidiary of Microsoft since 2018, which offers distributed version control. You may be wondering what the relationship between Git and GitHub is – short answer, GitHub hosts the central repository on the Internet. Repositories are also called repos. Developers use Git software to clone (make copy) the central repo from GitHub onto their local machine, and they add/update/ delete code to the local repo and track these changes again using Git. Once they have verified the code works fine, they push their local repo back to the central repo using Git, and the updates made on the local repo are merged with the central repo.

The long answer is, apart from being the hosting space for central repos, GitHub offers some other features like access control to determine in simple form as to who can view the central repo code, who can make a clone, who can add code to the repo, etc. Along with that there are a host of collaboration features such as issue tracker, bug tracker, wikis, CI/CD, notifications, etc. However, GitHub isn't the only company that offers hosting space for central repos; companies like Bitbucket and GitLab and products like Google Cloud Source Repositories, AWS CodeCommit, and Azure DevOps offer similar capabilities.

Two key features of Git are commits and branches. A commit is the snapshot of the Git repo; in simple words, it's like a checkpoint. Git creates a default branch called "Main" (used to be "Master" before) on which these commits are tracked. Developers can branch out from the main branch (or other branches) and add code there and, once it's complete, merge their branch into the main branch, thereby adding in their code to the main branch.

Let's take an example to understand this better by implementing a process to do our own "branch" and "commit" without Git. Say you have a file "Groceries.txt" in a directory named "Main," which contains the groceries you have to buy and has the text "Potatoes – 2lbs" and "Apples – 1lbs" in it. Let's say this version of file is saved in a subdirectory called A1. Then, you make another copy of the subdirectory called A2. In the Groceries file there, you update the quantity of Potatoes to "Potatoes – 4lbs"; add "Onions – 5lbs." Then, your roommate "Bretta" makes a copy of your "Main" directory on her local machine and renames the directory to "Bretta-update." She then makes the copy of the subdirectory A2 in it and names it B3. She adds in "Tomatoes – 2lbs" in the Groceries file in B3 and saves it. Then, she makes another copy of subdirectory B3 and names it B4. She updates the tomatoes to "Tomatoes – 1lbs" in the Groceries file there.

Feeling satisfied with the Groceries list, she shares her directory "Bretta-update" with you (say as a zip file). You open the last subdirectory B4 and review the Groceries file and see the updates and feel good that the list looks complete. So you copy all the subdirectories in "Bretta-update" directory and paste them in your "Main" directory, and you make a copy of the subdirectory B4 and name it A5. You let Bretta know that you have merged her updates and that the Groceries file in A5 subdirectory has the latest updated Groceries file. She then deletes the Bretta-update directory. If we map all the preceding actions to Git, the following is what makes a commit and a branch and is shown in Figure 1-10:

- Each subdirectory can be thought of as a commit as it is the snapshot of the files at that moment.

- The copy of "Main" directory and "Bretta-update" consisting of subdirectories A1, A2, B3, and B4 can be thought of as the branch of Main.

- Updates made on the "Bretta-update" branch didn't affect the Main branch, and only when they were merged did the changes reflect on Main.

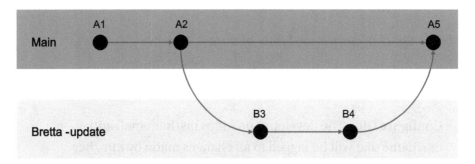

Figure 1-10. *A visual representation of commits and branches*

Now that we understand the macro view of how Git works, let's get into some details. We will learn of some common Git commands and develop a better understanding of how Git works. Figure 1-11 shows how Git commands are used to create a workflow by the engineers.

Note   You can skip the following section on Git commands and jump to the Git feature branch workflow section as you would never need to use Git in a nonengineering role. We added the section to give you an insight into the flow of Git commands.

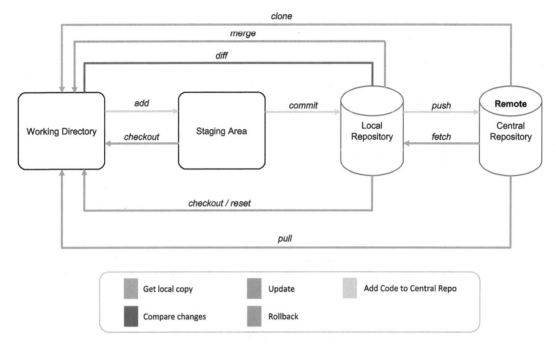

Figure 1-11. *Git commands and flow of data*

Initialize Git

1. **Configure Git** – The developer provides his/her email and a
   username that will be tagged to all changes made by him/her
   in the central repository to track ownership. This is done by the
   following commands:

   ```
   git config --global user.name <username>
   git config --global user.email <email>
   ```

2. **Clone the central repo** – The developer gets a copy of the central
   repo from a remote server by specifying the URL of the remote
   central repo in the following command. The developer then
   makes changes to source code files or adds/deletes files and
   folders.

   ```
   git clone <repo URL>
   ```

3. **Review commit history** – The developer can see the list of various commits made by different developers by the following command. It is used if the developer wants to check out an old snapshot of the repo or see when and who made a particular update to the code base. Each commit is uniquely identified by a commit Id which is an alphanumeric string.

```
git log
```

Example output from git log

```
commit a867b4af366350be2e7c21b8de9cc6504678a61b
Author: John Nash <johnn@gmail.com>
Date:   Fri Dec 3 18:59:41 2021 -0700

Added unit tests

commit 25eee4caef46ae64aa08e8ab3f988bc917ee1ce4
Author: John Nash <johnn@gmail.com>
Date:   Fri Dec 3 05:13:39 2021 -0700

Removed the alerts code

commit 0766c053c0ea2035e90f504928f8df3c9363b8bd
Author: John Nash <johnn@gmail.com>
Date:   Fri Dec 3 00:55:06 2021 -0700

Added Build instructions in README

commit 0d1d7fc32e5a947fbd92ee598033d85bfc445a50
Author: John Nash <johnn@gmail.com>
Date:   Thu Dec 2 23:56:08 2021 -0700

Added standard URLs for portability
```

Add Code to Central Repo

1. **Get status of repo** – Developer learns of the status of the repo, i.e., sees if there are any changes made to any files that are being tracked by Git through the following Git command. By default, Git tracks all files that were the part of the initial cloned repo for changes.

   ```
   git status
   ```

2. **Add changes to staging area** – Developer adds updated files/directories in the working directory to the staging area. Staging area can be thought of as a temporary storage where the draft of updated files is saved before they are committed (saved) to the local repo. It doesn't affect the repository in any way; it just tells Git that these changes from staging area should be included in the next commit. If developer makes additional changes to files that have been added to the staging area previous through git add, they will need to run the git add command again to bring the new set of changes to the staging area:

   ```
   git add <file name>
   git add <directory>
   ```

3. **Save changes in local repo** – Developer saves the files/directories from staging area into the local repo using the following command. They usually include a small message that describes what has been saved (committed).

   ```
   git commit -m "commit message"
   ```

4. **Save changes in central repo** – Developer then merges the updates made in the local repo with the central repo using the following command, making the central repo updated with his/her code:

   ```
   git push
   ```

Get Updates from Central Repo

1. **Update local repo** – As more than one developer works on the same code base, the central repo is updated frequently. Therefore, developers fetch updates from the central repo onto their local repo, so that it is up to date using the following command:

   ```
   git fetch <remote>
   ```

2. **Update working directory (from local)** – Developer updates the working directory with the updates fetched into the local repository using the following command:

   ```
   git merge
   ```

3. **Update working directory (from remote)** – Sometimes developers would want to not just update their local repo but also the files in their working directory such that edits/updates are made to the source code files in the central repo by other developers (collaborators) is reflected in the files they are working on. The following command does that, which is equivalent to git fetch + git merge:

   ```
   git pull <remote>
   ```

Reverting Changes

1. **Review an old snapshot** – Developer can check out any snapshot of the repo and see what the files and code were like at that time using the following command:

   ```
   git checkout <commit Id>
   ```

2. **Rollback** – There are times when the developers would like to reset to an old snapshot (commit) as in a case where there is a critical bug introduced in the code base and it's easier to roll back to a snapshot before the bug was introduced than fixing it. The developer can revert the repo to the snapshot of choice by specifying the commit Id (from Git log) in the following command:

   ```
   git reset <commit Id>
   ```

Branch Commands

1. **Create feature branch** – Developer creates a new branch to the Main branch after cloning the central repo on his/her local machine through the following command. This branch is used exclusively for the development of a given feature. Upon creation this branch can be thought of as a copy of Main branch.

   ```
   git checkout -b <feature branch name>
   ```

2. **Push feature branch to central repo** – Developer pushes the branch to the central repo using the following command:

   ```
   git push <remote> <feature branch name>
   ```

3. **Switch to another branch** – Developer can jump from one branch to another using the following command:

   ```
   git checkout <branch name>
   ```

4. **Merge branches** – Once the implementation of feature is done in the feature branch, the developer merges his/her feature branch into the Main branch, by first switching to the main branch and then merging the feature branch in the main branch through the following command:

   ```
   git checkout main
   git merge <feature branch name>
   ```

Note   Merges are generally done after the code in feature branch has been reviewed from senior developers or the central repo owners through a *Pull Request*.

---

5. **Delete a branch** – Once developers have merged the changes to Main branch, they delete the branch through the following command:

   ```
   git branch -d <feature branch name>
   ```

Compare Changes

1. **Compare changes made** – Developer can compare what has been added/updated/deleted from the source files by comparing two commits, branches, or files using the following commands:

   ```
   git diff <old commit Id> <new commit Id>
   git diff <branch1> <branch2>
   git diff HEAD <file path>
   ```

   Continuing with our earlier example with "Groceries.txt" file, let's say we run diff on commit A1 and A2, it will show the following output, where the "a" and "b" represent variants of the file in the two commits also represented by "-" and "+". Now we can see from the output that Potatoes has been updated from 2lbs to 4lbs between the two commits, Onions has been added and no change made to Apples.

   Example output from git diff

```
diff –git a/Groceries.txt b/Groceries.txt
index 5340ff32..t43gg23 100644
--- a/Groceries.txt
+++ b/Groceries.txt
@@ -1,2 +1,3 @@

-Potatoes – 2lbs
+Potatoes – 4lbs
Apples – 1lbs
+Onions – 5lbs
```

Git Feature Branch Workflow

Git supports collaboration among developers on the same code base (central repo) and increased productivity. There is a term for it, called "Git Workflow," which is a recommendation on how to use Git in a consistent manner to achieve productivity. There are multiple Git workflows developed over time, such as centralized workflow, gitflow workflow, forking workflow, and feature branch workflow, and the adoption of the git workflow is mostly based on team's preference and the product type they are building. We will focus on the Feature Branch Workflow as it's one of the most used workflows, especially for software products that are offered as Software as a Service (SaaS), which form the bulk of web and mobile software products. Feature branch workflow is also called GitHub Workflow or branch-per-issue workflow. Figure 1-12 shows two feature branches from the main branch.

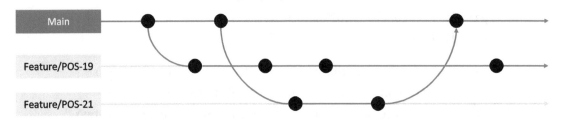

Figure 1-12. *Feature branch workflow for SaaS product*

The "Feature branch workflow" has the following two key features:

- **Branch per issue** – At a high level, an "issue" can be thought of as an article which documents the feature to be developed. It usually contains the gist of the problem and a high-level solution. Technically, an issue can be a feature, a bug, or an intermediate technical step. Usually, when product managers create issues, they put the user story there as a feature request. In the Feature branch workflow, each feature (issue) has its own branch, where the name of the branch is kept as the Issue Id like "Feature/POS-21" where POS-21 is the issue Id of the feature.

Note   Many user stories are not granular enough for agile development as a single feature branch. A user story is broken down into many To-Dos. A feature branch corresponds to one To-Do and is generally associated with one or multiple engineering tickets called tasks.

- **Pull request** – Once the implementation of a feature is complete in the feature branch, the feature developer prepares a request to pull in the code from the feature branch into the Main branch by opening a "Pull request" (called "Merge Request" on GitLab). Other developers on the team review the code in the branch to see if there are any problem(s) with the source code, which the feature developer is supposed to fix. Once everything has been verified, the team member merges the feature branch into the Main branch, and the Pull Request is marked complete. The feature branch is then generally deleted to reduce clutter in the repo.

To summarize, developers create a branch for each feature they develop, instead of adding code directly to the main branch. Once the developer has coded the desired functionality on the feature branch, it is merged with the main branch after getting it reviewed by other developers in the team through a pull request. Figure 1-13 shows how the pull request is completed.

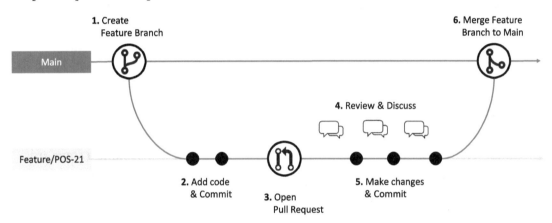

Figure 1-13. *Flow of the feature branch workflow with a pull request*

DevOps

Most software up until the early 2000s was *install based* where the end user would manually install the product on their desktop or mobile. It was critical for the software to go through a comprehensive QA cycle as it was difficult to generate another release. However, there was an uptick in development of SaaS products where the product is present in the cloud and accessed over the Internet by the end consumer through a front-end interaction medium like a web browser. The product engineering team would not only develop the product and its features but also deploy, run, and monitor them. Contrasting it with install-based software products, you can think in a SaaS product, the software that is being built by the company is also being installed and updated by that company, giving the end customer the benefit of having the latest features and bug fixes.

This required a new process to both speed up the delivery of the features such that it can be more agile and operating those features as operations become so critical to end customer experience. So came DevOps in the early 2010s, a combination of the words "Developers" and "Operations," which focuses on a set of practices to reduce the time it takes to release a feature (or even a small change) while ensuring it is of high quality. DevOps is complementary to agile process and has three key principles, namely, shared ownership, workflow automation, and rapid feedback.

DevOps actively controls the networking, compute, and storage capacities used by the service as well as manage the security and compliance of the operational processes. DevOps is also involved in the design of the product's architecture with respect to the hardware, networking, monitoring, scaling, backup/restore, disaster recovery, etc. DevOps has two core components, continuous improvement and continuous delivery (CI/CD) to improve the process of software development and make it available to customers, and monitoring and observability to streamline operations. Let's dive into these.

CI/CD

CI/CD is a core component of DevOps, and CI/CD pipelines have become a standard tool used by most product teams today. Before we get into understanding what and how CI/CD works, it's important we know about the following two areas:

1. **Software testing** – It is the process to verify that the software feature (or product) does what it is supposed to do. There are various types of software testing, and they are done in the following order:

   - **Unit testing** – Here individual parts of code that provide a specific functionality are tested against some predefined scenarios with inputs and expected outputs.

   - **Integration testing** – This tests that the interaction between interaction across components works fine. You may think of interfaces as APIs. If you don't know what APIs are, don't worry; we will learn of them in detail in the next chapter.

- **System testing** – This tests that the system (the product) as a whole is working fine including its subproducts. Its sole purpose is to exercise the full system and discover bugs if any.

- **User acceptance testing (UAT)** – Last test before product is released to the market. This tests if the feature or product meets the customer's requirements.

2. **Environments** – These refer to a collection of software and hardware that is required to build, deploy (think install), and run software products. These may contain servers, operating systems, databases, etc. The popular notion is to have four kinds of environments.

    - **Development** – This is the developer's computer on which she/he writes code for the product. All the testing done by the developer on the code she/he wrote also takes place here.

    - **QA** – The quality assurance (QA) environment is where extensive testing is done to ensure that the newly added code doesn't break anything in the product from an integration and system testing perspective. This helps to check that the product/feature meets the quality requirements in terms of security, performance, and functionality.

    - **Staging** – This is also called *preproduction* environment and consists of hardware and software that is very similar to the production environment. Once everything has been verified to work as expected on the development environment, the feature is pushed to staging environment. UAT and demo of the feature to the business stakeholders before releasing it to the end users are generally given from this environment.

    - **Production** – This is the software and hardware where the product is deployed from Stage environment. This is where the users use the product and its features. This is the most important environment as this is where customers consume the product and businesses make money.

Continuous Integration

Product teams want to deliver high-quality products and features, and software testing is a crucial input to deliver a high-quality product. There are two broad activities that are done for testing as follows by the engineering team:

1. Develop tests and automate them.

2. Run developed tests to prevent any regression (loss of existing functionality) due to new code changes.

In the Git feature branch workflow, the code is reviewed by other members of the team, as a part of the pull request; however, it would be great to also have these tests run and the results of those evaluated before the approval of the pull request. This is where *Continuous Integration* (CI) comes into play. It enables automated execution of the tests developed to identify regression issues without the engineers having to explicitly kick off these tests. It allows for a merge of the feature branch into main only if none of the tests fail.

CI is done by utilizing a CI system that could be a separate system (remove server running the CI system) or a part of version control system itself. The following is how a CI system works. Refer to Figure 1-14 to visually follow along the steps here:

1. On each pull request, the Git server (hosting the central repo) sends a notification to the CI server, running the CI software.

2. CI server clones the repo, checks out the feature branch, and merges it with the main branch.

3. CI server then builds the source code in a software product.

4. It runs the unit tests. These tests are created by the developer (or a test automation engineer) and are present in the repo.

5. It sends the test results back to the central repo hosting service (such as GitHub) where it is shared with the code reviewers and code author (feature branch owner).

6. If build is successful as reported by CI server, the pull request is allowed to merge to the main branch, else it is blocked.

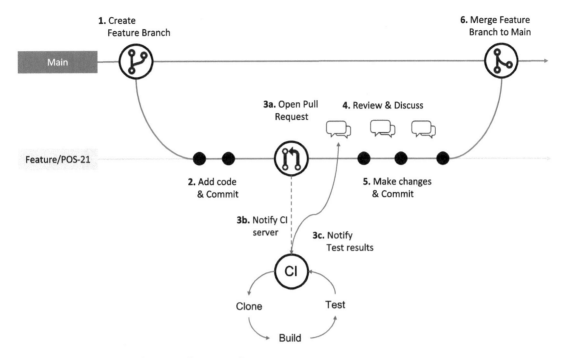

Figure 1-14. *Continuous integration process*

Continuous Delivery

CD is the next step in the CI/CD process, and it automates the release of the build (and sometimes the validated code) from the CI step into the repo on a staging environment. It runs the system tests and the automated user acceptance tests. Then, it performs some other tests like load testing to ensure the product can run smoothly in the peak user load it was designed for, i.e., number of concurrent users that can use the feature/product. If any test fails, the developer team is notified to fix the bugs. If tests pass, then the build is ready to be deployed in the production environment, i.e., released to the customers. The operations team can then take this build from the staging environment and deploy to the production environment.

Continuous Deployment

There is still a manual role involved in continuous delivery as someone must manually deploy the build from staging environment to the production. If after all the tests in the continuous delivery stage pass, the build is automatically deployed into production; then, that is called continuous deployment as shown in Figure 1-15.

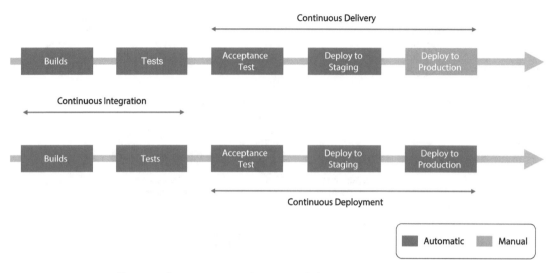

Figure 1-15. *Difference between continuous delivery and continuous deployment in CI/CD*

Depending on what is being deployed in production may dictate the use of the continuous delivery or continuous deployment. Internal product changes that are backward compatible and not impacting end customer's experience may be deployed immediately through the continuous deployment model. However, customer experience related changes that require customer communication such as release notes, announcements, etc., are not suitable for continuous deployment.

Customers often do not like to see unannounced changes to their UX. Hence, the decision on continuous delivery vs. continuous deployment is not a technical issue but more of a customer experience issue. For example, when it comes to enterprise software products, many enterprise customers do not want daily/weekly changes to the products they are using. So often, changes are batched into predictable scheduled release milestones.

There are many companies that offer CI/CD products that can be integrated with the version control system, such as Jenkins, TravisCI, CircleCI, etc. However, nowadays, central repository hosting companies such as GitHub and GitLab have also started to offer CI/CD solutions.

It may get daunting to get a complete picture of CI/CD among so many new concepts we learned. To make it clearer, refer to Figure 1-16 which gives a holistic picture of how engineering teams, Git, and environments are a part of the CI/CD process. Note how the product is deployed and run from the cloud providers AWS (Amazon Web Services) and GCP (Google Cloud Platform). We will learn more of the cloud in Chapter 2.

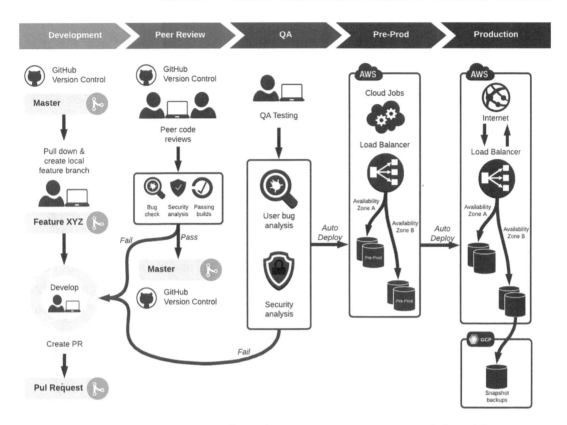

Figure 1-16. *A representation of a CI/CD process. Source: Lucidchart blog*

Monitoring and Observability

On October 4, 2021, at 15:39 UTC, the social network Facebook and its subsidiaries, Messenger, Instagram, WhatsApp, Mapillary, and Oculus, became globally unavailable for a period of six to seven hours because of a faulty configuration change.[7] Users on Twitter and Telegram (Facebook competitors) experienced slowdown response time, believed to be caused by people switching to these services from Facebook.[8] During the day of outage, the company shares dropped by nearly 5%, and the company lost at least $60M in advertising revenue. Mark Zuckerberg (CEO) and the company's CTO both wrote an apology for the downtime.

---

[7] www.theverge.com/2021/10/4/22709575/facebook-outage-instagram-whatsapp
[8] www.independent.co.uk/life-style/gadgets-and-tech/twitter-down-outage-not-working-b1932250.html

Mark Zuckerberg ✓
about 2 months ago

Facebook, Instagram, WhatsApp and Messenger are coming back online now. Sorry for the disruption today -- I know how much you rely on our services to stay connected with the people you care about.

👍 2.2M   💬 639K   ➤ 396K

This outage at Facebook is an extreme example; however, service disruptions are real, and besides bringing a bad customer experience, they also damage the brand and incur loss in revenue. It's important to track how our product is performing and if there is a degradation in anything, being able to understand what has caused it and fix it before it causes any major customer impact. Monitoring and observability is a core component of DevOps as it promotes the idea of pushing frequent code updates all the way into production and that needs good visibility in terms of performance and impact on the customer experience.

Monitoring is to watch and understand WHAT is the state of the system (software product) through predefined metrics and logs usually viewed on a dashboard. With efficient monitoring in place, engineers can quickly identify what has gone wrong. **Observability** is to understand WHY is this the state of the system (software product) by exploring/discovering patterns that are not predefined in advance. A good monitoring and observability system allows collecting metrics from the services of the software product and the underlying infrastructure running those services (CPU, memory, network, etc.), along with providing insights on these metrics and support for further analysis. The components of monitoring and observability are as follows. There are various products that can be used for monitoring and observability like Dynatrace, New Relic, SolarWinds, AppOptics, and cloud-specific ones like AWS CloudWatch, Google Cloud operations suite, etc.

Metrics

Metrics are the quantification of data. It is used to track performance or progress. To get a metric, one needs to clearly define what needs to be measured and how it should be measured. There are four basic metrics that are of interest to the DevOps teams:

1. **Latency** – This is the time between a request and the response from a service. Increase in latency points to degradation in customer experience.

2. **Errors** – Number of requests that don't return a successful outcome.

3. **Traffic** – Number of requests to the service.

4. **System state** – This is composed of other metric that helps with learning about the state of the system, usually CPU utilization, memory utilization, and network (data).

Logs

Logs record what happened when and by whom and therefore contain much more data than a metric. Logs are events from the system (infrastructure) or the product (application) that contain all the information produced by that event and saved on disk in the form of log files. All services that compose the product (more on services in Chapter 3) and the underlying infrastructure generate logs, and these logs are gathered and stored in a central location so that they can be searched easily for further analysis. Logs are semistructured (having some basic structure) for human readability. It is generally in a textual or JSON format with multiple fields. Logs will usually contain the timestamp (when), identifier(s) (who), source (service/infrastructure), and event details (what).

As an example, the following is how a web server log is saved using the "Common Log Format," where the information is which IP address made the request, userId of the person making the request, timestamp of request, and resource requested. HTTP 1.0 protocol is used with the GET method to get the resource dog.png, and the server responded with a success and sent back the dog image of size 2,320 bytes (2.3 KB):

```
127.0.0.1 user-identifier bella [15/Dec/2021:10:10:12 -0700] "GET /dog.png
HTTP/1.0" 200 2320
```

We need to be mindful while saving logs as there may be Personal Identifiable Information (PII) in the events which can be used to identify a specific individual or other similar information as financial data of the users that we shouldn't save in logs to protect our customers as well as to comply with regulations like General Data Protection Regulation (GDPR).

Traces

A trace is a user request's journey through all the different services of the software product. To do this each service log records the unique ID given to the request; that way the whole journey can be constructed based on the unique request Id and the timestamp in the log. More technically, traces in a distributed system (called distributed traces) are composed of spans, which encapsulate a named, timed operation representing a piece of the workflow from one microservice.[9] Traces are generally visualized in the form of a Gantt chart where span duration of the services is shown. In Figure 1-17, we can see how a distributed trace looks like for a request made by a user (through a push of some button) in a hypothetical system which has two services and a database involved in servicing that request.

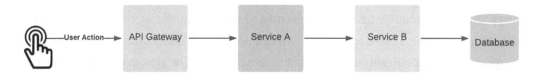

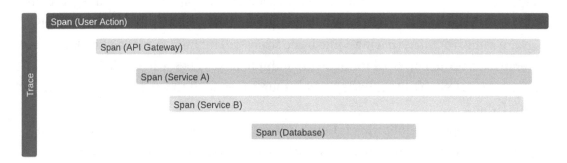

Figure 1-17. *A high-level understanding of how distributed traces are visualization. Source: Dynatrace*

Alerts

Alerts are a notification mechanism which lets the product team, usually DevOps engineers and others in a product team interested in a particular metric(s) or certain type(s) of logs, know when the system is not within its expected limits. The experts in

---

[9] www.dynatrace.com/news/blog/open-observability-part-1-distributed-tracing-and-observability/

the team may define thresholds (upper limit and/or lower limit) of the metric value, and as soon as the metric value breaches the threshold, an alert is sent out to the interested people through the defined alerting mode such as email, pager duty, slack, etc. The notification recipient can then quickly investigate what has happened, why, and remediate the issue before it causes severe customer impact.

Generation of alerting thresholds and dynamically adjusting the thresholds based on new data is often done using machine learning (ML). To understand this better, think of an ecommerce SaaS product like Amazon. Customer traffic will generally be high during the day than during the night. For this type of monitoring, a ML-based automatic threshold can learn the cyclic nature of the system behavior at different traffic volumes at different times in the day and create dynamic thresholds of different values throughout the day.

There are always human controls to adjust the sensitivity of the detection to control false positives and false negatives from ML-generated thresholds, as if the thresholds generated are too tight it may alert the team on a lot of false positives, and if the thresholds are defined too broad, they team may not get notified on real issues.

Testing in Production

We learned that there are some extensive automated tests performed as a part of CI/CD process; however, all of that is in preproduction environment. There is still a small risk that things may not pan out as planned in the production environment. Also, what if the product team wants to understand the impact the new feature will have on the product (system) metrics) and the product business metrics before rolling out the feature to all users? This can be solved if we can test our feature in production on a handful of users and continuously monitor the metrics, and if we see positive impact, we launch to everyone gradually. This is exactly what feature flags, canary releases, and A/B testing helps with.

Feature Flags

Feature flags, also known as feature toggles, are a software development and delivery technique that allow the product teams to activate and deactivate product functionality in the production environment at the flip of a switch from outside the source code, i.e., without having to change the source code or redeploy the application. Feature flags are not just there for customer-facing features. Feature flags are used to also control and try out different internal implementations such as new optimizations, new internal data flows, etc.

It is important to emphasize on the part of outside the code, as one may argue that they can comment the feature code and uncomment the code to get capabilities like the feature flag, however, that will take significant time to deploy it in product while going through the whole CI/CD process. Feature flags are saved as configuration outside the code and that controls activating or deactivating a functionality (feature) while the code is already running in production. This helps decouple deployments and feature releases by deploying the code for a particular feature in production, yet keeping it hidden from users until the product team doesn't feel like exposing the feature to the users.

Software products are not developed one to one with respect to the user-facing features. This is important for nonengineering team members to understand. The reality is that software is structured internally for reuse and reduction of redundancy. As a result, many user-facing features have shared elements that are developed and committed separately.

Feature flags are an asset to DevOps practice; if the developers only merge the feature branch with main branch when the feature is complete, there may be merge conflicts when multiple other developers on the same team may have already merged code that updates the source code that the developer merging the branch is also updating, which then will take time in resolving them and is a manual process. This is one reason why it is recommended that to be efficient with the DevOps practice, the product team should develop short-lived feature branches and activate the feature flags to expose the functionality to the users and test it there.

Feature flags run in production, and high caution should be taken while managing them. As a case in point, in 2012 Knight Capital Group, the largest trader in US equities with market share of around 17% on both NYSE and NASDAQ and trading on average $21 Billion daily repurposed a feature flag created for another reason and lost $440 Million in just 45 minutes.[10] Since the company had only $360 Million in assets, in those 45 minutes, the company went from being the largest trader in the US equities to being bankrupt. Luckily it was rescued by a set of external investors. Coming back to feature flags, the following is a flow of how feature flags are used:

---

[10] https://dougseven.com/2014/04/17/knightmare-a-devops-cautionary-tale/

1. Developers develop partial functionality and push code to production with the feature flag deactivated.

2. They keep pushing code to production (behind the deactivated feature flag) until the functionality is developed completely.

3. Product team identifies a small set of users who should be exposed to the feature. These groups of users are selected based on certain attributes such as geography, product usage time, account type, customers who signed up to be a part of the beta, etc.

4. Developers toggle the feature flag to active the feature(s) for the selected subset of users.

5. The team monitors the metrics closely. If metrics are not looking good, the feature flag is deactivated; else the feature is activated for more users and monitored continuously.

6. The team keeps repeating the preceding step until the feature has been activated for all the users.

7. Finally, the feature flag is removed from the source code in production and the configuration files once satisfied with the feature is released to everyone.

Canary Deployment

While feature flags expose a specific piece of functionality to the end users, canary deployments are used to expose the whole different version of the software product to a set of end users. As an example, canary deployments would be used to test out say the newer version of the product - version 11 with the existing version of the product - version 10, and monitoring if the metrics of interest are within range for the newer version before rolling it out to the broader user base.

Canary deployment takes its inspiration from the old coal mining industry. Coal mines would have carbon monoxide – a toxic, colorless, and odorless gas which is very hard for humans to detect and is referred to as "silent killer." To detect the presence of high level of carbon monoxide which might kill them, the miners would take the canary birds with them inside the coal mines. Since the birds have a rapid breathing rate, small size, and a high metabolism compared to the miners, the birds would die much before the miners would, and that would give a warning to the miners to evacuate the mine or put on their respiratory equipment.

Canary deployments work at the infrastructure networking layer. Generally, most SaaS products have multiple servers (web servers, application servers) that serve the user traffic as one server can only handle limited traffic load. The traffic first comes to a load balancer, which sends the traffic to the servers ensuring they are not overloaded. Canary deployments make use of this, where the product's new version (with the new feature) is only deployed to a small subset of servers. Then, a subset of live user traffic is redirected to this subset of servers and monitored. If metrics don't look good, the product version is rolled back and the previous version deployed again on that subset of servers. If metrics look good, more servers are updated to the new product version and more user traffic is exposed to the new version. This is done until all the traffic is now on the new version of the product. A recap of canary deployment is the following:

1. Developers deploy new product version (with new/updated features) to only a small subset of production servers.

2. DevOps team starts directing a subset of live user traffic (usually 5%) to this set of production servers running the new product version.

3. DevOps team monitors the metrics closely, and if metrics don't look healthy, they roll back the release to the previous stable version of the product on this subset of servers.

4. If metrics are healthy, they deploy new product version to more production servers and direct more traffic to the new product version (say 10% traffic now) and keep monitoring.

5. They repeat the preceding step and gradually increase traffic (5%, 10%, 25%...100%) until all the traffic is now on the new production version and all production servers have the recent product version.

Feature flags and canaries are so useful that they are the default way technology giants like Netflix, Reddit, and Google release features and products to market.

A/B Testing

While feature flags and canary deployments are strategies for deploying code into the production environments, A/B testing is more of a controlled experimentation technique for the UI layer which the product's users interact with. A/B test is conceptually an extension of feature flags and very often performed through feature flags too. As usual, let's take an example to understand this better.

Say Bella is a product manager at an ecommerce company and noticed that the conversion rate of the item description page of his ecommerce product isn't good. The conversion rate here is the % of people adding the item to their shopping cart. So, she works with the UX team and engineering team and develops a new version of the item description page (new layout, button theme, color palate, etc.). Figure 1-18 shows two versions of the same page with different element structure.

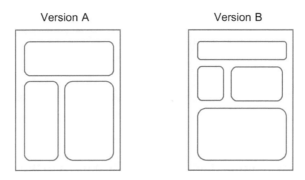

Figure 1-18. *Sample outline of two versions of a web page with significant changes in the UI elements – a good fit for A/B testing*

Now comes the time to deploy this new version to production. But the question lingers: Will the new page version have a better conversion rate than the existing page version? You may say, well let's use canary deployment and expose this new page version to a subset of live traffic and see if the conversion rate is higher or lower. If lower roll back, if higher roll it to everyone. However, there is a problem; you don't want to test this version out with your most important customers (most loyal, most revenue making, enterprise customers, etc.). Well in that case, you may recommend feature flags, and identify a target set of users and expose this new page version to only those users and test it. This is exactly the foundation of A/B testing. However, there is some bit of statistics involved. Let's go into the steps of setting up an A/B test to learn what's involved:

1. Product managers identifies a business metric that they would like to test and improve.

2. Product team develops a hypothesis on what changes (in the UI) can encourage the right user behavior and in turn improve the business metric.

3. Development team develops the new version of the page, essentially a feature behind a feature flag with that change, such as a different color or size of the button on a page, etc.

4. Data science team helps determine the minimum improvement the product manager would like to measure in the business metric between the versions of the page called effect size.

5. Data science team helps determine how many users should be exposed to the new versions of the page to be able to compare statistically if there is a significant improvement in the conversion metric with the new version.

6. And based on the daily average number of users that come to the original page version and the number of users needed on each version, they determine the length of the test.

7. Product team identifies and maps the target users to the new version's feature flag. The old version is called version A or the control, and the new version is called version B or test, hence the name A/B test.

8. The product team activates the feature flag, where users mapped to the feature flag get to see version B and all other users see version A. The feature flag is kept activated for the number of days determined earlier.

9. After the test has completed, the product manager measures the business metric for each version and compares them using a statistical test.

10. If version B shows statistically significant improvement compared to version A, then activate feature to all users; else, deactivate the feature and resume back to version A for all users.

Traditionally, the effect size, number of users, duration, etc., required data scientists to compute them; however, today most product teams utilize some in-house product to do A/B testing or use external products that provide A/B testing as a service, where all of this is computed automatically in the A/B test product.

Multivariate Testing

Most often we would not want to dramatically change the UI. We are rather more interested in testing how the interactions between multiple UI elements work together. This is what multivariate testing, also called multivariable testing, does. Multivariate testing has the same principle of statistical testing as A/B testing; just the setup of the experiment (test) is a little different.

Think of the different UI elements on a page exposed to customers as set of variables, where each UI element is a variable. These UI element variables can take multiple values, e.g., the title of the page (consider it variable one) may be styled as with value H1 or with value H2. Similarly, the right section of the page (second variable) may be styled with font "Arial" (let's call it A) or with font "Berlin Sans Fb" (let's call it B). In this case, we have two variables with two values, so we will get four versions with the combinations of these variables. To find out which of this version performs the best, we need to perform a multivariate test. Figure 1-19 shows the four versions of the page created by the combinations.

Version Number	Page Title	Section Font
1	H1	A
2	H1	B
3	H2	A
4	H2	B

These four versions are then tested just like how A/B testing is done, and the version which has the highest statistically significant improvement in the business metric is activated for all the customers. Although multivariate testing may seem the obvious choice to go after, it takes much more traffic (therefore much more time) to achieve statistical significance as compared to A/B tests, because of the number of variations being tested at the same time. As a thumb rule, if you have made dramatic change to the

UI or if you must determine the results of the experiment (test) soon, go with A/B testing else stick with multivariate testing. Optimizely, Mixpanel, and Google Optimize are some popular products to do A/B testing or multivariate testing.

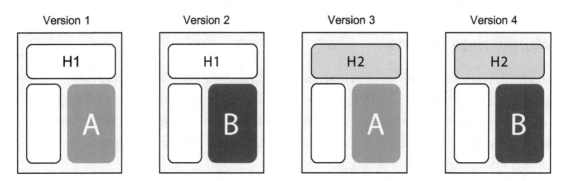

Figure 1-19. *Four versions of a web page formed by combinations of a change in the page title and a section – a good fit for multivariate testing*

Wrap-Up

This chapter has multiple related concepts around product development; let's quickly revisit what we learned. We started with learning what a product is and its various categories. Then, we learned that the product development is a multiple team effort while following a specific process. Process and people are highly coupled in product development and follow a development pipeline starting with the product manager creating a user story describing a user need and saving it into an issue tracker, i.e., the requirement gathering phase.

The UX then develops high fidelity designs showcasing how the UI should look like for the feature to the users (if it is a front-end facing feature) and adds it as an asset to the issue created by the product manager. The engineering teams (including architects) design the service architecture (system design) and divide up the work into engineering tasks, which will require to deliver that user story. The program manager starts tracking the progress on the issue and its constituent tasks through tools like Gantt charts and coordinates them among the teams.

The development team then pulls in engineering tasks to work on which would achieve the delivery of the issue (user story). For implementation, engineers create feature branches and develop code in them. Once coding is complete, they initiate a pull request which is reviewed by the engineering team. A CI pipeline is used to execute automated tests such that this part doesn't require manual intervention. If none of the tests fail and the reviewers approve the pull request, the branch is merged to the main branch.

There is more testing done in the QA and staging environments before the new feature is deployed in the production environment. The CD pipeline is used to automate the deployment of feature (or service) from one environment (infrastructure) to another all the way till production. Techniques such as canary deployments and feature flags are used for testing single functionality and versions of the product. There is monitoring and observability instrumentation put in place by the DevOps team who track metrics, logs, and traces for any issue. The product management team is generally interested in measuring the impact the feature had over the users and leverage techniques like A/B testing or multivariate testing to quantify any statistical improvement.

## CHAPTER 2

Cloud: On Demand Computing Resources for Scale and Speed

What Is the Internet

Let's ask ourselves what the Internet is and how it works. The Internet growth was explosive, and it seems impossible to escape it nowadays. Because the Internet has become such a large part of our lives, a good understanding is needed to use this new tool most effectively.

Since the Internet is a giant network, each computer needs to have a unique address, which comes in the form nnn.nnn.nnn.nnn where each of nnn is a number between 0 and 255. This address is called IP address, where IP stands for Internet Protocol.

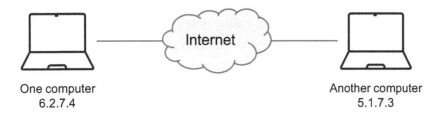

Figure 2-1. *Computers communicate over the Internet*

© Gaurav Sagar, Vitalii Syrovatskyi 2022
G. Sagar and V. Syrovatskyi, *Technical Building Blocks*, https://doi.org/10.1007/978-1-4842-8658-6_2

So when the computer is connected to the Internet, how does it talk to other computers? Let's say your computer has IP address 6.2.7.4 and another computer's IP address where you want to send the message is 5.1.7.3. And protocol stack is used for transmitting messages between computers. The protocol stack used on the Internet is referred to as the TCP/IP protocol stack because of the two major communication protocols used (IP and TCP), where IP directs packets to a specific computer using an IP address and TCP directs packets to a specific application on a computer using a port number. In addition to IP and TCP, protocol stack also includes a hardware layer which converts data to network signals, and an application protocol layer which is specific to applications such as WWW, email, FTP, etc. The stack works as shown in Figure 2-2.

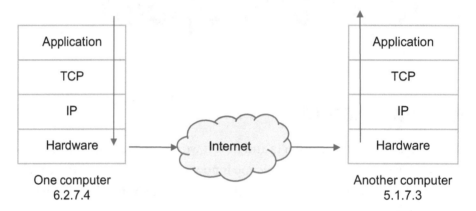

Figure 2-2. *Protocol stack*

The diagram demonstrates the path that message takes from computer with IP 6.2.7.4 to computer with IP 5.1.7.3. While taking this path, the message would start at the top of the protocol stack on the first computer and work its way downward, where it would be broken into chunks of data called packets, assigned a port at TCP level and assigned a destination IP at IP protocol level. Then, the packet goes through the physical layer and finally reaches its destination.

Let's see what is in between when packets travel from one computer to another. The first step is Internet service provider (ISP), which provides a physical connection to the Internet backbone for the client computers and contains a fleet of networking devices and servers. After packets traverse the ISP's local equipment, they are routed onto the ISP's backbone or a backbone the ISP buys bandwidth from. From here the packets will usually journey through several routers and over several backbones, dedicated lines, and other networks until they find their destination, the computer with address 5.1.7.3.

The Internet backbone is made up of many large networks which interconnect with each other and are known as network service providers or NSPs. These networks peer with each other to exchange packet traffic, and each is connected via network access points or NAPs. NSPs also interconnect at Metropolitan Area Exchanges or MAEs.

But how then packets find their way across the Internet? A router (network device) is usually connected between networks to route packets between them. Each router knows about its subnetworks and which IP addresses they use. When a packet arrives at a router, the router examines the IP address which was put there by the IP protocol layer on the originating computer. The router checks its routing table. If the network containing the IP address is found, the packet is sent to that network. If the network containing the IP address is not found, then the router sends the packet on a default route, usually up the backbone hierarchy to the next router. The process is then repeated, and hopefully the next router will know where to send the packet. If it does not, again the packet is routed upward until it reaches a NSP backbone.

But what if we don't know the IP address of the computer you want to connect to? But we want to connect to the server which is referred to as `www.anothercomputer.com`? The answer is domain name service (DNS). DNS is a distributed database which keeps track of computer's names and their corresponding IP addresses on the Internet, and contains multiple servers. No DNS server contains the entire database and only contains a subset of it, so when a DNS server does not contain the domain name requested by another computer, it redirects the requesting computer to another DNS server.

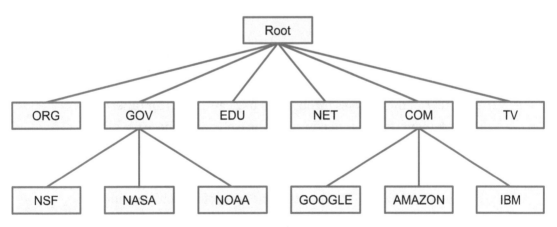

Figure 2-3. *Domain name service hierarchy*

The domain name service is structured as a hierarchy. At the top of the tree are the domain roots; some of the older, more common domains are seen near the top and so on.

Now let's describe some of the most common application layer protocols from protocol stack. The most commonly used services on the Internet is the World Wide Web (WWW), and the application protocol that makes the web work is hypertext transfer protocol or HTTP, which is the protocol that web browsers and web servers use to communicate with each other over the Internet. It is an application level protocol because it sits on top of the TCP layer in the protocol stack and is used by specific applications to talk to one another. In this case the applications are web browsers and web servers.

When you type a URL into a web browser, this is what happens:

1. If the URL contains a domain name, the browser first connects to a domain name server and retrieves the corresponding IP address for the web server.

2. The web browser connects to the web server and sends an HTTP request (via the protocol stack) for the desired web page.

3. The web server receives the request and checks for the desired page. If the page exists, the web server sends it. If the server cannot find the requested page, it will send an HTTP 404 error message. (404 means "Page Not Found" as anyone who has surfed the web probably knows.)

4. The web browser receives the page back and the connection is closed.

5. The browser then parses through the page and looks for other page elements it needs to complete the web page. These usually include images, applets, etc.

6. For each element needed, the browser makes additional connections and HTTP requests to the server for each element.

7. When the browser has finished loading all images, applets, etc., the page will be completely loaded in the browser window.

Under the application layer, there is a TCP layer. TCP is responsible for routing application protocols to the correct application on the destination computer, and for this port numbers are used. Applications on the computer use different port numbers (e.g., web servers commonly use port 80). When a packet arrives at a computer and makes its way up the protocol stack, the TCP layer decides which application receives the packet based on a port number. And TCP works like this:

- When the TCP layer receives the application layer protocol data from above, it splits data into smaller "chunks," and adds a TCP header to each chunk with the port number of the application the data needs to be sent to.

- And when the TCP layer receives a packet from the IP layer below it, data is read from the TCP header in the packet and sends the data to the correct application using the port number taken from the TCP header.

Notice that there is no IP address in the TCP header since TCP doesn't know anything about IP addresses, which is the job of the IP protocol.

IP's job is to send and route packets to other computers, similarly to TCP IP's wrapping packets received from TCP layer with headers containing destination IP address. After the IP header is added, a packet is sent over the Internet toward the destination.

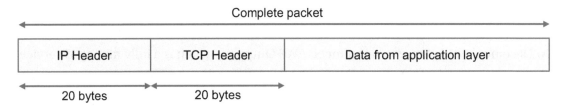

Figure 2-4. Packet components

History of Cloud and Relationship with the Internet

Let's now learn what the cloud is. The "Cloud" has always served as a metaphor for the Internet, where cloud symbols are generally used to signify the Internet on any diagram. The Internet, as a virtual space connecting users from all across the globe, is like a cloud, effectively sharing information via satellite networks. But cloud computing is something different and referred to cloud computing which is sharing of resources, information, and software through a network which in this case is the Internet. Cloud computing is the on-demand availability of computer system resources, especially data storage (cloud storage) and computing power, without direct active management by the user.

The term cloud was used to refer to platforms for distributed computing as early as 1993, when Apple spin-off General Magic and AT&T used it in describing their (paired) Telescript and PersonaLink technologies. And the use of the cloud metaphor for virtualized services dates at least to General Magic in 1994, where it was used to describe the universe of "places" that mobile agents in the Telescript environment could go.

The real evolution started in July 2002, when Amazon created subsidiary Amazon Web Services, with the goal to "enable developers to build innovative and entrepreneurial applications on their own." In March 2006, Amazon introduced its Simple Storage Service (S3), followed by Elastic Compute Cloud (EC2) in August of the same year. These products pioneered the usage of server virtualization to deliver IaaS at a cheaper and on-demand pricing basis. Then in April 2008, Google released the beta version of Google App Engine, which was positioned as PaaS (one of the first of its kind) and provided fully maintained infrastructure and a deployment platform for users to create web applications. Google Compute Engine was released in preview in May 2012, before being rolled out into General Availability in December 2013. Microsoft released Microsoft Azure in February 2010 which was announced in October 2008.

Some open source initiatives exist as well. In July 2010, Rackspace Hosting and NASA jointly launched an open source cloud-software initiative known as OpenStack. As an open source offering and along with other open source solutions such as CloudStack, Ganeti, and OpenNebula, it has attracted attention from several key communities. And in December 2019, Amazon announced AWS Outposts, which is a fully managed service that extends AWS infrastructure, AWS services, APIs, and tools to virtually any customer data center, colocation space, or on-premises facility for a truly consistent hybrid experience.

Cloud computing is the technology where companies offer different resources as services, mainly over the net. These companies are known as the "service providers," and the users are referred to as "subscribers." The subscribers are usually required to pay subscription fees on a typical per-use basis. The main categorization could be made by the types of services:

- **Infrastructure as a Service (IaaS)** – hardware infrastructure is the resource which is offered to users.

- **Platform as a Service (PaaS)** – where the service provider delivers a solution stack or a computing platform to the subscribers over the Internet.

- **Software as a Service (SaaS)** – when "software applications" are offered to users. The applications are accessible from various client devices through either a thin client interface, such as a web browser (e.g., web-based email), or a program interface.

The difference between the Internet and cloud is pretty clear. The Internet is a network of networks that provides software or hardware infrastructure to maintain and establish connectivity of computers across the globe, but the Cloud is a newer technology that offers various kinds of resources over the Internet. So the Cloud is a technology that makes use of the Internet as the medium of communication for the delivery of its services. Although it is possible to offer cloud services within organizations through local area networks (like Amazon Outposts), the Cloud generally operates internationally due to the Internet.

Motivations for Cloud Adoption

Cloud computing has become more and more popular, with more and more companies dropping their in-house solutions and moving to cloud. And companies who fail to adopt it will risk being erased from existence. Let's understand what is driving this move and why the cloud is so attractive. The benefits of deploying applications in the cloud are

- **It is cost-effective** – When adopting the cloud, the enterprise can keep to the minimum or eliminate completely associated capital expenses because no on-site data center is required (i.e., no physical servers, hardware, software, electronic depreciation, etc.), no electricity and cooling, etc. With the savings on capital expenses, physical data center setup, and maintenance, the much-needed fund can be used elsewhere, and the firm can have more time to focus on their core business.

- **On-demand access** – Resources in the cloud can be easily stored, retrieved, recovered, or processed with just a couple of clicks. Users can get access to their works on the go, 24/7, via any devices of their choice, in any corner of the world as long as you stay connected to the Internet. On top of that, all the upgrades and updates to the underlying hardware and systems are done automatically, off-site by the service providers, therefore saving time and team effort in maintaining the systems and tremendously reducing the IT team workloads.

- **Endless probabilities** – Cloud provides a wide variety of services, applications, and ways to use them:

  - Software as a Service (SaaS)

  - Infrastructure as a Service (IaaS)

  - Platform as a Service (PaaS)

  Customers can create public, hybrid, private network access, locations of data center, etc. Options are plentiful and completely customizable.

- **Adaptability** – Since cloud has a wide variety of services, it can be applied and adapt to almost any use case and any change. For example, the firm can choose to rump up to 10,000 web users 10 times during a Christmas sale instead of 1,000 daily target. Other examples companies can choose to increase storage temporarily to accommodate for additional flow of data, switch between private and public network, all of these can be done easily in the cloud.

- **No mess, no fuss collaborations** – Consistent location of files, resources for team collaboration, and easy access. Consistently see one version of the file, share real-time feedback, thus improving productivity, minimize errors, guarantee customer satisfaction, the list goes on.

- **Data security** – The service providers ensure along with all the new and exciting features entail an update in security through audit and compliance. All activities on the cloud will also be closely monitored and frequently audited by a third party to ensure that security standards are met.

- **Get ahead in the game** – There has been a steady increase of demand for migrating to cloud computing for small, medium, and large sectors of the economy. By taking advantages like swift services, cost- and time-efficient, eco-friendly, and fuss-free collaborations among employees, adopting cloud computing can put companies one step ahead of those who still incline with traditional computing.

One of the most important benefits in the cloud for organizations is cost optimization. Cloud providers continue to strengthen their native optimization capabilities to help organizations select the most cost-effective architecture that can deliver the required performance. There is also a big market for third-party cost optimization tools, which concentrate on higher-quality analytics that can maximize savings without compromising performance, providing independence from cloud providers.

A lot of large enterprises also do not want to be dependent on a single cloud provider and often choose at least two to be used simultaneously (e.g., Amazon AWS and Microsoft Azure), which is called multicloud. Although application portability between clouds is nice to have for organization, the main considerations when doing multicloud are focused on procurement, functionality, and risk mitigation than on portability.

One of the important obstacles in the way for cloud adoption for organizations is the lack of IaaS skills. Today's cloud migration strategies tend more toward "lift-and-shift" than toward modernization or refactoring, which do not develop native-cloud skills. Thus, enterprises looking to migrate workloads to the cloud work with managed service providers that have a proven track record of successful migrations within the target industry.

Companies more and more adopt the policies to prefer clouds called a cloud-first policy, which means they're deploying new applications using public cloud services by default. These policies are often IT-driven initiatives, presenting numerous financial, security, and digital transformation benefits, but also driven by business owners who are more focused on reaching customers and reducing complexities in bringing new products to market.

Cloud Delivery Models

To leverage cloud services, we must understand the different types of cloud computing models. The three standard models most widely used are Infrastructure as a Service (IaaS), Platform as a Service (PaaS), and Software as a Service (SaaS). And these models offer increasing abstraction; they are thus often portrayed as layers in a stack: Infrastructure, Platform, and Software as a Service. Let's look at these delivery models in more detail.

Infrastructure as a Service (IaaS)

Traditionally, a company's IT infrastructure was built on-premises. This meant that companies had to constantly invest in expensive hardware like servers and storage and ensure everything stays up to date. As technology grew, companies turned to cloud service providers to help with managing their IT infrastructure.

IaaS enables businesses to access virtualized computing resources from cloud servers. It consists of online services that provide high-level APIs used to abstract various low-level details of underlying network infrastructure like physical computing resources, location, data partitioning, scaling, security, backup, etc.

The key offerings in IaaS are usage of virtual machines and/or containers, which run in the provider's configured networks. IaaS clouds often offer additional resources such as a virtual machine disk-image library, raw block storage, file or object storage, firewalls, load balancers, IP addresses, and virtual local area networks.

These are some of the benefits which IaaS provides:

- **Greater flexibility** – IaaS allows access to infrastructure services on-demand. Infrastructure can be scaled to support business growth and reduced when needed.

- **Cost savings** – Physical hardware does not need to be bought every time upgrade is required. Computing infrastructure is provided on a subscription basis, meaning the vendor is the one responsible for infrastructure management.

- **Reliability** – Assets are stored in a remote data center, where it's managed by cloud service providers. This service model all but eliminates the threat of a single point of failure.

IaaS is a highly expandable and lucrative service as outsourcing data centers, cloud components, and servers annihilate the necessity for establishing an in-house infrastructure. This service model can aid in upscaling and downscaling infra service on-demand. IaaS is a good fit for almost all companies from start-ups to very big corporations. Smaller companies benefit from accessing resources that are expensive to build on their own, while big companies benefit from reducing the complexity of managing their own data centers with people and hardware.

Platform as a Service (PaaS)

Such a model allows companies to create, run, and manage software used for application development without the on-site infrastructure. Platforms are provided and maintained by third-party cloud providers. And client companies do not worry about infrastructure operations such as provisioning and backups, which is done for them.

Let's look into some of the benefits of PaaS which include

- **Improved efficiency** – Since the PaaS provider handles commonly used technologies such as servers, databases, and middleware, businesses can spend more time focusing on developing, testing, and deploying applications on top of these technologies.

- **Simplicity** – PaaS provides clients a set of development tools, making it easy and convenient to develop, test, and host applications in the same environment.

- **Elasticity and scalability** – With PaaS clients can easily scale by requesting additional capacity such as increasing the number of databases. Additionally clients can get easier access to new technologies (middleware, queues) without investing in learning how to manage or scale these technology pieces.

Thus, PaaS enables users to emphasize their application resources and effectively manage their data as the rest of the things will be handled efficiently by the vendors. Since the platform is web-accessible, remote development units can have ready access to all the assets ubiquitously. This, in turn, will help them to improve their product development life cycle, resulting in more agile product delivery.

Software as a Service (SaaS)

SaaS is the most well known of these cloud service models to end clients. That's because most people use SaaS applications every day, and when people talk about "the cloud," they're often talking about SaaS applications like Google Drive, Dropbox, or even Netflix.

The SaaS model provides clients with a full functional model that is run and managed by cloud providers. And typically it is accessed via browser with the added convenience of not downloading and installing any applications, because the cloud provider takes care of that.

The most important benefits of the model are

- **Lightweight** – For end clients running SaaS applications does not require as many resources as running on-premises software.

- **No need for software updates** – Since cloud providers manage updates and versioning of software, every user typically works on the same up-to-date software.

- **Pay as you go** – Since premium SaaS applications use the subscription model, it means that clients don't have to worry about buying and renewing software licenses.

SaaS is sometimes referred to as "on-demand software" and is usually priced on a pay-per-use basis or using a subscription fee. Cloud applications also differ from other applications in their scalability – which can be achieved by cloning tasks onto multiple virtual machines at runtime to meet changing work demand. To accommodate a large number of cloud users, cloud applications can be multitenant, meaning that any machine may serve more than one cloud-user organization.

The pricing model for SaaS applications is typically a monthly or yearly flat fee per user, so prices become scalable and adjustable if users are added or removed at any point. SaaS gives a business the potential to reduce IT operational costs by outsourcing hardware and software maintenance and support to the cloud provider. This enables the business to reallocate IT operations costs away from hardware/software spending and from personnel expenses toward meeting other goals.

SaaS is the superset of both PaaS and IaaS as it offers the entire package from infrastructure, middleware, and OS to applications deployed over the Web, which can be seamlessly accessed, invariant to time, place, and platform. This fully developed cloud service model encourages businesses to get going amid the COVID-19 pandemic and respond expeditiously to it as well as scale business operations remotely.

Comparison of the Three Service Models of Cloud Computing

So how to decide what service model is right for the use case? All three cloud models provide businesses with an excellent alternative to on-premises solutions. But each cloud computing model comes with its own benefits and drawbacks. Choosing the right option for the organization depends largely on the needs and what it hopes to gain from migrating to cloud services.

Figure 2-5 demonstrates different levels of support and client involvement required based on the selected service model. It is important to understand that it is not mutually exclusive models, but models rather represent different separation of responsibilities between client and cloud service provider. You can think of IaaS to PaaS to SaaS progression as increase of cloud service provider responsibilities in an attempt to solve more and more common use cases for clients and provide such solutions "out of the box," given client needs align with such common use cases:

1. The SaaS model works "out of the box" with service providers managing the whole stack starting from networking till the applications layer. But SaaS might not provide the full flexibility and customization for all the use cases clients need. SaaS provides common capabilities, but bigger companies tend to have unique business requirements that are not satisfied by SaaS. In such cases customization is built on top of SaaS, effectively turning it into a PaaS model.

2. The PaaS model requires clients to be a bit more involved, which typically means developing and managing its own data and applications. PaaS has similar drawbacks as SaaS, namely, providing clients the most commonly used features and might not satisfy unique business cases clients have. PaaS also is more expensive to use from a money perspective in comparison with running the software on IaaS on your own.

3. The IaaS model requires the most from the client, but at the same time, it is the most flexible. It requires the client to manage everything starting from the virtualization layer, which means O/S,

middleware, runtime, data, and applications. Drawbacks might come in cost, since pricing is often set up in a way that continuous using of resources can become expensive, so clients need to manage their IaaS cost carefully to avoid cost overrun.

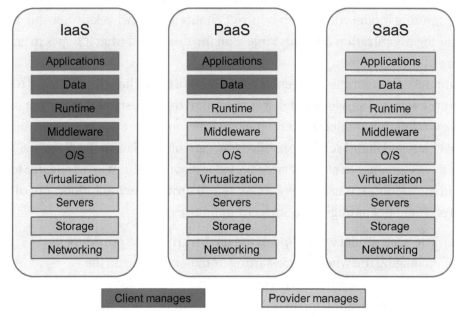

Figure 2-5. *Managing responsibilities between client and cloud service provider*

Common instances of the corresponding SaaS, PaaS, and IaaS models:

1. **SaaS** – Dropbox, Microsoft Office 360, Salesforce, Slack, JIRA

2. **PaaS** – AWS RDS, Azure SQL Database, Amazon AWS Elastic, Microsoft Azure AppFabric, Google App Engine, Force.com

3. **IaaS** – Amazon EC2, Microsoft Azure, Google Cloud Platform, DigitalOcean

When Should You Use IaaS?

One of the common use cases is when an organization needs computing power, but does not have time or resources to upgrade it, or trying to reduce cost in the future, and IaaS can help here. Some additional reasons might include

- Organization requires rapid deployment and/or reduction of infrastructure based on the business performance.

- Access to greater computing power is required to pursue current or future digital strategies, but the organization doesn't want to own the infrastructure.

- Organization doesn't have the IT personnel to manage the infrastructure while pursuing other high-value projects.

With the choice of the service provider, the decision on the type of service model needs to be made:

- A private cloud, which will be used exclusively by the organization. It offers companies more flexibility and control over their infrastructure, but it's more expensive.

- A public cloud, which would be used by multiple organizations. It is cheaper and provides customers powerful computing power, but companies have less control over their configurations.

- Or a hybrid approach, which uses both public and private infrastructure. It offers the best of both worlds, but it can be significantly more challenging to implement and maintain.

Some organizations opt to use a private cloud for security reasons. While that doesn't mean that the public cloud is not secure, accessing the cloud environment is fundamentally different. The private cloud is accessed through private network links, whereas the public cloud isn't. We will discuss deployment models more in detail shortly.

When Should You Use PaaS?

PaaS is best bet when an organization requires a flexible computing platform for developing and testing applications and software. And whether the company simply implements agile methodologies or specializes in software development PaaS can help.

PaaS provides tools to quickly build, test, and deploy applications so you can develop iteratively and modify software based on customer feedback.

Let's list some reasons for using PaaS model:

- Projects require the use of technologies such as databases, middleware, etc.

- Business model requires shorter development cycles.

- Solution is required that enables scaling an application as needed, without putting a strain on internal resources.

One potential caveat when choosing a PaaS approach is service provider lock-in. Most providers have their own proprietary technology variations that are not available outside of the provider, which can make it challenging to migrate from one platform to another.

When Should You Use SaaS?

SaaS is the model for companies that need applications, but don't have a need for developing such software in-house. So in such case SaaS is a great excellent solution for small- and medium-sized businesses that

- Need business productivity software

- Do not have the expertise to develop required software

- Do not want to deploy and manage vendor provided software on-premise or in a private cloud

One of the caveats to know is that SaaS solutions prioritize configuration over customization. Most vendors develop SaaS applications with the aim of serving as many customers as they can. While clients can configure these applications to suit their unique needs, they probably won't be able to customize them if a one-of-a-kind software solution is needed.

Cloud Deployment Models

A cloud deployment is an installation of hardware and software that is accessible over the Internet on a specialized platform. Platforms are coming as one of the delivering models described previously: Software as a Service (SaaS), Platform as a Service (PaaS), Infrastructure as a Service (IaaS), and other possible hybrid solutions. Each of these different solutions is offered to end users, businesses, and other providers so that they can perform specific tasks.

Good understanding of the four deployment models is important to make an optimal choice for each specific use case. These models are public cloud, private cloud, community cloud, and hybrid cloud. These are not the only cloud deployment models, but they are certainly the most popular.

Public Cloud Deployments

Public cloud deployments are performed on public servers that are available over the Internet or through a VPN service. All of the hardware such as VM hosts and network equipment belongs to the service owner. The service owner maintains and manages all of the available resources. This makes it far less onerous to operate IT infrastructure for companies that do not want to invest heavily in hardware and software.

Additional advantage of this type of deployment is that there is no need to hire additional people to support service components, which is again taken care of by service providers. Most popular cloud service providers allow for easy and streamlined ways of provisioning resources and scaling them up/down. But there are some things to be considered, especially in the area of privacy and data segmentation, which is a very real concern for many organizations. Usually it is quite acceptable to use public cloud infra even for the majority of government uses, which demands high degrees of compute/storage/networking isolation, as long as good practices are utilized. But some extreme needs with high regulatory requirements would require private cloud solutions. Some additional concerns may come from the connection speed, since end users or services will need to connect to that service, so the minimum connection speed will need to be confirmed.

The benefits of public cloud deployments are as follows:

- **Easy to manage** – The great thing about having a managed service is that there is very little for you and your team to do on the maintenance front. The setup is taken care of, and there is no need to develop your own tools as this is also accounted for.

- **Cost** – The way services are billed means that you don't pay for items that you don't use. You can pay more when you need more resources, and then scale back when that levels out again. It is also much cheaper to use resources in a different region in the world without having to first build up a data center in that region.

- **Performance and reliability** – Uptime is the main concern that most businesses have. If your systems are down, then your business suffers. Many of these cloud providers offer exceptional uptime and service availability.

The disadvantages of public cloud deployments are as follows:

- **Less control** – You are not in control of the systems that host your business applications. In the unlikely event that a public cloud platform fails, you do not have access to ensure continuity as would be the case with a traditional server room or data center environment.

- **Privacy and security** – Segmentation needs to be carried out to the highest standard to ensure that there is no cross contamination between clients that are using the same hardware on a public cloud.

- **Cost** – Cost might be not only advantage but disadvantage as well, which depends on how cloud resources are used. While noncontinuous usage cost is lower with public cloud, continuous usage is much more expensive. In case continuous usage is needed, the typical solution is instead to prepay (reserve) the resources with a commitment for a certain period (i.e., of 1/2/3 years), much like a lease agreement.

- **Simple environments** – Most organizations have specific requirements for tailor-made services. Many cloud platforms offer only common functionality with little to no customization opportunities.

The largest cloud service providers today include Amazon Web Services, Microsoft Azure, Alibaba Cloud, Google Cloud, and IBM. There are a range of providers to choose from, both large and small, each offering its own menu of services.

However, there are some workloads that simply won't work in the public cloud - for example, legacy applications that are too difficult or risky to migrate. As such, the private cloud remains a critical part of your cloud strategy.

Private Cloud Deployments

The private cloud deployment model is the exact opposite of the public cloud deployment model. It's a one-on-one environment for a single user (customer). There is no need to share your hardware with anyone else. But although there are differences between public and private cloud platforms in terms of access, underneath the hood there isn't all that much to differentiate the two.

The distinction between private and public cloud is in how you handle all of the hardware. It is also called the "internal cloud," and it refers to the ability to access systems and services within a given border or organization. The cloud platform is implemented in a cloud-based secure environment that is protected by powerful firewalls and under the supervision of an organization's IT department. The private cloud gives the greater flexibility of control over cloud resources.

A company might choose to have their cloud infrastructure on premise or hosted at a data center. In either case the company usually owns the infrastructure. The systems that run on a private cloud are designed and maintained by the company's own staff. Access is strictly controlled so that only authorized users have access to the private cloud's resources. A great thing about this type of cloud platform is that there are opportunities to integrate the cloud services into your organization's own infrastructure.

Pros of private cloud deployments are

- **Increased control** – Access to the administration and configuration of the back-end infrastructure that powers the private cloud would be limited, which gives you more control.

- **Customization** – If there is a new business case or a new requirement, it can be developed and deployed in-house, giving you more options than a publicly available cloud.

- **Higher security** – Many security services could be incorporated in order to secure your private cloud. Two-factor authentication is far more secure when combined with security best practices such as complex passwords and mandatory password changes.

- **Cost** – Similarly to public cloud cost is both a benefit and drawback depending on use case. For very large companies because for continuous usage scenarios, it would be much cheaper to build in house than it is to hire others to do this work

Cons of private cloud deployments are

- **Learning curve** – To take advantage of being able to customize your private cloud, you need the right technical skills. Developers, cybersecurity experts, and DevOps professionals are all roles that you need to fill in order to effectively develop a solution on your private cloud.

- **Cost** – All but the largest companies in the world can afford to set up their own private cloud infrastructure. The hardware costs alone are prohibitively expensive for most companies. There's also the cost of keeping skilled staff and other infrastructure costs. This is a cloud deployment method that is aimed at large organizations and not SMBs.

- **The lack of elasticity** – It takes time (even if it is cheaper) to acquire additional resources (buy servers, networking, etc.) when the need expands.

Community Cloud Deployments

Community cloud shares infrastructure between several organizations from a specific community with common concerns (security, compliance, jurisdiction, etc.), whether managed internally or by a third party, and either hosted internally or externally. The costs are spread over fewer users than a public cloud (but more than a private cloud), so only some of the cost savings potential of cloud computing are realized. So by sharing the infrastructure between multiple companies, community cloud installations are able to save their members money. Data is still segmented and kept private, except in areas where shared access is agreed upon and configured.

The main benefits are the shared costs and the increase in opportunities to collaborate in real time across the same infrastructure. Uniformity of best practices will help to increase the overall security and efficiency of these setups, so they rely quite heavily on effective cooperation between tenants.

Pros of community cloud deployments are

- **Cost** – The main benefit of using community cloud is that there are cost savings. This is because all of the users that access the community cloud will share the costs to create desired experience.

- **Security between tenants** – In such cases security policies are usually aligned, and thus if everyone follows the same standards, then the community cloud model is very secure.

- **Enhanced collaboration** – When there is a shared goal, then having everyone on the same platform creates more opportunities to work together toward the same objectives.

And cons of community cloud deployments are

- **Technical requirements** – A community cloud has to agree upon what are requirements to the shared cloud. This means that each stakeholder must have their own technical resources available to enforce the policies.

- **Data isolation** – Security and segmentation is difficult to maintain.

- **Rarity** – This model is not widely used yet, so there are not too many resources available for people to learn from or well-known examples.

Hybrid Cloud

Hybrid cloud is a composition of a public cloud and a private environment, such as a private cloud or on-premise resources, that remain distinct entities but are bound together, offering the benefits of multiple deployment models. So it is a cloud computing service that is composed of some combination of private, public, and community cloud services, from different service providers. A hybrid cloud service crosses isolation and provider boundaries so that it can't be simply put in one category of private, public, or community cloud service. It allows one to extend either the capacity or the capability of a cloud service, by aggregation, integration, or customization with another cloud service.

Hybrid clouds can also partition different services onto different cloud models. Sensitive data can be stored on a private cloud, user functions can be placed on a public cloud, and collaborative projects with strategic partners can be offloaded onto a community cloud.

Pros of hybrid cloud deployments are

- **Flexibility** – This type of deployment is very flexible. You can pick the best parts of each cloud type and integrate it into your solution.

- **Scalability** – You are not limited to any one platform and so to its limitations. This means that you can scale with the demand of your users.

- **Cost** – If executed correctly companies don't need to spend time and money migrating legacy software to the public cloud, can utilize the elasticity of the public cloud for workloads that are not continuous, and utilize private cloud for continuous workloads that are cost-efficient and predictable.

Con of hybrid cloud deployments is

- **Data isolation** – If you are using a combination of public and private services, you have to make sure that all of your data has been properly separated. This can increase the security, compliance, and auditing requirements of your business.

Varied use cases for hybrid cloud composition exist. For example, an organization may store sensitive client data in house on a private cloud application, but interconnect that application to a business intelligence application provided on a public cloud as a software service. This example of hybrid cloud extends the capabilities of the enterprise to deliver a specific business service through the addition of externally available public cloud services. Hybrid cloud adoption depends on a number of factors such as data security and compliance requirements, level of control needed over data, and the applications an organization uses.

It could be challenging to select the right deployment model; thus, many different considerations need to be taken into account, and the number of providers and vendors that offer cloud-hosting services and products is growing steadily. So to successfully deploy your own cloud infrastructure, it is important to know about these models and corresponding benefits and disadvantages they bring.

Virtualization

What is virtualization? In computing, virtualization is the process of creating a virtual version of something at the same abstraction level, including virtual computer hardware platforms, storage devices, and computer network resources. So virtualization is a technology that lets you create useful IT services using resources that are traditionally bound to hardware. It allows you to use a physical machine's full capacity by distributing its capabilities among many users or environments.

Imagine you have three different physical servers where you run three different services with different purposes. One could be a web server, second a mail server, and third one some legacy server for legacy backward compatibility. And each server is used at 20% of the capacity, which is a fraction of its potential. But since all the applications are important (including legacy one), you need to run all the three physical servers to host them.

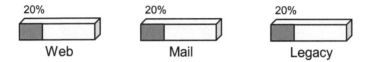

Figure 2-6. *Before virtualization*

And traditionally it was always easier to add a separate server to run a separate purpose process/application, 1 server, 1 OS, and 1 task. But with virtualization, you can split one server into two unique ones that can handle independent tasks, so, for example, the legacy apps can be migrated to the mail server. It's the same hardware; you're just using more of it more efficiently.

Figure 2-7. *With virtualization*

With the right security approach in mind, you could split the server again so it could handle web server task which would increase server use from 40% further to 60%. Once you do that, the now empty servers could be reused for other tasks or retired altogether to reduce maintenance costs.

Virtualization began in the 1960s, as a method of logically dividing the system resources provided by mainframe computers between different applications. An early and successful example is IBM CP/CMS. The control program CP provided each user with a simulated stand-alone System/360 computer. But it was not widely adopted until the 2000s.

The technologies that enabled virtualization, like hypervisors, were developed in the 1970s to give multiple users simultaneous access to computers that performed batch processing. Batch processing was a popular computing style in the business sector that ran routine tasks thousands of times very quickly (like payroll).

Over the next few decades, other solutions grew in popularity to the many users/ single machine problem. One of those solutions was time-sharing, which isolated users within operating systems, which led to other operating systems like UNIX, and eventually Linux. But during all this time, virtualization remained a largely unadopted, niche technology.

In the 1990s most enterprises had physical servers and single-vendor IT stacks, which didn't allow legacy apps to run on a different vendor's hardware. As companies updated their IT environments with less-expensive commodity servers, operating systems, and applications from a variety of vendors, the problem of underused physical hardware was becoming more and more visible – each server could only run one vendor-specific task. And it was the time when virtualization started taking off, and it was a solution for the following problem: companies could partition their servers and run legacy apps on multiple operating system types and versions. With the adoption of virtualizations, servers are used more efficiently with associated reduction in cost.

Virtualization's widespread applicability helped reduce vendor lock-in and made it the foundation of cloud computing, which is so widely used across enterprises today that specialized virtualization management software is often needed to help keep track of it all.

Types of Virtualization

There are several different types of virtualization which are widely used; let's discuss them in more detail.

Hardware Virtualization

Hardware virtualization is the creation of a virtual machine that acts like a real computer with an operating system. Software executed on these virtual machines is separated from the underlying hardware resources. As an example, a computer that is running Linux may host a virtual machine that looks like a computer with the Microsoft Windows operating system, and Windows-based software can be run on the virtual machine.

Terms host and guest machine are respectively used to refer to a machine which is used by virtualization and the virtual machine itself.

Types of hardware virtualization are

- **Full virtualization** – Almost complete simulation of the actual hardware to allow software environments, including a guest operating system and its apps, to run unmodified.

- **Paravirtualization** – The guest apps are executed in their own isolated domains, as if they are running on a separate system, but a hardware environment is not simulated. Guest programs need to be specifically modified to run in this environment.

So how does hardware virtualization work? The important component is a software called hypervisor, which is computer software, firmware, or hardware that creates and runs virtual machines. A computer on which a hypervisor runs one or more virtual machines is called a host machine, and each virtual machine is called a guest machine. The term hypervisor is a variant of supervisor, a traditional term for the kernel of an operating system: the hypervisor is the supervisor of the supervisors, with hyper- used as a stronger variant of super-.

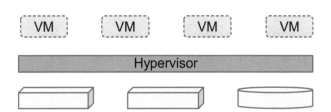

Figure 2-8. *How virtualization works*

Hypervisor separates the physical resources from the virtual environments – the things that need those resources. Hypervisors can run in the operating system or on the hardware directly, and they take physical resources of the server and divide them between virtual environments so they can use them. Resources are partitioned as needed from the physical environment to the many virtual environments. Users work with and run operating systems, applications, and processes within the virtual machine.

OS-Level Virtualization

It is an operating system (OS) paradigm in which the kernel allows the existence of multiple isolated user space instances, which could be called containers, zones, partitions, virtual environments, etc., depending on the implementation.

Such instances may look like real computers from the point of view of programs running in them. A computer program running on an ordinary operating system can see all resources (connected devices, files and folders, network shares, CPU power, quantifiable hardware capabilities) of that computer. However, programs running inside of a container can only see the container's contents and devices assigned to the container.

Operating system–level virtualization is commonly used in virtual hosting environments, where it is useful for securely allocating finite hardware resources among a large number of mutually distrusting users. System administrators may also use it for consolidating server hardware by moving services on separate hosts into containers on the one server.

Other typical scenarios include separating several programs to separate containers for improved security, hardware independence, and added resource management features. The improved security provided by the use of a chroot mechanism, however, is nowhere near ironclad.

With operating system virtualization, or containerization, it is possible to run programs within containers, to which only parts of these resources are allocated. We will cover containerization in more detail in further sections.

Desktop Virtualization

Not to be confused with operating system virtualization, desktop virtualization allows a central administrator (or automated administration tool) to deploy simulated desktop environments to hundreds of physical machines at once. Desktop virtualization also allows admins to perform mass configurations, updates, and security checks on all virtual desktops.

Desktop virtualization implementations are classified based on whether the virtual desktop runs remotely or locally, on whether the access is required to be constant or is designed to be intermittent, and on whether or not the virtual desktop persists between sessions.

Virtualization is employed to present independent instances to multiple users and requires a strategic segmentation of the host server and presentation at some layer of the host's architecture.

There are several types of desktop virtualization:

- **Remote desktop virtualization** – Remote desktop virtualization implementations operate in a client/server computing environment. Application execution takes place on a remote operating system which communicates with the local client device over a network using a remote display protocol through which the user interacts with applications. All applications and data used remain on the remote system with only display, keyboard, and mouse information communicated with the local client device, which may be a conventional PC/laptop, a thin client device, a tablet, or even a smartphone.

- **Application virtualization** – Application virtualization improves delivery and compatibility of applications by encapsulating them from the underlying operating system on which they are executed. A fully virtualized application is not installed on hardware in the traditional sense. Instead, a hypervisor layer intercepts the application, which at runtime acts as if it is interfacing with the original operating system and all the resources managed by it when in reality it is not.

- **User virtualization** – User virtualization separates all of the software aspects that define a user's personality on a device from the operating system and applications to be managed independently and applied to a desktop as needed without the need for scripting, group policies, or use of roaming profiles.

- **Local desktop virtualization** – Local desktop virtualization implementations run the desktop environment on the client device using hardware virtualization or emulation.

Benefits of Virtualization

Virtualizing resources lets administrators pool their physical resources, so their hardware can truly be commoditized with a wide set of associated benefits. So the advantages of utilizing a virtualized environment include the following:

- **Lower costs** – Virtualization reduces the amount of hardware servers necessary within a company and data center. This lowers the overall cost of buying and maintaining large amounts of hardware.

- **Easier disaster recovery** – Disaster recovery is very simple in a virtualized environment. Regular snapshots provide up-to-date data, allowing virtual machines to be feasibly backed up and recovered. Even in an emergency, a virtual machine can be migrated to a new location within minutes.

- **Improved productivity** – Fewer physical resources result in less time spent managing and maintaining the servers, although there could be an increase in complexity due to the introduction of an additional (virtual) layer to manage. Tasks to expand physical infrastructure that can take days or weeks while adding virtual machines on existing servers can be done in minutes. This allows staff members to spend the majority of their time on more productive tasks, such as raising revenue and fostering business initiatives.

Virtualization provides companies with the benefit of maximizing their output. Additional benefits for both businesses and data centers include the following:

- **Single-minded servers** – Virtualization provides a cost-effective way to separate email, database, and web servers, creating a more comprehensive and dependable system.

- **Expedited deployment and redeployment** – When a physical server crashes, the backup server may not always be ready or up to date. If this is the case, then the redeployment process can be time-consuming and tedious. However, if the data center is virtualized, then the process is quick and fairly simple. Virtual backup tools can expedite the process to minutes.

- **Better for the environment** – Companies and data centers that utilize copious amounts of hardware leave a large carbon footprint; they must take responsibility for the pollution they are generating. Virtualization can help reduce these effects by significantly decreasing the necessary amounts of cooling and power, thus helping clean the air and the atmosphere. As a result, companies and data centers that virtualize will improve their reputation while also enhancing the quality of their relationship with customers and the planet.

- **Easier migration to the cloud** – Virtualization brings companies closer to experiencing a completely cloud-based environment. Virtual machines may even be deployed from the data center in order to build a cloud-based infrastructure. The ability to embrace a cloud-based mindset with virtualization makes migrating to the cloud even easier.

- **Lack of vendor dependency** – Virtual machines are agnostic in hardware configuration. As a result, virtualizing hardware and software means that a company does not need to depend on a vendor for these physical resources.

But virtualization does not come without limitations or caveats, and it is important to consider all the upfront costs if converting to virtualization. The necessary investment in virtualization software, as well as hardware that might be required to make the virtualization possible, can be costly, especially for older hardware. But it is where cloud service providers can offer a solution, when by moving into cloud organizations effectively adopt virtualization as well.

There is also software licensing that needs to be considered when moving ahead with virtualization. Converting to virtualization takes time and may come with a learning curve. Implementing and controlling a virtualized environment demands each IT staff member to be trained and possess expertise in virtualization.

There are also security risks involved with virtualization. A common target for attacks is crucial business data, and the chances of experiencing a data breach significantly increase while using virtualization.

Virtual Machine Management

A VM management system is a software that interfaces with virtual environments and the underlying physical hardware to simplify resource administration, enhance data analyses, and streamline operations. There are different VM management systems, but they are mostly represented by an uncomplicated user interface, streamline the virtual machine (VM) creation process, monitor virtual environments, allocate resources, compile reports, and automatically enforce rules.

It depends on how big and diverse the environments are or on how experienced the IT team is, but VM management software might make life a lot easier. Large enterprise-wide deployments use VM management software to help their systems be successful since they cannot depend on single (or more) system administrators to manually manage systems anymore.

Someone needs to tell hypervisors what to do in order to provision VMs. And that is usually a combination of the three following responsibilities:

- **Provisioning** – Processing resource requests, creating templates, and configuring VMs

- **Compliance** – Securing and monitoring systems, identifying issues, and validating user access

- **Operations** – Retiring or reclaiming unused or underused physical resources, investigating bugs, and projecting future needs

Managing virtual environments seems pretty straightforward, they contain physical hardware and VMs, but it can get complicated if there are too many instances.

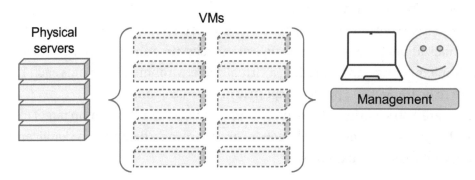

Figure 2-9. *VM management*

Even if simple maintenance tasks are easy, spreading them out to large amounts of instances could be overwhelming to do manually. Imagine an easy analogy with a hotel, where every room is a VM, each of it needs to make sure to watch over smaller issues like that lights are off, doors are locked, and water isn't left running in each room. These are simple tasks that can become really, really time-consuming. But what if outlets, faucets, and locks were synced to an app that automatically turned the lights off, locked the doors, and checked pipe flow in empty rooms after guests checked out. In such a case, the job of maintaining rooms becomes much easier. So similarly with VM management, software can take some of that burden off IT professionals' shoulders so they can solve big, enterprise-wide problems.

Companies have different requirements based on a company's unique business situation, IT stack, and experience level. It is a lot to consider when it comes to choosing the right VM management tools. But the right tools do exist, and the best of them unify heterogeneous environments in a vendor-neutral and scalable solution – giving IT admins greater efficiency without increasing operational expenses. Some of these tools are VMware VCenter Server, SolarWinds Virtualization Manager, Microsoft Hyper-V, IBM Turbonomic, and others.

Containerization

Containerization is the packaging together of software code with all its necessary components like libraries, frameworks, and other dependencies so that they are free from interference from other applications that may use incompatible libraries and dependencies. The software or application within the container can run consistently in any environment and on any infrastructure. The container acts as a computing environment surrounding the application and keeping it independent of other containers, making it a fully functional and portable computing environment.

Coding on a one platform or operating system historically was making it difficult to move software around since the code might not then be compatible with the new environment due to different required dependencies (such as library versions). By packaging up an application in a container, dependencies are included and not mixed with other container dependencies. This makes the running of containers predictable across platforms and infrastructures.

The ability to isolate application execution has been supported by operating system for a long time, but it was not until Docker introduced Docker Engine in 2013. Docker created a container orchestration software by providing convenient and easy to use application isolation within the operating system for developers. It also provided a universal approach for packaging, which then accelerated the adoption of container technology.

Containers provided a benefit of being lightweight and portable solution to run software removing the need for a separate operating system for each application and allowing multiple applications to run on the same operating system, yet still achieving application level isolation.

Container Architecture

Containers are isolated from one another and bundle their own software, libraries, and configuration files; they can communicate with each other through well-defined channels. Because all of the containers share the services of a single operating system kernel, they use fewer resources than virtual machines. Containers are software programs and do not require an operating system to be installed into it. All applications within a container run in the user space of the OS which allows applications to communicate with the CPU without passing through the guest operating system and then the hypervisor. As a result, containers offer better performance.

Containers replicate the file system and enable users to run applications in a secure environment. All of the resources and the files run within the container file system. The environment variables along with the libraries are stored within the containers. This promotes faster execution of instructions in containers when compared to the hypervisor based instances.

Containers are launched by a container engine. Subsequently a container engine can launch a number of containers. The containers have a file-based configuration system. These files can be versioned, backed up, and monitored.

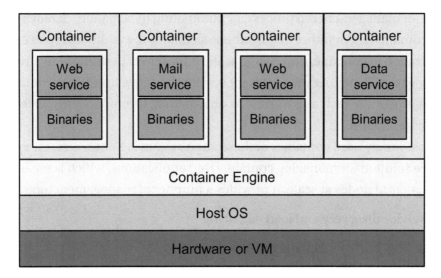

Figure 2-10. *Container architecture*

Containers are represented by image files, which hold the entire information that the containers need to execute. All containers can share the same OS; therefore, they can all share the same kernel. As a result, the boot-up time is faster. This design increases efficiency in container-based architecture.

Containers and Microservices

Since containers are often used to package single functions that perform specific tasks, usage of container-based infrastructure encourages the usage of microservices. This allows developers to focus on working on a specific area of an application, without impacting the app's overall performance. Microservices and containers work well together, as a microservice within a container has all the portability, compatibility, and scalability of a container.

Container Management

When a company relies on containers to quickly deploy and update applications, it is necessary to use container management systems, such as Kubernetes and Docker Swarm, which are designed to handle the rapid changes in DevOps strategy. Containers need management services because a vast number of containers can become too complex for an IT team to handle.

Container management is a process for automating the creation, deployment, and scaling of containers. Container management facilitates the addition, replacement, and organization of containers on a large scale. It makes orchestration, security, and networking easier. Container management systems handle a number of containerized application processes, such as governance, automation, layered security, extensibility, and enterprise support.

The most widely used container orchestration system is Kubernetes, an extensible, open source solution for managing containerized applications, which is meant to manage clusters of nodes at scale. It provides a number of management tools, such as

- Service discovery and load balancing

- Rollout and rollback automation

- Storage orchestration

- Configuration management

While simple container hosting (such as Docker) is sufficient for very basic private setups based in a single data center. However, the cloud architecture of most organizations demands an orchestrated approach, such as that provided by Kubernetes. Organizations can also choose to use managed Kubernetes services from their cloud provider, such as AWS EKS or Azure Kubernetes Service.

There are a number of benefits that effective container management provides:

- **Ease of setup** – Container management includes storage, security tools, schedulers, monitoring systems, and more, significantly reducing hosting setup complexities.

- **Simplified administration** – Good container management makes it easier for IT teams to administer and keep up with their containerized environments, as well as decreasing the time and resources needed for DevOps processes.

- **Automation** – Container management automates a number of processes, from load balancing to orchestration.

- **Continuous health checks** – Container management platforms like Kubernetes provide automatic health checks on apps, monitoring your environment for containers that have failed or stalled.

Container management provides a variety of benefits but also comes with some challenges. One of which is security, since the container's lightweight package makes it more vulnerable to hacking, as well as dependencies such as API servers, and monitoring tools make containers more vulnerable to attack. But there are technologies, however, which are integrating containers within other IT systems to improve the security potential of containers. Some additional challenges for moving to containers infrastructure could be

- **Learning curve for engineers, who have not worked with containers yet** – One solution could be just engaging with a service provider to deploy containers on a managed service.

- **Storage required for container images** – Again a number of managed solutions exist on cloud providers, such as AWS ECR.

- **Troubleshooting** – Since containers are dynamically deployed to different hosts based on suitability at a given time, they often switch between hosts, which adds an additional step to troubleshooting. Additional container monitoring tools will be needed.

Kubernetes is the most widely used container management software, and there are many tools that exist that collaborate with Kubernetes to provide specific aspects of container management, such as Mesos, D2iQ, and Docker's swarm mode.

Since Kubernetes is the most popular solution to container management, let's talk a bit more about how it works. A Kubernetes cluster consists of at least one control plane and at least one worker node (typically a physical or virtual server). The control plane has two main responsibilities. It exposes the Kubernetes API through the API server and manages the nodes that make up the cluster. The control plane makes decisions about cluster management and detects and responds to cluster events. The smallest unit of execution for an application running in Kubernetes is the Kubernetes Pod, which consists of one or more containers. Kubernetes Pods run on worker nodes.

The control plane purpose is to control communications, manage nodes, and keep track of the state of a Kubernetes cluster:

- It exposes Kubernetes API.

- Contains a key-value store where all data for the Kubernetes cluster is stored.

- Kube scheduler, which watches for new Kubernetes Pods with no assigned nodes and assigns them to a node for execution based on resources and policies.

- And Kube controller-manager, which is responsible for control functions.

Kubernetes nodes also consist of several components:

- **Kubelet** – An agent that makes sure that the necessary containers are running in a Kubernetes Pod.

- **Kube proxy** – A network proxy that runs on each node in a cluster to maintain network rules and allow communication.

- **Container runtime** – The software responsible for running containers.

Kubernetes is the most popular solution because it provides all the benefits of container management listed previously and it is cost-efficient, API-based, and easily integratable into CI/CD and has a large ecosystem.

Infrastructure as Code

Infrastructure as Code (IaC) is the managing and provisioning of infrastructure through code instead of through manual processes. IaC was developed and gained popularity as the result of the difficulty posed by utility computing and second-generation web frameworks. In 2006, the launch of Amazon Web Services' Elastic Compute Cloud created widespread scaling problems in the enterprise that were previously experienced only at large, multinational companies. The need to deploy large and complicated infrastructure setup was growing, and that is why the thought of modeling infrastructure with code, and then having the ability to design, implement, and deploy application infrastructure with known software best practices appealed to both software developers and IT infrastructure administrators. The ability to treat infrastructure as code and use the same tools as any other software project would allow developers to rapidly deploy applications.

With IaC developers write configuration files which contain infrastructure details and specifications. Via configuration files it is easy to edit and distribute configurations. It also ensures that you provision the same environment every time. With this approach it is also easy to document details and changes, which could be just part of the configuration file itself.

Also configuration files would be a subject for version control just like any other software source code file. IaC also allows the division of the infrastructure into modular components that can then be combined in different ways through automation.

Automating infrastructure provisioning with IaC means that developers don't need to manually provision and manage servers, operating systems, storage, and other infrastructure components each time they develop or deploy an application.

There are two types of IaC: declarative and imperative. And the difference between the declarative and the imperative approach is essential "what" vs. "how":

- **Declarative IaC** defines the state of the system, including what resources you need and any properties they should have, and an IaC tool will configure it for you. A declarative approach also keeps a list of the current state of your system objects, which makes taking down the infrastructure simpler to manage.

- **Imperative IaC** in turn defines the specific commands needed to achieve the desired configuration, and those commands then need to be executed in the correct order.

As you see the declarative approach focuses on what the eventual target configuration should be; the imperative focuses on how the infrastructure is to be changed to meet this. Many IaC tools use a declarative approach and will automatically provision the desired infrastructure. If you make changes to the desired state, a declarative IaC tool will apply those changes for you. An imperative tool will require you to figure out how those changes should be applied.

The value of IaC can be seen into three measurable categories:

- **Cost** – While using IaC, a significant cost reduction can be achieved. It aims at helping not only the enterprise financially but also in terms of people and effort, meaning that by removing the manual component, people are able to refocus their efforts on other enterprise tasks.

- **Speed** – Infrastructure automation enables speed through faster execution when configuring your infrastructure and aims at providing visibility to help other teams across the enterprise work quickly and more efficiently.

- **Risk** – Automation removes the risk associated with human error, like manual misconfiguration; removing this can decrease downtime and increase reliability.

Especially with cloud computing, the number of infrastructure components has grown, and more applications are being released to production on a daily basis, and infrastructure needs to be able to be spun up, scaled, and taken down frequently. IaC can help the organization to manage IT infrastructure needs while also improving consistency and reducing errors and manual configuration.

Also the outcomes and attributes of IaC help the enterprise move toward implementing a culture of DevOps, the combined working of development and operations. IaC takes away the majority of provisioning work from developers, who can execute a script to have their infrastructure ready to go. DevOps relies on ongoing automation and continuous monitoring throughout the application life cycle, from integration and testing to delivery and deployment. And IaC helps DevOps in the following ways:

- Aligning development and operations teams through a DevOps approach leads to fewer errors, manual deployments, and inconsistencies.

- The same deployment process is used for every environment (dev, QA, production).

- Removes the need to maintain individual deployment environments with unique configurations that can't be reproduced automatically.

- Infrastructure can go through the same CI/CD pipeline as an application does during software development, applying the same testing and version control to the infrastructure code.

Server automation and configuration management tools can often be used to achieve IaC. There are solutions specifically for IaC such as AWS CloudFormation, Chef, Puppet, Terraform, Red Hat Ansible Automation Platform, Saltstack, and others.

Serverless Computing

Serverless computing is a cloud computing model in which the cloud provider allocates machine resources on demand, taking care of the servers on behalf of their customers. Although servers are still used by service providers, the fact of its use and implementation is hidden from clients, and developers of serverless applications are not concerned with capacity planning, configuration, management, maintenance, fault tolerance, or scaling of containers, VMs, or physical servers.

In serverless computing resources are provided on a per-use basis. A company that gets back-end services from a serverless vendor is charged based on their computation and does not have to reserve and pay for a fixed amount of bandwidth or number of servers, as the service is autoscaling. Serverless computing allows developers to purchase back-end services on a flexible "pay-as-you-go" basis, meaning that developers only have to pay for the services they use.

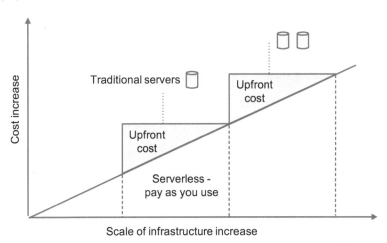

Figure 2-11. *Cost of serverless vs. traditional deployment*

Serverless computing can simplify the process of deploying code into production. Serverless code can be used in conjunction with code deployed in traditional styles, such as microservices or monoliths. Alternatively, applications can be written to be purely serverless and use no provisioned servers at all.

Serverless vendors offer compute runtimes, also known as Function as a Service (FaaS) platforms, which execute application logic but do not store data. FaaS allows developers to execute small pieces of code on the network edge. With FaaS, developers can build a modular architecture, making a code base that is more scalable without having to spend resources on maintaining the underlying back end.

The first "pay-as-you-go" code execution platform was Zimki, released in 2006, but it was not commercially successful. In 2008, Google released Google App Engine, which featured metered billing for applications that used a custom Python framework and was the first abstract serverless computing offering but could not execute arbitrary code. PiCloud, released in 2010, offered FaaS support for Python. AWS Lambda, introduced by Amazon in 2014, popularized the abstract serverless computing model. It is supported by a number of additional AWS serverless tools such as AWS Serverless Application Model (AWS SAM) Amazon CloudWatch, and others.

Let's understand what are the advantages and what are the disadvantages of the serverless compute.

The advantages are

- **Lower costs** – Serverless computing is generally very cost-effective, as traditional cloud providers of back-end services (server allocation) often result in the user paying for unused space or idle CPU time.

- **Simplified scalability** – Developers using serverless architecture don't have to worry about policies to scale up their code. The serverless vendor handles all of the scaling on demand.

- **Simplified back-end code** – With FaaS, developers can create simple functions that independently perform a single purpose, like making an API call.

- **Quicker turnaround** – Serverless architecture can significantly cut time to market. Instead of needing a complicated deploy process to roll out bug fixes and new features, developers can add and modify code on a piecemeal basis.

Disadvantages of serverless compute are

- **Performance** – When code which is deployed on serverless architecture used infrequently, it can suffer from greater response latency. It is because the cloud provider typically "spins down" the serverless code completely when not in use.

- **Resource limits** – Is not suited to some computing workloads, such as high-performance computing, because of the resource limits imposed by cloud providers and also because it would likely be cheaper to bulk-provision the number of servers required for constant computations.

- **Monitoring and debugging** – Diagnosing performance or resource usage problems could be difficult to debug. And the environment in which the code runs is typically not open source, so its performance cannot be accurately replicated in a local environment by developers.

- **Security** – There are usually far more moving pieces underneath the serverless service which creates a larger attack surface than traditional architectures. This is amplified by the fact that provider use the same architecture for the entire network and a single flaw or vulnerability can be applied globally.

- **Privacy** – Many serverless function environments are based on proprietary public cloud environments, and it does not give companies full control over privacy mechanisms, just as with hosting in traditional server setups.

- **Vendor lock-in** – Serverless computing is provided as a third-party service. Applications and software that run in the serverless environment are by default locked to a specific cloud vendor Therefore, serverless can cause multiple issues during migration.

Serverless computing continues to evolve as serverless providers come up with solutions to overcome some of its drawbacks. For example, some serverless service providers solve performance (cold start of not used code) by spinning up serverless functions in advance, during the TLS handshake during connection.

Cloud Storage

Cloud storage is a cloud computing model that stores data on the Internet through a cloud computing provider who manages and operates data storage as a service. The data is stored by the cloud provider on the physical storage layer which spans multiple servers, sometimes in multiple locations. Cloud storage is delivered on demand with just-in-time capacity and costs, which eliminates buying and managing the client's own data storage infrastructure. This gives agility, global scale, and durability, with "anytime, anywhere" data access.

Cloud computing was invented by Joseph Carl Robnett Licklider in the 1960s with his work on ARPANET to connect people and data from anywhere at any time.[1] First remote storage was observed in 1983 when CompuServe offered its consumer users a small amount of disk space that could be used to store any files they chose to upload. In 1994, AT&T launched PersonaLink Services, which was an online platform for personal and business communication and entrepreneurship and was one of the first to be all web-based. Amazon Web Services introduced their cloud storage service AWS S3 in 2006, and has gained widespread recognition and adoption as the storage supplier.

How does cloud storage work? Cloud storage is provided by a cloud storage vendor who owns and operates data storage capacity and delivers it over the Internet in a pay-as-you-go model. Cloud storage vendors also manage capacity, security, and durability for their clients.

Cloud storage heavily utilizes virtualized infrastructure to gain near-instant elasticity and scalability. There are three types of cloud storage: a hosted object storage service, file storage, and block storage. Each of these cloud storage types offers their own unique advantages. Also many vendors offer complementary services designed to help collect, manage, secure, and analyze data at a massive scale.

Object Storage

Object storage is a computer data storage that manages data as objects. All data is stored in one large repository which may be distributed across multiple physical storage devices, instead of being divided into files or folders. Each object typically includes the data itself, a variable amount of metadata (different accompanying information to the main data), and a globally unique identifier. The metadata is added to each object, which makes it possible to access data with no hierarchy.

What are the benefits of object storage?

- **Good data analytics** – Object storage is stored with metadata, and with this level of classification for every piece of data, the opportunity for analysis is very good.

- **Infinite scalability** – Clients can keep adding data as long as they want. There's usually no limit.

---

[1] "A History of Cloud Computing." ComputerWeekly. www.computerweekly.com/Articles/2009/06/10/235429/A-history-of-cloud-computing.htm

- **Fast data retrieval** – Due to the categorization structure of object storage, and the lack of folder hierarchy, you can retrieve your data much faster.

- **Reduction in cost** – Due to the scale-out nature of object storage, it's less costly to store all the data.

- **Optimization of resources** – Because object storage does not have a filing hierarchy, and the metadata is completely customizable, there are far fewer limitations than with file or block storage.

Object storage systems allow retention of massive amounts of unstructured data in which data is written once and read once (or many times). Object storage is used for purposes such as storing objects like videos and photos on Facebook, songs on Spotify, or files in online collaboration services, such as Dropbox.

Network File Storage

File storage stores data in folders. This method, also known as hierarchical storage, simulates how paper documents are stored. When data needs to be accessed, a computer system must look for it using its path in the folder structure. It is the most familiar way of organizing data since it is how files are organized on personal computers.

The data is separated into pieces giving each piece a name. The data is easily isolated and identified. Taking its name from the way a paper-based data management system is named, each group of data is called a file. The structure and logic rules used to manage the groups of data and their names is called a file system.

Block Storage

A block is a sequence of bytes or bits, usually containing some whole number of records, having a maximum length, a block size. The process of putting data into blocks is called blocking, while deblocking is the process of extracting data from blocks.

Block storage splits a file into separate data blocks, and stores each of these blocks as a separate data unit. Each block has an address, and so the storage system can find data without needing a path to a folder. This also allows data to be split into smaller pieces and stored in a distributed manner. Whenever a file is accessed, the storage system software assembles the file from the required blocks.

Cloud Security and Networking

Cloud security is the technology, policies, services, and security controls to protect data, applications, and environments in the cloud. It focuses on

- Ensuring the privacy of data across networks

- Handling the unique cybersecurity concerns of businesses using multiple cloud service providers

- Controlling the access of users, devices, and software

A lot of organizations now host their data and applications using cloud service providers, such as Google Cloud Platform (GCP), Amazon Web Services (AWS), and Microsoft Azure (Azure). Cloud security is a shared responsibility between these cloud service providers and their customers. The level of responsibility between client and service provider is dependent on the model of cloud used: Software as a Service, Platform as a Service, or Infrastructure as a Service.

Table 2-1 provides the breakdown of responsibilities based on the model.

Table 2-1. *Vendor and User responsibilities*

Service model	Vendor responsibility	User responsibility
SaaS	Application security	Endpoints, user and network security; misconfigurations, workloads and data
PaaS	Platform security, including all hardware and software	Security of applications developed on the platform. Endpoints, user and network security, and workloads
IaaS	Security of all infrastructure components	Security of any application installed on the infrastructure (e.g., OS, applications, middleware). Endpoints, user and network security, workloads, and data

Threats and Need for Security

There are some unique cloud security challenges and risks which drive the need for security when cloud solutions are used:

1. **Data breaches** – One of the top concerns for companies today. Data breaches occur differently in the cloud than in on-premise attacks. Malware is less relevant. Instead, attackers exploit misconfigurations, inadequate access, stolen credentials, and other vulnerabilities.

2. **Visibility** – Often companies utilize two or more cloud providers to meet their business or operational needs, and it creates a lack of visibility of the entire cloud environment. Decentralized controls and management, which create blind spots, which are endpoints, workloads, and traffic that are not properly monitored.

3. **Dynamic workloads** – Applications deployed on the cloud are made up of many workloads like VMs, containers, kubernetes, microservices, serverless functions, databases, etc. If not properly secured, each of those workloads makes the application and organization vulnerable to breaches.

4. **Misconfigurations** – Moving fast makes applications vulnerable to misconfigurations, which is today the number one vulnerability in a cloud environment. Misconfigurations create wrong privileges on accounts, not enough logging, and other problems that increase probabilities of data breaches, cloud breaches, and insider threats.

5. **Unsecured APIs** – APIs allow applications to communicate with each other over the Internet or a private network and transfer data, either internally or to partners, suppliers, and customers. So problems with APIs, when they are exposed or hacked, lead to data breaches, exposing financial and other critical data.

6. **Unauthorized access** – Granting more access and permissions than needed to employees is a common occurrence which increases identity-based threats. Also relying on default access

controls of cloud providers could become an issue especially in multicloud or hybrid cloud environments.

7. **Security compliance and auditing** – Cloud compliance and governance, along with industry, international, federal, state, and local regulations, is complex but cannot be ignored. To address them organizations need a comprehensive cybersecurity strategy designed around vulnerabilities specific to the cloud.

Data Centers and the ISPs

We have talked about how the Internet works earlier in the chapter, and also talked about cloud deployment models and associated risks due to exposure of applications and data to the Internet. But where does physically all the application and data reside in the cloud? It resides in the huge sets of servers organized in data centers. Data center is a building, a dedicated space within a building, or a group of buildings used to house computer systems and associated components, networking equipment.

One of the earliest examples of a data center is the huge computer rooms of the 1940s, with very early days computer, ENIAC. It was complex to operate and maintain, and required a special environment in which to operate. The boom of data centers came during the dot-com bubble of 1997–2000. Companies needed fast Internet connectivity and nonstop operation to deploy systems and to establish a presence on the Internet. And installing such equipment was not viable for many smaller companies.

Modern data centers have a large network which interconnects all the servers inside the data center. The network itself connects to other data centers, sometimes directly if they are close enough (a group of data centers), or via using an Internet service provider's (ISP) infrastructure.

Companies who own data centers have the capital and expertise to be their own ISP. Still, depending on the situation, it can be more economical for an ISP and data center to collaborate with each other. For instance, Google provides ISP services, but also has a lot of peering agreements with companies who cooperate in distributing information.

Virtual Private Networks and Access Control Lists

Companies often want to have the convenience of the cloud and the benefits of the separate private network at the same time. The answer to this need is virtual private networks. A virtual private network, or VPN, is an encrypted connection over the

Internet from a device to a private network that is not publicly accessible. It extends a private network across a public network and enables users to send and receive data across shared or public networks as if their computing devices were directly connected to the private network.

Because the traffic is encrypted between the device and the network, traffic remains private as it travels. An employee can work outside the office and still securely connect to the corporate network. Even smartphones and tablets can connect through a VPN. All the major cloud providers (AWS, Azure, GCP, and others) provide the ability to create VPNs as part of their core offering.

Virtual private networks may be classified as follows:

- **Remote access** – A remote access VPN securely connects a device outside the corporate office. These devices are known as endpoints and may be laptops, tablets, or smartphones. This configuration is analogous to connecting a computer to a local area network.

- **Site-to-site** – A site-to-site configuration connects two networks. As an example it connects the corporate office to branch offices over the Internet. Site-to-site VPNs are used when distance makes it impractical to have direct network connections between these offices. Dedicated equipment is used to establish and maintain a connection. Think of site-to-site access as network to network.

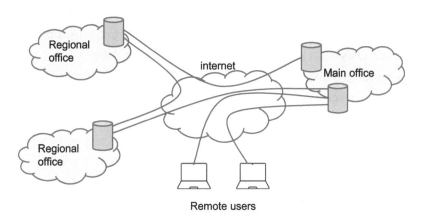

Figure 2-12. *VPN*

Access control lists are actively used in combination with VPN and control which traffic can come in or come out from the server or network part. More generally access control list (ACL) is a list of permissions associated with a system resource (object) which it controls, like in the situation with VPN it is network connection.

Access control list provides rules that are applied to port numbers or IP addresses that are available on a host. ACLs contain a list of hosts and/or networks permitted to use the service. Access control lists can generally be configured to control both inbound and outbound traffic, and in this context they are similar to firewalls.

Firewalls and Load Balancers

Let's look now into what a firewall is. A firewall is a network security device that monitors incoming and outgoing network traffic and decides whether to allow or block specific traffic based on a defined set of security rules. A firewall typically establishes a barrier between a trusted network and an untrusted network, such as the Internet.

The term firewall originally referred to a wall intended to confine a fire within a line of adjacent buildings which was applied in the late 1980s to network technology.

Firewalls are the key component in any security infrastructure, but setting up a firewall is a complex and error-prone task. A network may face security issues due to configuration errors.

Likewise load balancer is a key component for the scalability of the service and its purpose to efficiently distribute incoming network traffic across a group of back-end servers. Modern high-traffic websites must serve hundreds of thousands, if not millions, of concurrent requests from users or clients and return the correct text, images, video, or application data, all in a fast and reliable manner. To cost-effectively scale to meet these high volumes, modern computing best practice generally requires adding more servers. Load balancer sits in front of your servers and routing client requests across all servers capable of fulfilling those requests in a manner that maximizes speed and capacity utilization and ensures that no one server is overworked.

Both firewalls and load balancers are important concepts which we will cover in more details in the following chapters.

Identity and Access Management

Identity and access management is the core component in cloud security. And it is required to secure digital assets. There are two parts to it: authentication and authorization.

All the major cloud providers have a robust offering to perform identity and access management effectively. As an example AWS IAM provides fine-grained access control across all of AWS. You can specify who can access which services and resources, and under which conditions. IAM allows you to

- Apply fine-grained access control

- Establish permissions, guardrails, and data perimeters across your organization

- Achieve least-privilege permissions

- Automatically scale fine-grained permissions

Identity and access management is a very critical component to the security of a company's cloud solution, and we will look into it in more detail in Chapter 6.

Service Quality Metrics (SLAs)

A service-level agreement (SLA) is a plain-language agreement between service provider and customer (whether internal or external) that defines the services which are delivered, the responsiveness that can be expected, and how to measure performance. SLAs define contractually agreed-upon terms for services including things like uptime and support responsiveness, for instance, promising customers 99.9% service uptime or a response from support within 24 hours.

SLAs describe quality-of-service (QoS) features, guarantees, and limitations of one or more cloud-based IT resources. SLAs use service quality metrics to express measurable QoS characteristics. For example:

- **Availability** – Uptime, outages, and service duration

- **Reliability** – Minimum time between failures, guaranteed rate of successful responses

- **Performance** – Capacity, response time, and delivery time guarantees

- **Scalability** – Capacity fluctuation and responsiveness guarantees

- **Resiliency** – Mean time to switchover and recovery

Service providers use these metrics to constantly measure service to verify compliance with SLA guarantees. Each service quality metric is ideally defined using the following characteristics:

- **Quantifiable** – The unit of measure is clearly set, absolute, and appropriate so that the metric can be based on quantitative measurements.

- **Repeatable** – The methods of measuring the metric need to yield identical results when repeated under identical conditions.

- **Comparable** – The units of measure used by a metric need to be standardized and comparable. For example, a service quality metric cannot measure smaller quantities of data in bits and larger quantities in bytes.

- **Easily obtainable** – The metric needs to be based on a nonproprietary, common form of measurement that can be easily obtained and understood by cloud consumers.

Service-level agreements are also defined at different levels; there could be

- **Customer-based SLA** – An agreement with an individual customer group, covering all the services they use. For example, an SLA between a supplier (IT service provider) and the finance department of a large organization for different financial services like payroll system and billing system.

- **Service-based SLA** – An agreement for all customers that use corresponding services. For example, an AWS S3 service provides availability guaranties to all the users.

- **Multilevel SLA** – The SLA is split into the different levels, and each addresses different sets of customers for the same services, in the same SLA.

- **Corporate-level SLA** – Covering all the generic service-level management (SLM) issues to every customer throughout the organization.

- **Customer-level SLA** – Covering all generic service-level management issues in relation to the particular customer group, for all used services.

- **Service-level SLA** – Covering all service-level management issues for the specific service, related to specific customer groups.

It usually depends on the service, but some common metrics to monitor could be

- **Service availability** – The amount of time the service is available for use. This may be measured by time slot, with, for example, 99.5% availability required between the hours of 8 a.m. and 6 p.m., and more or less availability specified during other times. Ecommerce operations typically have extremely aggressive SLAs at all times; 99.999% uptime is a not uncommon requirement for a site that generates millions of dollars an hour, like amazon.com.

- **Defect rates** – Counts or percentages of errors in major deliverables. Production failures such as incomplete backups and restores, coding errors/rework, and missed deadlines may be included in this category.

- **Technical quality** – In outsourced application development, measurement of technical quality by commercial analysis tools that examine factors such as program size and coding defects.

- **Security** – In these hyperregulated times, application and network security breaches can be costly. Measuring controllable security measures such as antivirus updates and patching is key in proving all reasonable preventive measures were taken, in the event of an incident.

- **Business results** – Increasingly, IT customers would like to incorporate business process metrics into their SLAs. Using existing key performance indicators is typically the best approach as long as the vendor's contribution to those KPIs can be calculated.

How should you select metrics to monitor as part of SLA? Usually they need to use best practices and requirements that will maintain service performance and avoid additional costs. It is important to choose measurements that motivate the right behavior and ensure that it measures what is actually under your control. For example, it would be a mistake in choosing the SLA to penalize the service provider for delays caused by the client's lack of performance, also by choosing measurements that are easily collected and done so automatically.

Specifically cloud computing, since it is shared resources SLAs span across the cloud and are offered by service providers as a service-based agreement rather than a customer-based agreement. SLAs for cloud services focus on characteristics of the data center and include characteristics of the network to support end-to-end SLAs.

Wrap-Up

In this chapter we learned that there are different cloud delivery models, which differ in the level of responsibilities between client and cloud provider. The most flexible model when a cloud provider serves the infrastructure on which a client can deploy the application is Infrastructure as a Service, and it is a good choice for a wide variety of use cases. Starting from there cloud providers build more managed solutions providing the additional functionality in the form of platform in Platform as a Service model and further providing out-of-the-box applications in Software as a Service model. As responsibilities shift toward service providers (IaaS ➤ PaaS ➤ SaaS), the model usually allows clients to get to the working state of the product faster to start serving their customers, but it becomes less flexible and either would not work for special use cases or would require a lot of customization.

We learned about cloud deployment models. The ease of use of public cloud deployment is attractive where companies can just not bother with their own hardware and infrastructure. The main considerations, especially with large enterprises, come to the decisions related to cost. The cost can be both a benefit and drawback for public cloud and for private cloud depending on use cases and the patterns of resource usage. Careful considerations are required for taking one or another decision. A possible solution could be a hybrid cloud where depending on use case either public or private cloud can be used for one or another service.

We learned about virtualization and containerization, which revolutionized the ways how software is delivered. Kubernetes, a container management system, is the most popular way to manage and deploy the applications within containers. The raise of serverless computing (i.e., AWS lambda) provides a convenient way to solve request-driven use cases, when, for example, we need to run a code based on request or trigger from the user as opposed to long continuous calculations.

In the next chapter, we would learn how to build the application in a modular and scalable way using the components and solutions which are commonly deployed in the cloud nowadays.

## CHAPTER 3

System Design: Architecting Robust, Scalable, and Modular Applications

In this chapter we will talk about how the modern software applications are built and what problems they are solving and optimized for. The biggest and most complicated solutions are naturally built by the leading companies in the industry (Amazon, Google, Facebook, and others), since they need to solve large problems which are demanded by their business.

Monolithic Applications

Let's imagine we want to build a product, an ecommerce website, sometime in the early 2000s. The site would take orders from customers, verify inventory and available credit, and ship them. The small group of developers (usually even just a single one) would start coding a website and incorporate functionality in a single application which would work as a web server. There will be implemented UI, back-end logic, and data access layer all in a single application. As the product grows, the developer(s) will add additional functionality like identity verification, order history, feedback listener, etc. By keeping adding more and more functionality to a single application, we inevitably use so-called monolithic architecture. And it is a way how majority (if not almost all) applications were built relatively recently.

© Gaurav Sagar, Vitalii Syrovatskyi 2022
G. Sagar and V. Syrovatskyi, *Technical Building Blocks*, https://doi.org/10.1007/978-1-4842-8658-6_3

So what is a monolithic application? Monolithic applications are designed to handle multiple related tasks. They're typically complex applications that encompass several tightly coupled functions. They usually consist of a single application layer that supports the user interface, the business rules, and the manipulation of the data all in one. The data itself could be physically stored in a remote location, but the logic for accessing it is part of the application.

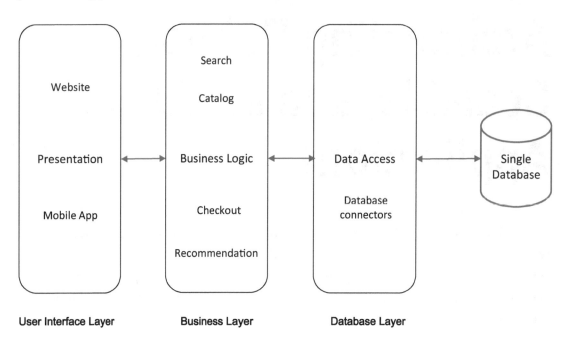

Figure 3-1. *Monolithic architecture for ecommerce websites*

Any early years ecommerce website could be a good example of a monolithic application (Figure 3-1). The user interface is an integral part of the application. The business logic, such as searching and checkout, is also part of the application. The data access routines, to manipulate the contents of the database, are also part of the application.

By the nature of having "everything in one," the monolithic application can become a single point of failure, which can easily become a problem for a product especially when scaling due to an increasing number of customers and under the heavy load. For example, problems in noncritical data processing can bring down the whole application, or making a change in one part of the application can cause unpredictable changes in behavior in another part.

Another big problem with monolithic applications is a slow development cycle: slow builds, slow test validations, and slow and complicated deployment process.

While all current leading IT companies started with monolithic applications, all of them have moved to service-oriented and microservices architectures, which represent a model of separated services in charge of a single logical function and talk to each other based on established contracts.

Scaling

What do companies need to do when the load on the system keeps increasing? The answer is to scale the capabilities to sustain the increased load. Scaling resources can include any combination of adjustments to CPU and physical memory (different or more machines), hard disk (bigger hard drives, less "live" data, solid-state drives), and/or the network bandwidth (multiple network interface controllers, bigger NICs, fiber, etc.).

Two main approaches are vertical and horizontal scaling. Scaling horizontally and scaling vertically are similar in that they both involve adding computing resources to your infrastructure. There are distinct differences between the two in terms of implementation and performance:

- **Vertical scaling** implies replacing servers with higher capacity ones, which increase corresponding available resources for application and thus allow it to sustain higher load.

- **Horizontal scaling** implies adding more servers on which application runs and thus reaching the same goal of increased resources.

In many respects, vertical scaling is easier because the logic really doesn't need to change and you're just running the same code on higher-spec machines. When taking decisions about what approach to take, there are a lot of factors which need to be considered such as performance, flexibility, and cost. The difference in operational complexity. It is less complex to operate fewer instances. The more instances there are, the higher probability of failure on some of the instances leading to a degraded runtime environment.

The most common flow is to start with the vertical scaling until the reasonable cost and efficiency level and expand horizontally afterward, given the application is built with such capabilities. And in practice you do not need to choose between the two as both horizontal scaling and vertical scaling go together, since you often need to scale up the fleet of horizontally scaled services.

In a lot of cases, application is developed without scaling in mind, so by the time of need for horizontal scaling, it needs to be refactored and broken down in smaller pieces. But in the modern development, especially by the leading companies in the industry, application is designed in a stateless way from the very beginning, since horizontal scaling is the only feasible solution to sustain the loads such systems receive. The ease of horizontal scaling comes from better infrastructure support such as autoscaling from cloud vendors, managed container runtimes, and advancement of stateful services like various databases, which allowed many applications to become stateless enabling their horizontal scaling.

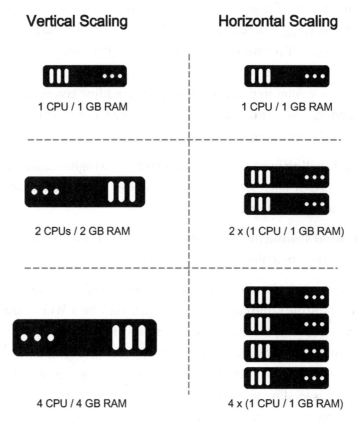

Figure 3-2. *Application scaling*

Issues with Monoliths

Monolithic architectures have their own benefits like simplicity of initial development, time to market, simplicity of testing, deployment, and scaling, and are often the right choice for brand new projects with a small and focused team. But it has a number of issues as the products grow over time:

- **Time to market** – Although the development of the monolithic system is fast in the beginning, it slows down when code base grows due to a lot of interdependencies. Also refactoring (improving code readability and maintainability) is hard to do with a large single code base.

- Deployments and scaling require the whole monolith to be redeployed; even a small fix in one particular area of the code base requires a full-scale deployment process.

- Coding languages usually should be the same across the monolithic application which sets additional limitations for developers.

- Low readability and maintainability since usually a lot of code being produced in a single code base with multiple people having access to it.

Need for Service-Oriented System Design

Business demands of large companies are usually very big scoped, with large scale, reaching millions of customers around the world. No surprise that the systems the teams are building there are very complex and efficient.

And while historically the majority of the application starts in a monolithic way. This is a way how software is naturally progressing; first a small application is built to solve some use cases and keep building up on to solve more and more use cases, adding functionality and expanding the application until it becomes relatively big and contains functionality to handle multiple tasks.

In the monolithic systems, it is best practice to create layers and modularity. There was no modularity between layers, and there were no possibilities to reuse components from other applications. So the first improvement to the monolithic architecture was modules that are reusable within the monolith. The execution and deployment was still in a single logical executable, and so it still was a monolithic system.

The next step was the introduction of a public API, so the external processes were able to communicate with the application. This was done by creating a variety of proprietary or customized message formats and protocols, such as .NET Remoting, WCF, sockets, and many others.

Then, the trend of designing applications as a suite of fine-grained services is called microservices, which is based on the idea to create and operate a bigger system with single-responsibility services. And this became a standard in the design of Enterprise Applications. The technologies used in the single services are independent, providing the possibility for individual teams to create and own services with different sets of external dependencies. For example, the clients of a data service do not need any information on the actual database where the data sits and neither do they have a dependency on the framework used by the data team. All they need is to have an interface to call into for the required data.

Key Characteristics of Distributed Design

Distributed system is a collection of components located on different servers that coordinate and work together in order to achieve a common goal. They are usually able to fail independently and are autonomous computers linked by a network to share information, communicate, and exchange information easily. The key characteristics of such systems are

1. **Heterogeneity** – In distributed systems components can have variety and differences in server configurations, network, operating systems, written in different programming languages, etc.

2. **Openness** – Distributed systems are open in terms of communicating and integrating. The interfaces for components must be standardized and published so the new components could be easily integrated into a distributed system.

3. **Scalability** – Is the main reason the distributed systems are built. They are easily scalable; more computers can be added to the network to sustain the increased load on the system. If properly designed, increased demand on the system can be achieved by simply adding components without actual changes to the code.

4. **Fault tolerant** – In the distributed system, anything can fail, like hardware failure on individual servers or network issues. So it should be designed in a way that failures of the individual elements do not bring down the whole system.

5. **Concurrency** – Multiple servers can be accessed at the same time by multiple servers, responding to which would require sharing of multiple resources. The system should be able to concurrently execute multiple requests, effectively communicate between its components, and effectively share available resources such as data, software (files, and data objects), and hardware (disks and printers).

6. **Transparency** – Distributed systems should be perceived by users as a whole rather than as a collection of independent components. Transparency could be of different forms, like transparency of access (how a system is accessed by user), transparency of location (accessed from anywhere), and maybe others.

Considerations and Trade-Offs

One of the most important questions the team should ask when starting solving a problem is: do we need a distributed design? The answer to this question is not obvious; there are a lot of cases when building a distributed system is not reasonable and a lot of considerations should be taken in account with different trade-offs.

One of the biggest considerations is the complexity of a distributed system. Such systems are legitimately harder to build, and significantly harder to understand and operate. Another big consideration is dependencies between services. As service depends on others and these other services must serve multiple use cases, it is slow and difficult to ask for new features on the dependent services. This often leads to inefficient implementation or delays in the project, which is a major drawback with service-oriented design, and especially with microservices.

Performance and Scalability

Performance of a distributed system is a composition of its elements. Each service of a distributed system needs to be performant. And while achieving efficiency in usage on machine resources is similar for distributed and monolithic systems, for distributed comes an additional aspect, which is efficiently communicating between distributed components. And a wrong configuration or inappropriate usage of local resources of a single layer could be a bottleneck and make the whole distributed system low performant.

Latency and Throughput

When comparing latency, a time it takes for the system to respond to a user, one of the main limitations is the network calls. There are basic rules at play when it comes to distributed systems, which consists of many elements located on different servers across the network. To answer on request most distributed systems involve multiple components and multiple underlying calls over the network. A monolith has no network latency after receiving a request, as all calls are local. Even in a perfectly parallelizable world, the monoliths will have lower latency.

The same is true for throughput. Data needs to be sent between servers, and also all the infrastructure induces a certain overhead. If the workload cannot be scaled to multiple instances, a monolith can deliver a higher throughput.

Availability and Consistency

The availability of a monolithic system basically boils down to the actual server it runs on. Despite modern machines being pretty great, they still expected to fail with some expected frequency per year. This can stack up to the large amount of toil for bringing the servers back, and toil is there since we are building a monolithic system, stirring a state on the server and some expensive procedure required to start it back. And the second problem is quite a long time to recover for a monolithic server, which usually involves long startup procedures.

Distributed systems achieve a higher level of availability, which is one of the main goals to build a distributed system. The cost of bringing back failed servers of distributed systems is similar to monolithic design, but since usually there are more servers, the operation to recover might be needed more often, and solving this problem is achieved by a lot of cost and complexity to get into this state such as dedicated state stores, replication, and consensus. Modern ops practices, like infrastructure as code, immutable infrastructure, containers, and serverless, reduce the toil even more. Distributed systems can also be placed closer to users, which makes them more available in the case of network partition events.

Both monolithic and distributed systems can achieve strong consistency by choosing to use certain data stores with strong consistency. Consistency is implemented using choices of data storage layer: ACID or not. A monolithic operation + the use of an ACID storage achieves strong consistency. An operation spanning multiple services generally cannot achieve strong consistency and uses eventual consistency or have very complex retry/undo logic. Distributed systems are mostly trading off consistency for higher availability and fault tolerance.

Actually building and operating distributed systems that do better than monolithic systems on all these properties is difficult. That is why distributed systems are mostly built for products beyond the initial stages in the industry, since building and maintaining a proper operating distributed system requires big resources and established infrastructure.

Microservices

Microservices architecture, or simply microservices, is a distinctive method of developing distributed software systems that focus on building single-function modules with well-defined interfaces and operations.

The trend for microservices continues to grow in popularity since more and more enterprises look to become more agile and follow the example of leading tech companies. Amazon, Google, Twitter, PayPal, and other leaders in the tech industry have all evolved from monolithic to microservices architecture.

Microservices externalizes the modules inside one monolithic application to their own independent monoliths, a suite of small services, each running in its own process and independently deployable. Microservices could be built independently and owned by different teams, could be written in different programming languages, and use different data storage techniques, making as a result systems that are scalable and flexible.

The microservices architecture of the same ecommerce website (from Figure 3-1) might look as shown in Figure 3-3.

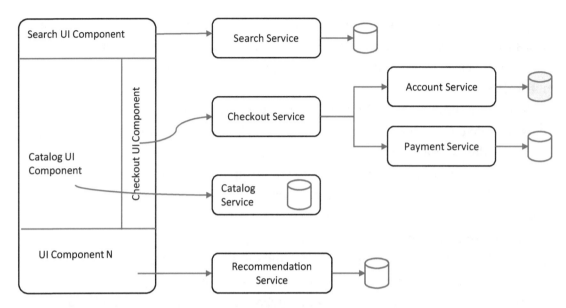

Figure 3-3. *Microservices architecture of ecommerce site*

Here you can see how the whole product becomes a composition of individual services like Search Service, Checkout Service, Account Service, and others. Web service is also separated from back-end services each of which performs its own specific role. And when we have several separate microservices, it is important to understand now how they will be communicating.

Communication Style

Microservices are separately built and possibly in different programming languages, so how can they communicate with each other? They communicate with each other via standardized interfaces, and as long as one service can craft requests in the specified format recognized by another service, the communication is possible. There are several different technologies which are used to design the communication interfaces for services, such as SOAP, REST, RPC, and GraphQL, each of them has its own cons and pros as well as recommendation for use in different situations[1].

---

[1] www.altexsoft.com/blog/soap-vs-rest-vs-graphql-vs-rpc/

SOAP

Simple object access protocol (SOAP) is an XML-formatted and highly standardized communication protocol released by Microsoft in 1999. Once REST was introduced (2000), they were used in parallel, but slowly over years, SOAP lost its popularity, but still it is used in legacy systems or when highly secured data transitions are required like in payments.

So how does SOAP work? It is an XML data format with strong types, and since the message is very structured, it makes SOAP the most verbose format among all mentioned above. The format is written in Web Services Description Language (WSDL) and composed of

- An envelope tag that wraps every message (<env:Envelope>)

- A header with specific information (<env:Header>)

- A body containing the request or response (<env:Body>)

An example SOAP envelope to fetch last trade price would look like this:

```
<SOAP-ENV:Envelope
xmlns:SOAP-ENV="http://schemas.xmlsoap.org/soap/envelope/"
SOAP-ENV:encodingStyle="http://schemas.xmlsoap.org/soap/encoding/">
<SOAP-ENV:Body>
      <m:GetLastTradePrice xmlns:m="Some-URI">
          <symbol>DIS</symbol>
      </m:GetLastTradePrice>
   </SOAP-ENV:Body>
</SOAP-ENV:Envelope>
```

```
With the corresponding response from server:
<SOAP-ENV:Envelope
  xmlns:SOAP-ENV="http://schemas.xmlsoap.org/soap/envelope/"
  SOAP-ENV:encodingStyle="http://schemas.xmlsoap.org/soap/encoding/"/>
  <SOAP-ENV:Body>
      <m:GetLastTradePriceResponse xmlns:m="Some-URI">
          <Price>34.5</Price>
      </m:GetLastTradePriceResponse>
   </SOAP-ENV:Body>
</SOAP-ENV:Envelope>
```

115

There are reasons why SOAP has lost its popularity. It is heavyweight (due to verbose XML structure), is narrow specialized, and has tedious message updating, requiring effort to add or remove the message properties. Although there are still pros like built-in error handling, which specifies return errors and its explanations, and a number of security extensions, which meet an enterprise-grade transaction quality, it provides privacy and integrity inside the transactions while allowing for encryption on the message level.

REST

Representational state transfer (REST) is a software architectural style for implementing web services defined by a set of architectural constraints and intended for wide adoption.

Original definition of REST is pretty strict and not observed by most implementations. Hence, a separate term is used for systems meeting all original REST criteria: HATEOAS. REST protocol implementation is usually characterized by the following constraints:

- **Data-oriented interface style** – Data is first-class citizen, and the number of verbs used by a vendor needs to be uniform. Best practice is not to create new verbs.

- **Stateless** – Is an ideal characteristic which is almost never observed, which means that all the state information to handle the request are contained within the request itself.

- **Client-server architecture** – Independent evolution of both client and server sides.

- The ability for servers to provide executable code to the client via the response.

The main attribute of the protocol is that with each response, a REST API provides metadata linking to all the related info about how to use the API. That's what enables decoupling the client and the server. As a result, both API provider and API consumer can evolve independently without hindering their communication.

An example for client requesting user information with ID 12345 via RESTful API:

```
HTTP GET http://www.myexampleapplication.com/users/12345
```

And the corresponding response will be

```
{ id: 12345,
  username: 'admin',
  email: 'admin@myexampleapplication.com }
```

As any other protocol, REST has its own pros and cons. The pros are that

- The client and server are decoupled, abstracting implementation details to better identify and sustain its properties, which lets REST to be flexible, evolving over time while remaining a stable system.

- Discoverability, again an ideal characteristic which is not observed by most REST implementations, which mean that no external documentation is required to understand how to interact with the REST API, which is described in protocol itself.

- Supports multiple communication formats (JSON, XML, etc.).

While the cons of REST are

- No single defined REST structure, so how to model resources will depend on use case making protocol simple in theory, but difficult in practice.

- Big messages since REST responses contain metadata for the client to understand all about the state of the application.

- Often designed that responses contain not enough data, which creates the need for the follow-up requests.

- Lack of strong types and type checking, which complicates compilation level validation and testing.

REST is the best applicable in the management use cases, when design is focused on management of objects in the system, and REST helps such APIs to have strong discoverability and good documentation.

One of the examples for REST API would be a management of user entity, where different HTTP methods would create(POST), update(PUT), read(GET), or delete(DELETE) corresponding resource entry:

- User creation operation

```
POST /services/user
...
{
  "user_id": "12345",
  "email": "example.user@host.com",
}
```

- User update operation to change email to example.user@
  myexample.com:

```
PUT /services/user
...
{
  "user_id": "12345",
  "email": "example.user@myexample.com",
}
```

- Delete user with 12345 user id would erase the user from the system:

```
DELETE  /services/user?user_id=12345
```

- And read user details (email address, first and last name, etc.)
  would be

```
GET / /services/user?user_id=12345
```

RPC

Remote Procedure Call is a request-response protocol that allows for remote execution of a function in a different context.

So how does RPC work? When a client invokes a remote procedure, it serializes the parameters and any additional information and sends the message to the server over the network. The server receives the message, deserializes parameters, and executes locally requested procedure. The results of execution serialized into the message as well and sent back to the client. The server's and client's stubs perform the serialization and deserialization of the parameters.

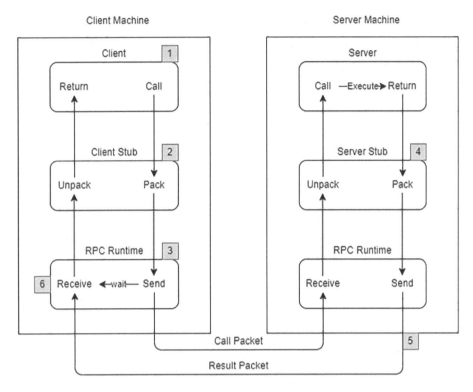

Figure 3-4. *RPC request and response flow*

Before looking into the RPC use cases, let's understand what are pros and cons of this protocol. The pros are

- **Simplicity** – Conceptually all that RPC does is calling an endpoint and getting a response.

- **Easy to extend** – When we need to add new functionality, we just need to write a new function, put it behind the endpoint, and provide the client with the mock interface to call it.

- **Performance** – RPC calls have lightweight payloads, so the load on the network is low which provides the high performance.

But RPC has its cons as well:

- **Tight coupling between systems** – There is a tight coupling between client and server systems in case of using remote procedures which does not allow for any abstraction layer. It also impacts the collaboration between teams making it hard to have a

119

loosely coupled team, since clients are either exposed too much to implementation details and worry too much about side effects or lack information on how to use endpoints.

- **Low discoverability** – It is impossible for clients to introspect the APIs, as opposed to verbose ways in REST.

- **Duplication** – Since it is easy to add functions, it often leads to situations when instead of refining the interface or changing the existing ones, a ton of new overlapping functions gets created.

RPCs are currently widely used especially by the big companies where they often use high-performance varieties of RPC for internal services communications. Such internal communications require messages to be clear and short, and so RPCs are widely used in Google (gRPC), Twitch (twirp), Facebook (Apache Thrift), and others.

Other more concrete use cases of RPC usage are Command APIs. These are types of APIs which are designed for receiving commands from remote clients, for example, for chat systems commands like join a channel, leave a channel, and send a message, where an RPC-like style of messages makes it small, tight, and quite easy to use.

Another use case would be a single client specific API, where direct integration between remote systems is required, where we do not need to transmit a lot of metadata over the network (i.e., in REST), do not need verbosity and discoverability benefits of other protocols, and simply aim for high efficiency.

GraphQL

GraphQL is a language for querying databases from client-side applications which was created by Facebook in 2012 for internal use for their mobile applications to reduce network usage due to its specific data-fetching capabilities.

When rest was created in 2000, the client applications were relatively simple, but since then APIs have gotten more complex and data-driven affected by factors like increased mobile usage, which created a need for more efficient data loading, varieties of clients and expectations for faster development. GraphQL is positioned as a more modern alternative to REST to address these factors since it allows for requesting specific data that a client needs, departing from the fixed data structure approach.

The GraphQL ecosystem is expanding with libraries and powerful tools like Apollo, GraphiQL, and GraphQL Explorer and used in production by hundreds of other organizations like Credit Karma, GitHub, Yelp, PayPal, etc.

So how GraphQL works? First you start with defining the schema, which describes all the possible calls you can make and return types for these calls, which is a hard part since it requires strong typing in the Schema Definition Language (SDL). But having a schema allows a client to validate requests before sending to the server making sure the requests would be accepted and accordingly formatted. When a request reaches the server, it gets interpreted against the schema and resolved with the response for the client. When a client sends one massive query to the server, it gets a JSON response with all the data being asked for.

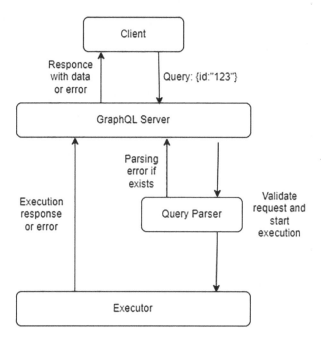

Figure 3-5. *GraphQL high-level diagram*

Being the most recently invented protocol, you might expect a number of benefits it can provide, and the main pros are[2]

- **Fetching data with a single API call** – This is the main difference with REST (and other protocols). GraphQL is not designed to operate over individual endpoints like REST, where multiple calls are required to get all the data needed. GraphQL focuses on the task itself; in this case, a developer can request the needed data with just one API call.

---

[2] www.altexsoft.com/blog/engineering/graphql-core-features-architecture-pros-and-cons/

- **Typed schema** – Developers can see what the schema can query and how the data is set up there. Based on that, they can easily add new fields to existing queries through a GraphQL IDE.

- **Detailed error messages** – Similarly to other protocols, GraphQL provides details to errors that occurred.

- **A standard method to request data subsets** – Opposite to REST where requesting a subset of data requires custom design for the calls with query parameters. Here in GraphQL, it has a standard way of specifying subsets eliminating the need to design something proprietary for this capability.

- **No versioning, which is not really a requirement but best practice** – By using a single, evolving version, GraphQL APIs give apps continuous access to new features and encourage cleaner, more maintainable server code. Although cases exist where versioning must take place as semantics of the data may change.

- **Permissions and additional operations** – GraphQL allows for selectively exposing certain functions while preserving private information and, in addition to CRUD, brings in subscriptions, which allows clients to receive real-time messages from the server.

Despite being the most modern protocol of all, GraphQL also has its own disadvantages:

- **Performance issues on complex queries** – GraphQL query can encounter performance issues if a client asks for too many nested fields at once, so some limiting to prevent inefficient requests might be required (max depth, no recursion, etc.)

- **Complexity** – To effectively use GraphQL, a lot of predevelopment study is required, like learning the Schema Definition Language.

GraphQL is rising in popularity and the ecosystem is growing at a high speed. Libraries for GraphQL are offered in multiple languages; there are GraphQL servers, clients, and gateways, including growing IDE support and multiple useful tools.

GraphQL is best applicable to the use cases such as mobile API, where the optimization is important for network performance, or complex systems where we can hide the complexity of multiple systems behind the exposed API.

So which pattern to choose when considering your use case? There is no single answer as you might know and depends on the goals of development and resources to spare. But knowing all the trade-offs helps to choose the right approach for each particular use case. For example, SOAP is strongly typed, but security features help in payments, booking, and billing systems, RPC is great for internal communication but not for public API, and REST is easy to set up with lots of standardized tooling, but may be inefficient to represent behaviors as side effects. And GraphQL is good with client data fetching, but still complex on the server side to fulfil the requests with efficiency.

API Documentation

Let's suppose you've built your product, have chosen communication protocol type, i.e., REST, and exposed your endpoints via API gateway. And now you expect clients to use your APIs, integrated with your product to achieve their business goals. In order to do so, client's developers need to understand how to use your API, what objects are exposed and which operations with what parameters could be called, and what side effects happen for the calls. Exactly for this reason, API documentation should be provided.

So what is API documentation? API documentation is a technical content manual which describes all the information needed to work with API. It contains details about the functions, classes, return types, arguments, and more, often supported by tutorials and examples.

There are two main parts of any API documentation:

- **API specification** – Such as OpenAPI spec, SOAP, and Protocol Buffers can be generated by tools against the API producer (server side). API specification is then consumed by the caller programs and developers to build software code.

- **API description** – Additional content aiding the caller developer to understand the behavior of the APIs.

API documentation has a direct impact on adoption and usage providing a number of benefits to the product:

- **Saves time and effort going in support** – Good documentation will decrease the time developers spend adopting the API; they will find the answers on how the API is supposed to be used from documentation and via reaching out to the support. It saves your team hours responding to support emails and calls.

123

- **Improves user adoption** – Having good documentation will improve the experience of developers who use it. And people adopt products they enjoy, and the same is true for API with good documentation.

- **Increases awareness** – As with any product, your satisfied customers will become your advocates. The network effect would benefit the product the more customers use your API and the more they like it.

- **Easier maintenance** – Good documentation helps product maintenance. It helps your intended audience know the details of your resources, methods, and their associated requests and responses, making maintenance and updates quicker.

There are no real downsides to providing documentation with your API, apart from possibly the effort spent to create one, but the benefits and impact of it are more than enough to justify the effort, and especially documentation generation tools reduce the effort required if adapted. There are many ways to write API documentation, from manual compiling corresponding text to tools which automate these processes (there are a lot of them on the market), and from simply written by developers (in startups) to complicated processes involving tech writers and multiple approvers (in enterprises). But no matter the process of writing documentation, a good product treats API as another UX with the customer. An API program is used to provide a holistic location to educate the customer on how to use the APIs with API specification, API descriptions, how-to, examples, and mocking service to try out the APIs.

API Measures (Latency, Availability, Robustness)

So now we have developed APIs with proper documentation and want to serve our customers. But how do we know that APIs' performance will be up to customers' expectations? For that we would need to measure key API metrics such as latency, availability, and robustness.

Why is it important to measure different aspects of APIs? Stress testing before launch to ensure the APIs perform as expected under the load while ongoing measuring of metrics would inform us if APIs' behavior degrades. For example, if APIs' latency is too high, customers would not be able to rely on them in time-sensitive operations, or if APIs have low availability customers will not be able to include it into the workflows with high reliability requirements. Also, API usually goes with some set of SLAs (service level agreements), which describe to customers operational guarantees, for example, what uptime percent we would provide.

So what are metrics out there to monitor for APIs? The metrics are usually split between operational and business metrics. The former intend to give information on how APIs are doing from a technical point of view and latter to indicate business growth or usage.

The main operational metrics are[3]

- **Availability** – Is the uptime percentage of the API which is usually included in API SLAs and usually presented in terms of 9s: three nines, four nines, etc. This means the percentage of time the service is up and operational, for example, three nines – 99.9% uptime which is no more than 8.77 hours of downtime per year. It is most commonly measured via some kind of ping service.

- **Latency** – One of the most important metrics for customer experience, and often tracked in multiple ways, such as max, average, or percentile latencies. These metrics are an important indication of the overall health of your service.

- **Errors** – Usually as errors per certain period of time and it is a number of APIs calls that returned errors, which also usually split between caused by wrong input (expected errors) and unexpected errors of service itself.

- **Requests per minute** – Important operational metrics which gives you indications and patterns of the load on your service. It could be different based on day of week/year and helps plan your capacity/scaling of your infrastructure.

---

[3] www.moesif.com/blog/technical/api-metrics/API-Metrics-That-Every-Platform-Team-Should-be-Tracking/

The other class of metrics is business oriented; they could be dependent on your use case:

- **API usage growth** – Should measure longer intervals (unlike requests per minute), for example, growing month over month to understand real trends. It is an important business metric which gives valuable insights into future planning.

- **Top customers by usage/load/spend** – If you wish to understand how the APIs are used, it is often beneficial to track the usage by the biggest customers (especially in b2b scenario). You may track how your top 10–20 customers use your APIs and may have breakdown by endpoints/operations.

- **Unique API consumers** – Together with share amounts in API usage, it is important to track the number of unique customers/consumers. This will give the information on how the user base is growing and are you over-indexing on a single big consumer (and thus creating vulnerability).

Use Case: Building a RESTful API

Let's design a simple RESTful API for listing and searching for products at the Internet store. We need to make sure that the base URL of our API is simple and easily readable.

First we start with the API endpoint for listing and getting details of products:

```
/products/
```

Note since REST is data driven and not behavior driven, we are using just noun in REST notation and not /getAllTheProducts/. Hence, there are no verbs outside a small standard set of verbs for CRUD of data.

Then, we will use the HTTP methods to do the operations on this endpoint:

- **GET /products/** – Would simply return the summary of all the products.

- **GET /products/1234** – Will return details on the product with id = 1234 and will return error if record is not found.

- **POST /products/** – With the JSON body {name: Table, price: 123} would create a new product with the name "Table" and price 123 (e.g., USD as default) and will return id for the new product.

- **PUT /products/1234** – With the JSON body {price: 142} would find a product with id=1234 and update its price to 142 and will return error if record is not found.

- **DELETE /products/1234** – Will delete a product with id = 1234 and will return error if record is not found.

We can extend GET /products/ API with the additional parameters to implement search functionality. For example, /products?name='QWE' will look for products named 'QWE' and return a list if found.

We can introduce pagination in GET /products/ to make return lists more manageable and not overstretch the system when we have a lot of products:

```
GET /products/limit=25&offset=50
```

While designing responses of our API, we also need to carefully return appropriate error codes if anything goes wrong or the input is not correct.

There are a set of common used error codes, and just using 200 on success and 500 on error might be not enough, so we can implement the following error codes:

- **200 OK** – Common code to show that the operation is successful.

- **201 CREATED** – We will return on successful POST method.

- **400 BAD REQUEST** – Will be used when JSON payload for POST and PUT is incorrect.

- **401 UNAUTHORIZED / 403 FORBIDDEN** – Will be used if the user is not authorized into the system.

- **404 NOT FOUND** – Will be used on GET, PUT, and DELETE if specified product with ID is not found.

- **500 and/or 502** – For internal server errors, we should not return this explicitly.

We also need to introduce versioning into our URL; this will help with subsequent upgrades and evolution of our API, since all the breaking changes would be implemented in new version and not break existing users:

```
/v1/products
```

So as you might notice when designing an API, you want to create as clear communication as possible with your client. Explicit and transparent usage of endpoints, parameters, and error codes would help to create manageable and readable APIs.

Database

Almost no system, product, or service is created without some way of storing data. Information about users, related products, or history of operations and simply logging all are examples of data you might want to store. And the most common way of storing the data is databases.

So what is a database? A database is a software system for managing collection of data. A database is typically designed so that it is easy to store and access information. Usually a good database is crucial to any product, and thus the right selection of one is very important. The database stores all the pertinent details and is usually quite difficult to change the type of database used later.

The first database was created in the early 1960s by Charles Bachman. It was known as the Integrated Data Store, or IDS which was shortly followed by the information management system, a database created by IBM. Both of them were the navigational databases, which required users to navigate through the entire database to find the information they wanted. Navigational databases have two models: the hierarchical model and the network model. In the hierarchical model (which was developed by IBM), data is organized like a family tree, where each data entry has a parent record, starting with a root record. And the network model (released by Conference on Data Systems Languages) allowed a record to have more than one parent and child record.

Most probably the most influential event in the history of databases happened in the 1970s when E. F. Codd released his paper "A Relational Model of Data for Large Shared Data Banks." The paper introduced the concept of relational databases. A relational database manages data by types and type-to-type relationships and is searchable using a declarative syntax. Relational databases are also more space-efficient, meaning reduced data storage costs. IBM then released their take on a relational database. Known as System R, it was the first in the history of databases to use structured query language (SQL).

In the 1980s the navigational models faded, and it was a time for relational databases growth and commercialization. Also it was a time when SQL became the standard language used for databases, which we still use today. Another database type was invented in the 1980s which is an object-oriented database management system. They would manage data as objects and classes with tight integration with object-oriented programming languages.

In the 1990s the creation of the Internet (World Wide Web) has driven the development of databases due to demand for client-server applications. And one of the most important database of decades was created in 1995 – MySQL, an open source relational database management system.

In the 2000s the NoSQL (not only structured query language) databases were introduced. NoSQL databases are useful for unstructured data, and they saw a growth in the 2000s in the variety of use cases where low latency writes and data volumes requirements cannot be fulfilled by relational databases. This development was important because NoSQL allowed for faster processing of larger, more varied datasets, by relaxing and eliminating various data consistency and flexible data access capabilities of relational databases.

In the 2010s was the rise of big data. It increased a need to collect, organize, and process huge amounts of data which created a push on new types of databases for different use cases to become even more available, reliable with high performance. Today, there are a variety of databases and data stores ranging from relational, document, key value, time series, and analytical to support various use cases.

Relational Database Management System

Let us recap what a relational database is. Relational database uses a structure that allows identifying and accessing data in relation to another piece of data in the database. And quite often such data is organized into tables.

With data organized in tables, each table can be considered as a type or set of data with the same characteristics, which usually have multiple columns and lots of rows; each row can be considered as an instance of the type with each column being an attribute of the type. Columns are labelled with names and have specific data types. Each row in turn corresponds to a single data record which is represented by values per each column definition.

Here is an example of a "user" database table:

Id	Name	Age	Country
1001	Alex	21	United States
1002	Anna	34	Ireland
1003	John	57	Australia

Relational databases are often used for their guarantees for storing data, the one of the most important one called ACID (atomicity, consistency, isolation, durability) which intended to guarantee data validity despite errors, power failures, and other mishaps. And in the context of databases, a sequence of database operations that satisfies the ACID properties (which can be perceived as a single logical operation on the data) is called a transaction.

Characteristics of ACID properties are[4]

1. **(A) Atomicity** – Transactions in databases are often composed of multiple statements (i.e., changes to different tables and rows). Atomicity guarantees that each transaction is treated as a single "unit," which either succeeds completely or fails completely, so there is never a partial inconsistent change to the database.

2. **(C) Consistency** – It means that any data written to the database must be valid according to all defined rules. This prevents database corruption by an illegal transaction (but does not guarantee that a transaction is correct).

3. **(I) Isolation** – Transactions are often executed concurrently (e.g., multiple transactions reading and writing to a table at the same time). Isolation ensures that concurrent execution of transactions leaves the database in the same state that would have been obtained if the transactions were executed sequentially.

4. **(D) Durability** – Durability guarantees that once a transaction has been committed, it will remain committed even in the case of

[4] Haerder, T.; Reuter, A. (1983). "Principles of transaction-oriented database recovery". ACM Computing Surveys. 15 (4): 287

a system failure (e.g., power outage or crash). This usually means that completed transactions (or their effects) are recorded in permanent storage (i.e., hard drive).

Replication

We already know that data is the core of almost any product or service, and the importance of data persistence is high. If data is lost due to any type of failure, it usually impacts a lot on product reputation. That is why replication, as a method to make data storage more resilient, is very important.

So what is data replication? Data replication is the process of storing data in more than one site or node and is very useful in improving the availability of data. It is simply copying data from a database from one server to another server so that all the users can see the same data at some point without any inconsistency. The result is a distributed database in which users can access data relevant to their tasks without interfering with the work of others. There could be full replication, when whole data is replicated between database hosts, and there could be partial replication when only the most important data is replicated.

How does replication work? Database replication can be a continuous process when data keeps replicating for every change or single operation at some points in time to replicate the whole database. The replication logic tries to make sure that additions and deletions performed on the data at any given location are automatically reflected in the data stored at all the other locations.

And there are several ways to replicate databases with corresponding pros and cons, so the choice is usually dependent on the type of data, intended usage, and product needs.

There are two main approaches for replication if we look at the problem from the timing point of view, in particular when the replication operation should happen in regard to the mutation operation on the data:

- **Synchronous** – Replication happens during the time of the main mutation operation and is considered as a part of that transaction. This means the user will not receive any confirmation from the server about the success (or failure) of the operation until the replication completes. So in such cases when users receive a successful response, it means the data is persistent on multiple servers and the changes are available on all servers. Synchronous is usually slower but more reliable, used when consistency of data is the top priority.

- **Asynchronous** – Replication happens after or during the main operation but not tied to it. Users will receive a response from the server with the result of operation without checking or waiting for the replication process. Asynchronous is faster, but there can be read after write inconstancy.

There are also several types of database replication based on the type of server architecture:

- **Single primary architecture** – It is when a single master host is receiving all the mutation calls and replication is happening to one or several read-only hosts. This type of replication is often synchronous and the most classical one.

- **Multiple primaries architecture** – The architecture when several hosts receive mutations and replication happens between them as well as to multiple read-only hosts. This model is usually needed when hosts are distributed by multiple locations.

- **No primary architecture** – Every server that can receive writes and serve as a model for replication. This is often supported by NoSQL databases such as Cassandra, HBase, and DyanmoDB. It offers very high flexibility, but replication could be a challenge where data can be partitioned and not all server handles all data.

As with everything else, there are advantages and disadvantages to using database replication models. Among the advantages is load reduction, since reads can happen from multiple hosts, efficiency, and high availability – the main reason for replication. And among disadvantages are possible data inconsistencies if there are problems with replication and more complicated and costly server architecture.

In the early days, all the replication started as synchronous in favor of data constancy over latency. Today, various options exist providing trade-offs between consistency and performance.... Using the right type of replication is usually an exercise to balance between data consistency and performance and mainly driven by the use case of the product.

Federation

Let's now understand what federation concept in the world of databases is. Federation is a software process that allows multiple databases to function as one, and this concept is technically part of data virtualization. With federation, a virtual database takes data from a range of sources (i.e., other databases) and converts them all to a common model, which provides a single source of data for consuming applications[5].

---

[5] www.tibco.com/reference-center/what-is-a-data-federation

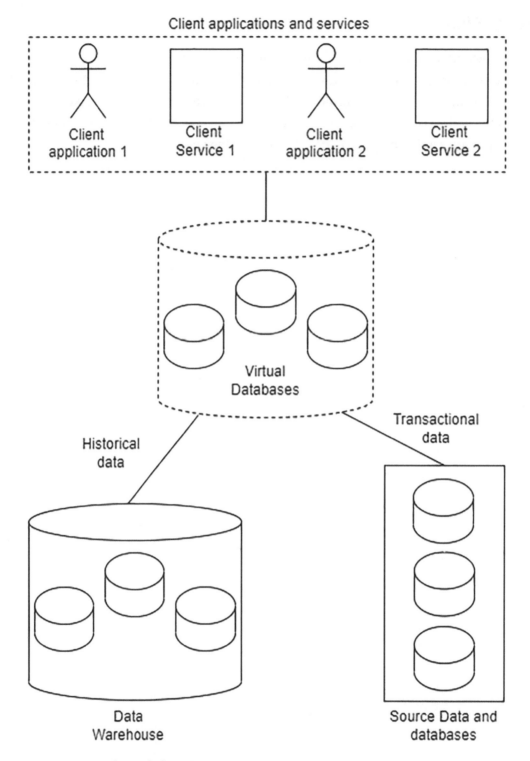

Figure 3-6. *Database federation*

In practice to end users and client applications, data sources appear as a single collective database in the database system. Users and applications interface with the federated database that is managed by the federated server. The federated system processes SQL statements as if the data from the data sources were ordinary relational tables or views within the federated database.

There are multiple benefits of setting up federated database:

- **No extra storage space required** – For federated server (apart from host itself), no additional space is required since data is not stored but served from the underlying sources.

- **A single source of truth** – It would be a single source of truth for the underlying data. Most recent data would be fetched which means less errors, happier customers, and more reliable business information.

- **Fast data access** – The access to underlying data sources is usually quite fast, often involving just a single intermediate step, given the underlying data source is built to support the query use case of the top caller.

But there are some negatives in data federation model:

- **Schema changes** – Underlying database may change its schema, but such change is not reflected in the federation layer.

- **Slow data access** – Mismatch of capabilities for the federated queries (OLAP) against underlying database (OLTP). While the query can be run, it is slow and causes load on the underlying system. The federation layer is also not always optimized to perform the complex query breakdown and pushdown logic into the underlying database causing slow data processing.

- **Lack access** – Often the databases are private to a service and not exposed to allow external entities outside of the service to access it directly.

- **Security and access control** – Security and access control are often enforced inside the application layer. Accessing the database directly may violate these requirements.

- **Impacting other use cases** – If the same underlying database is used for federation use cases and other use cases, the database can be overloaded and cause production issues.

- **Cost of the added layer of infrastructure** – Getting a single point of access for all underlying data comes with additional cost.

So how does the data federation usually look inside organizations? There are often multiple databases and separate data silos that are hard to access, and fragmented access to data could make business information inconsistent and unreliable. In such situations data federation brings all the data together. The control of the original databases remains with the division or branch, ensuring continued accuracy. This makes the implementation far more supported, with more political buy-in throughout all levels of the organization.

Organizations usually have tens of databases. Advancements in technology development push custom-built platforms out of use, and no one piece of software will ever meet all business requirements. As legacy systems are retired, data still needs to be accessed. Organizations incorporate data warehouses, cloud and on-premises, and data integrations. And it is the situation where data federation shines becoming a seamless system satisfying all requirements. Although usually it is quite difficult to set up a proper data federation with security and performance since it requires each underlying participant to build and support dedicated databases of the right type for the use case, the right amount of capacities, and the right access control. There are limited cases where this makes sense, primarily when the use case for federated access is the same use case for underlying database.

Denormalization and Sharding

Design of tables and relations between them in the relational database could be very different case by case and heavily dependent on the type of data you want to store and requirement for the product or service.

When you considering should you repeat the same information across the tables, there could be two extremes: repeat nothing and rely on relations between tables and joins, and repeat as much information as possible so every time you can just query a single table and set all that you need. In reality the design of the database lies somewhere in between.

Normalization is the process of reorganizing data in a database so there is no redundancy and data dependencies are logical. The opposite process, when you replicate information between tables and thus reduce dependencies between them, is called denormalization.

There are two goals of the normalization process: eliminating redundant data (e.g., storing the same data in more than one table), identifying shared information, and establishing relationships ensuring data dependencies make sense (only storing related data in a table). Both of these make it easier to develop applications to update information in a consistent manner.

There are a series of guidelines for organizing your database which are called the normal forms. They are numbered from 1 to 5 and called NF1, NF2, ... , NF5. And the forms progress from the least demanding NF1 to the very strict NF5. We will not go deep into these forms, but just list the common normalization steps applied to the database:

- Eliminate duplicative columns from the same table.

- Create separate tables for each group of related data, and identify each row with a unique column or set of columns.

- Create relationships between these new tables and their predecessors through the use of foreign keys.

- Remove columns that are not dependent upon the primary key.

- Every determinant must be a candidate key.

- Relations should not have multivalued dependencies.

And depending at which step you stop you end up in one or another normal form. And while database normalization is often a good idea, there are a lot of cases where deliberately violating the rules of normalization is a good practice.

And while normalized databases are space-efficient and make it easier to perform consistent updates, there is a big drawback to it. Queries against normalized databases which require collecting data from multiple tables via joins are often very slow. So when a product is growing and load on the database becomes more demanding often to improve the database performance, it needs to be denormalized. In short it is a process to combine normalized tables into one.

In case of a rapid increase in read requests in a database, denormalization brings a lot of benefits, but it has drawbacks as well. Let's describe the advantages of denormalization:

- **Increased query execution speed** – Since there is no need to use joins between tables, it is possible to extract the information from a single table, which is much faster.

- **Creating queries is much easier** – It is much easier to write a query which gets data from a single table, then crafting multijoin requests.

- **Easy to compute aggregated data** – It is easier to create statistics (i.e., average sales, number of customers) and include them in one table than to retrieve them by joining multiple tables.

- **Reduction of the number of tables in a database** – When properly denormalized the number of tables can be reduced, thus simplifying architecture.

But denormalization has disadvantages too:

- Tables would have a lot of data redundancy and possible duplication; the size of query processing could increase.

- Writes are slower as more data are written for a partial change.

- There will be increased cost to inserts and updates, since these operations, unlike in properly normalized databases, would need to touch more than a single record to perform the operation due to data duplication.

- Since data is duplicated, it may end up in an inconsistent state after multiple mutations. This is not an acceptable state and would be a bug, but since data is duplicated, it is easier to forget all the places the update has to take place.

Overall the majority of the big corporations have taken the path to use both normalized and denormalized approaches based on use cases, for example, normalized representations for updates and generate denormalized for read access only. Other systems use a combination in the same database: normalizing some fields while keeping others denormalized.

But how can we scale relational databases when single host processing power is not enough? The answer is sharding data. What is database sharding? It is a database horizontal partitioning – the practice of separating one table's rows into multiple different tables, known as partitions. Each partition has the same schema and columns, but also entirely different rows. And the data held in each partition should be unique and independent of the data held in other partitions[6]. Such partitioning can be done either by application between multiple independent database servers and databases that aren't aware of it or by one logical database cluster with multiple servers, where the database still needs to keep track of the shards as a whole and has limits on how much sharding it can support. Only when application level partitioning is implemented can it scale out horizontally without limit.

When sharding the tables got broken down in smaller independent parts, called logical shards. Then, these logical shards are served from different database instances where they can be modified or can be read together as well. Each database instance can contain multiple logical shards. The shards should be autonomous and don't share any of the same data or computing resources. In some cases it may make sense to replicate certain tables into each shard to serve as reference tables.

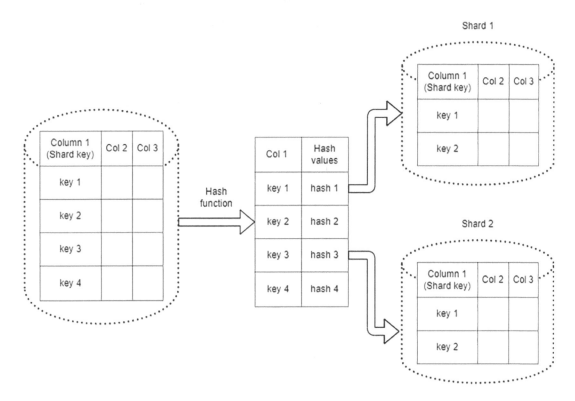

Figure 3-7. *Partitioning process*

---

[6]www.digitalocean.com/community/tutorials/understanding-database-sharding

As with anything else, let's explore the pros and cons of database sharding. The benefits would be

- **It helps with scaling** – Via sharding you can implement the horizontal scaling by adding more hosts to the database setup.

- **It helps with relational database simplicity** – It is quite simple to have a relational database on a single machine and then scale it up as necessary by upgrading its computing resources and then via sharding.

- **It speeds up in query response times** – When a call is directed to a single shard, it will be much faster to search through a single shard and then through the whole database.

- **It makes application more reliable** – An outage in the sharded database will likely affect only some subset of shards, and application will be at least partially available.

The drawbacks of sharded database would be

- **Difficulty** – It is quite difficult to implement sharding properly. If done incorrectly, there's a significant risk that the sharding process can lead to lost data or corrupted tables.

- **Dealing with shard unbalancing** – Sometimes one shard grows way faster than others, which creates uneven pressure on database hosts. The database would likely need to be repaired and resharded to allow for a more even data distribution.

- **Hard to go back** – Once a database has been sharded, it can be very difficult to return it to its unsharded architecture.

- Sharding is not natively supported in all databases.

- Slower query when data is required from multiple shards.

- Database cluster supporting sharding is more complex to operate and have degraded performance when some shards are down.

Now after you assessing sharding pros and cons and wanting to ahead, you need to understand sharding architectures, which represents how the data is being distributed between the shards:

- **Hash-based sharding** – Use a value taken from a new record, such as a customer's ID number, a client application's IP address, or a ZIP code, and plug it into a hash function to determine which shard the data should go to. What is good about this approach is that it distributes data evenly across shards and the needed shard can be found algorithmically as long as you know the corresponding key.

- **Range-based sharding** – Sharding data based on ranges of a given value. One of the main benefits of range-based sharding is that it allows queries of data using a range condition such as from A to B. Also it is relatively simple to implement. Every shard holds a different set of data, but they all have an identical schema as one another, as well as the original database. For example, if you shard on range prices of some product, you can create shards (0–49.99; 50–99.99; etc.). But range-based sharding doesn't protect data from being unevenly distributed, leading to the aforementioned database hotspots.

- **Directory-based sharding** – It involves creating and maintaining directory lookup tables which hold mapping information between data and corresponding shards. The main appeal of directory-based sharding is its flexibility and allows you to use any type of algorithm for sharding data (as opposed to only hash function in key based). But the need to connect to the lookup table before every query or write impacts the performance.

So should you apply sharding or not? Sharding is usually done when a single database hits its limitations like fast growth of data or increased volume of writes and reads, but you still want to use the current database solution and are not ready to evolve to a different system.

So in such cases, sharding can be a great way to keep growing your product or service and keep up with increasing load. But it also adds complexity and creates more potential failure points for your application.

NoSQL Systems

When your product or service rapidly expands and there is more and more demand on the database that even sharding your SQL solution is a stretch for the load, the answer might be in moving to some NoSQL solution if business use case allows.

The term NoSQL was used by Carlo Strozzi in 1998 to name his lightweight Strozzi NoSQL open source relational database that did not support the standard structured query language (SQL) interface, but was still relational. The expansion of NoSQL systems picked up ~10 years later with the emergence of an increasing number of nonrelational, distributed data stores, including open source clones of Google's Bigtable/MapReduce and Amazon's DynamoDB.

There a lot of ways to classify NoSQL systems, but the most common classification are as follows[7]:

- **Key-value store databases** – Where data is represented using a distributed hash table, such that each possible key appears at most once in the collection. Examples of such databases are Amazon DynamoDB and Redis.

- **Document store** – The data treated as a "document" with the assumption that all the structure is encapsulated in it, with the examples of such databases are MongoDB and Apache CouchDB.

- **Wide-column databases** – They use tables, rows, and columns, but unlike a relational database, the names and format of the columns can vary from row to row in the same table. It can be interpreted as a two-dimensional key–value store, with the examples of these databases being Apache Cassandra and HBase.

- **Graph databases**, which are designed for data whose relations are well represented as a graph consisting of elements connected by a finite number of relations. Examples of data include social relations, public transport links, road maps, network topologies, etc. Examples are Neo4j and Apache Giraph.

---

[7] Strauch, Christof. "NoSQL Databases". pp. 23–24. 27 August 2017.

And since most NoSQL databases lack the ability to express business entity relationships natively and easily, they require database schema to be designed differently to represent business entities and relationships. In practice when dealing with SQL databases, design requires to get as much data as possible in a single query, but with NoSQL multiple queries are often acceptable. It is common to do several queries to get the desired data since NoSQL queries are generally faster than SQL queries.

Let's look in more detail at different NoSQL database types.

Key-Value Store

Key-value stores are the least complex of the NoSQL databases. They are, as the name suggests, a collection of key-value pairs internally stored as a distributed hash table. This simplicity makes them the most scalable of the NoSQL database types, capable of storing huge amounts of data. The value in a key-value store can be anything: a string, a number, but also an entire new set of key-value pairs encapsulated in an object. An example of key-value store would be data about a person ("key" : "value"):

```
"name" : "Joe Smith"
street: "782 Southwest St."
city: "Seattle"
state:  "WA"
```

So how does the key-value database work? Key-value databases use compact, efficient index structures to be able to quickly and reliably locate a value by its key, making them ideal for systems that need to be able to find and retrieve data in constant time. It allows programs or users of programs to retrieve data by keys, which are essentially names, or identifiers, that point to some stored value. Key-value databases are defined simply, but can be extended and optimized in a lot of ways. There is no global list of common features between different key-value store implementations, but there are a few common ones:

- Retrieving a value (if there is one) stored and associated with a given key

- Deleting the value (if there is one) stored and associated with a given key

- Setting, updating, and replacing the value (if there is one) associated with a given key

143

This is the bare minimum key-value store should support. Of course many advanced and mature databases would support a lot of additional features (e.g., DynamoDB).

It is also important to understand use cases when using a key-value store is the right option; among them are

- Real-time random data access, for example, user session attributes.

- Caching – key-value store suits caching use cases very well (i.e., Memcached).

- Or in general application logic is well suited for simple key-based queries.

Although key-value databases are quite simple in theory, a lot of them have expanded functionality and powering a wide variety of use cases. The main drawback though is that it is very slow to retrieve related information. Hence, it is suited only for situations when the data are used separately and do not require retrieval of many keys per operation.

Document Store

The next popular type of NoSQL databases are document stores. Document stores are one step up in complexity from key-value stores: a document store does assume a certain document structure that can be specified with a schema. This type of database comes through as the most natural in a lot of cases, since the purpose is to store document-like data. Newspapers or magazines, for example, contain articles, which to be stored in relational databases needs to be broken down and represented in certain formats, while with document stores they can be stored largely as is in its own format.

The central concept of a document-oriented database is the notion of a document. While each document-oriented database implementation differs on the details of this definition, in general, they all assume documents encapsulate and encode data in some standard format or encoding. Encodings in use include XML, YAML, JSON, etc[8].

Documents in a document store are roughly equivalent to the programming concept of an object. Databases allow different types of documents in a single store, allow the fields within them to be optional, and often allow them to be encoded using different encoding systems. For example, the following is a document, encoded in JSON:

---

[8] Drake, Mark. "A Comparison of NoSQL Database Management Systems and Models". DigitalOcean. 9 August 2019

```
{
    "FirstName": "Joe",
    "Address": "782 Southwest St.",
    "Hobby": "fishing"
}
```

or it can be encoded differently, using XML format:

```
<contact>
    <firstname>Joe</firstname>
    <address>
      <type>Home</type>
      <street>782 Southwest St.</street>
    </address>
    <phone type="Cell">(123) 456-7890</phone>
  </contact>
```

They both share some information but also have unique elements. Unlike a relational database where every record contains the same fields, leaving unused fields empty, there are no empty "fields" in either document (record) in the preceding example. This approach allows new information to be added to some records without requiring that every other record in the database share the same structure. Often additional information is stored with the document which is metadata. That metadata may be related to facilities the data store provides for organizing documents, providing security, or other implementation-specific features.

The document database in its basic supports at least CRUD operations (Create, Read, Update and Delete). And documents are accessed in the database using unique keys. This key is a simple identifier (or ID), typically a string, a URI, or a path. Typically the database retains an index on the key to speed up document retrieval, and in some cases the key is required to create or insert the document into the database.

The feature where document store differs the most from key value is retrieval. Beyond the simple key-to-document lookup that can be used to retrieve a document, the database sometimes offers an API or query language that allows the user to retrieve documents based on content (or metadata), and obtaining just a subset of the document. For example, you may want a query that retrieves all the documents with a certain field set to a certain value. The set of query APIs or query language features available, as well as the expected performance of the queries, varies significantly from

145

one implementation to another. Likewise, the specific set of indexing options and configuration that are available vary greatly by implementation.

Wide-Column Databases

A wide-column database is a type of NoSQL database that extends key-value store in that the value is another structure made of column keys and values. In a wide-column database, the names and format of the columns can vary across rows, even within the same table.

Wide-column stores, also called extensible record stores, store data in records with an ability to hold very large numbers of dynamic columns. Since the column names as well as the record keys are not fixed, and since a record can have billions of columns, wide-column stores can be seen as two-dimensional key-value stores.

Wide-column stores are schema-free as document stores; however, the implementation is very different. And wide-column stores must not be confused with the column-oriented storage in some relational systems. This is an internal concept for improving the performance of an RDBMS for OLAP workloads and stores the data of a table not record after record but column by column.

Benefits of a wide-column NoSQL database include

- **Speed of querying** – Each data element can be referenced by the row key and a column range scan. Getting to the row key is fast like a key-value store. Obtaining the column values can be done by sequential scanning or range scan based on a condition of the column name.

- **Scalability** – The data is stored in individual rows which can be sharded or partitioned across multiple servers.

- **Flexible data model** – There is still the concept of rows, but reading or writing a row of data consists of reading or writing the individual columns. A column is only written if there's a data element for it.

So what is the wide-column database use case? Wide-column databases are ideal for use cases that require a large dataset that can be distributed across multiple database nodes, and the values can be ordered within that row for sequential access:

- Log data

- Time-series data, such as device monitoring or financial trading data

- Attribute-based data, such as user preferences or product features

- Real-time analytics

Most popular examples of wide-column databases are Cassandra, HBase, and Microsoft Azure Cosmos DB.

Graph Databases

Graph database is very useful in situations when your data has flexible and ad hoc relationships that cannot be easily expressed through data types and connections that resemble graphs. And it is because such databases use graph structures for semantic queries with nodes, edges, and properties to represent and store data. The graph relates the data items in the store to a collection of nodes and edges, the edges representing the relationships between the nodes. The relationships allow data in the store to be linked together directly and, in many cases, retrieved with one operation. Graph databases can manage distinct and heterogeneous relationships per data object rather than per data types compared to a relational database. Relationships can be intuitively visualized using graph databases, making them useful for heavily interconnected data[9].

The underlying storage mechanism of graph databases can vary. Some depend on a relational engine and "store" the graph data in a table; others use a key–value store or document-oriented database for storage, making them inherently NoSQL structures.

Let's understand how graph databases portray the data. A graph database is a database that is based on graph theory. It consists of a set of objects, which can be a node or an edge.

---

[9] Yoon, Byoung-Ha; Kim, Seon-Kyu; Kim, Seon-Young (March 2017). "Use of Graph Database for the Integration of Heterogeneous Biological Data". Genomics & Informatics. 15 (1): 19–27.

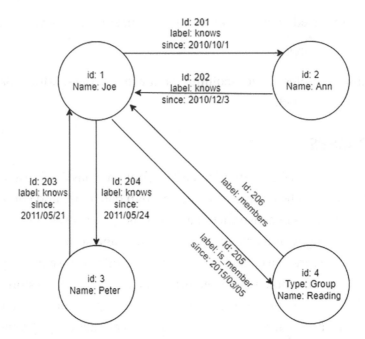

Figure 3-8. *Graph database*

- **Nodes** – Represent entities or instances such as people, businesses, accounts, or any other item to be tracked. They are roughly the equivalent of a record, relation, or row in a relational database, or a document in a document-store database.

- **Edges** – Termed graphs or relationships, are the lines that connect nodes to other nodes, representing the relationship between nodes. The edges can either be directed or undirected. In an undirected graph, an edge connecting two nodes has a single meaning. In a directed graph, the edges connecting two different nodes have different meanings, depending on their direction.

- **Properties** – Are information associated with nodes. For example, if Wikipedia were one of the nodes, it might be tied to properties such as website, reference material, or words that start with the letter w, depending on which aspects of Wikipedia are germane to a given database.

Graph databases are a powerful tool for graph-like queries, for example, computing the shortest path between two nodes in the graph. And graphs are flexible, meaning it allows the user to insert new data into the existing graph without loss of application functionality. There is no need for the designer of the database to plan out extensive details of the database's future use cases.

And there are multiple types of graphs that can be categorized; among them are

- **Social graph** – This is about the connections between people.

- **Intent graph** – This deals with reasoning and motivation.

- **Consumption graph** – Also known as the "payment graph," the consumption graph is heavily used in the retail industry.

- **Interest graph** – This maps a person's interests and is often complemented by a social graph.

- **Mobile graph** – This is built from mobile data.

As you can see, there are a lot of real-life use cases where representing the data as a graph makes a lot of sense and provides certain benefits. With the increase of importance and desire to provide corresponding solutions, the development of graph-oriented DBs is on the rise, and there are a lot of graph-oriented databases to choose from.

API Gateway and Service Discovery

Now let's suppose your product has grown to multiple services with the chosen communication style based on your use case. Say you use REST as the communication protocol and expose APIs of five+ microservices to your customer, like authentication service, account management service, read, update and notification services, and more.

Each service API has the need to handle common capabilities such as authentication, authorization, rate limiting, and monitoring. Additionally, you would want an API gateway to provide a single, unified API entry point across several or all of internal APIs. API gateway is an API management tool which will sit between clients and your services acting as a reverse proxy which accepts all calls to internal services and returns the appropriate responses. A microservice-based architecture may have from 10 to 100 or more services, and API gateway can help provide a unified entry point for external consumers, independent of the number and composition of internal microservices.

Most enterprise APIs are deployed via API gateways. It's common for API gateways to handle common tasks that are used across a system of API services, such as user authentication, rate limiting, and statistics.

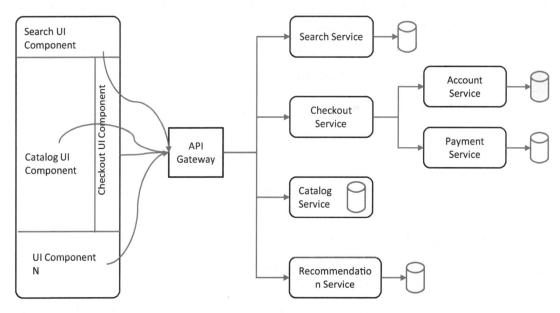

Figure 3-9. *Introduction of API gateway to ecommerce microservices architecture*

In Figure 3-9 you can see the introduction of API gateway to our ecommerce microservices architecture which hides the service layer for clients and presents a unified access point.

Additionally we could also have API gateways in front of Account Services, Payment Services, and others. The collection of API gateways, when used one per service, forms a service mesh to allow centralized control of service-to-service communication.

So let's understand why to use API gateway and what benefits it provides. Among the main benefits are

- An additional layer of security to your microservices. API gateways protect your APIs from overuse and abuse and help to prevent malicious attacks by providing an additional layer of protection from attacks such as SQL injection, XML Parser exploits, and denial-of-service (DoS) attacks.

- It prevents exposing internal details to external clients. API gateway will separate public APIs from internal microservice APIs allowing relatively painless subsequent changes to internal infrastructure, adding additional capabilities like analytics and monitoring tools, monetization, and authentication.

- It enables support for mixing communication protocols. API gateway can provide an external, unified API protocol across all communications while allowing teams to choose what best fits the internal architecture. For example, a common choice would be exposing externally REST API, but internally microservices would communicate with each other using gRPC.

- Decreased microservice complexity by abstracting common infrastructure like authorization, access control, and rate limiting.

There are also some drawbacks from using API gateway which should be considered before using, such as

- More complex deployment process vs. just deploying your service which now would require coordination with API gateway.

- API gateway can become a bottleneck in architecture of the product, so it needs to be built/architectured with scalability in mind.

- Configuration of the routing logic must be managed during deployment, to ensure proper routing from the external API to the proper microservice.

But overall an API gateway is a useful concept which breaks client requests into multiple requests, routes them to the right places, produces a response, and keeps track of everything. It often simplifies development and helps products to scale, so no wonder that all of the leading tech companies have API gateway as part of architecture in their products and solutions.

Service Registry, Authentication, and Authorization

Since API gateway is an interface to a large set of services for whom it acts as an entry point, the API gateway needs to know how to call such services. To help with this problem, we introduce a service registry which is an essential part of a microservice-based architecture.

Service registry is a catalogue of services, which stores and provides information on live endpoints of services behind API gateway. When a client needs to send a request to a service, the service registry provides the information about the endpoint in which the service is live. Service registry is tracking and storing information on multiple locations where microservices are available, updating states of instances going live and taking down.

Service registry provides multiple benefits for our architecture by becoming a documented single point of truth, validated and agreed upon by all parties involved. In addition the service itself can be easily designed to be a separate microservice itself used by API gateway for resolving user request paths.

Also API gateway usually is the ideal point for any common operations which should be performed on any user request such as authentication (AuthN) and authorization (AuthZ).

Authentication is the process of verifying who you are and making sure you are who you say you are, while authorization is the process of verifying that you have access to something.

When a user tries to access information, the authentication process begins, and this process usually requires some sort of user credentials to identify that the user is the one who he claims to be.

After that comes authorization, which is the process of determining that the authenticated user can perform the action (read data, store information, etc.).

Both these processes can become quite complicated in large systems, where each service must also perform authorization by returning only authorized data. We will cover the topic in more detail in one of the next chapters, but for the purpose of building microservices architecture for our ecommerce website, they could be represented as a separate service that is called by the API gateway on every request to validate if the user has the correct authentication and authorization.

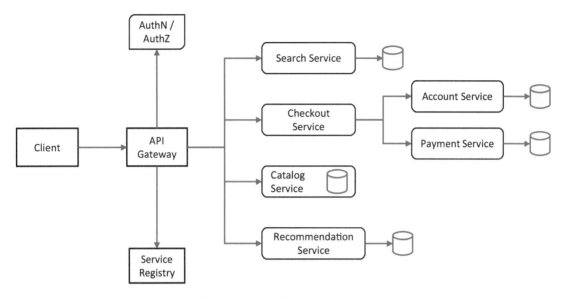

Figure 3-10. *Introduction of AuthN/AuthZ and service registry*

Content Delivery Networks (CDNs)

Let's say you've built service and exposed APIs, put in place proper monitoring and keep growing. At some point you realized from metrics that your customers are international now, but with this the max and average latency started crawling up, especially on heavy operations which involves transmitting large amounts of content, such as audio and video, over the network. The reason for it is your content being served from a single place and being transmitted over half of the planet to your customers. And content delivery network is a solution specifically designed to help services scale in such situations.

So what is CDN (content delivery network)? It is a geographically distributed group of servers which sits on the communication path with the user and provides fast delivery of Internet content. CDN does not really host the content and does not replace the web host, but you can think of it as a distributed cache sitting across the globe and serving heavyweight content to the customers[10].

So how exactly does CDN work? It is a network of services to quickly and reliably deliver content to clients. In order to improve speed and connectivity, a CDN will place servers at the exchange points between different networks and are often placed at Internet exchange points.

---

[10] www.cloudflare.com/learning/cdn/what-is-a-cdn/

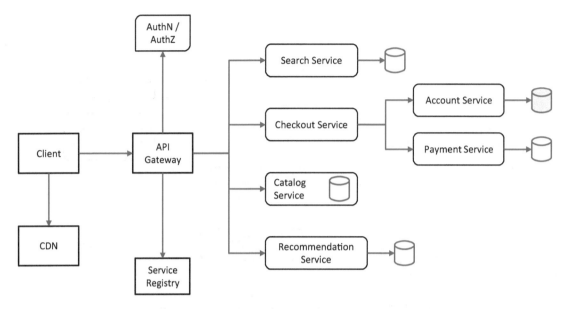

Figure 3-11. *Introduction of content delivery network*

CDN provides a number of benefits and improves latency, reliability, and redundancy of the service or product. Let's discuss some of them:

- **Improves load times for websites** – Direct impact to the latency, since content is served from close to customer locations web pages load much faster, which helps with customer satisfaction and retention.

- **Reduce network bandwidth cost** – Since heavyweight content is not served from central locations and thus it reduces the bandwidth traffic and cost. (Although CDN will cost as well, so it might be evened out in a lot of cases.)

- **Increase of availability and redundancy for content** – Media is distributed and deep cached in multiple locations, which reduces the load on websites which in turn helps its availability.

Usage of CDN is very widespread in the top technological companies. As soon as your service or product archives high volume and you serve media content, CDM becomes almost mandatory in order to scale and sustain load.

Load Balancer and Reverse Proxy

When scaling up the application, you generally want to avoid situations when one host receives way more calls than another since it might create situations when one host dies from load while another could still serve all the request. Load balancers are used to mitigate such situations in modern applications.

What is a load balancer? Although load balancing can be done toward any types of resources such as computers, a computer cluster, network links, central processing units, or disk drives, most commonly when we speak about building production systems, it is referred to efficiently distributing incoming network traffic across a group of back-end servers, also known as a server farm or server pool[11].

Load balancer sits in front of your servers and routes client requests to all servers which can take the requests, often trying to achieve efficiency and maximizing capacity. It performs important functions like distributing client requests or network load efficiently across multiple servers, ensuring high availability and reliability by sending requests only to servers that are online, and providing the flexibility to add or subtract servers as demand dictates.

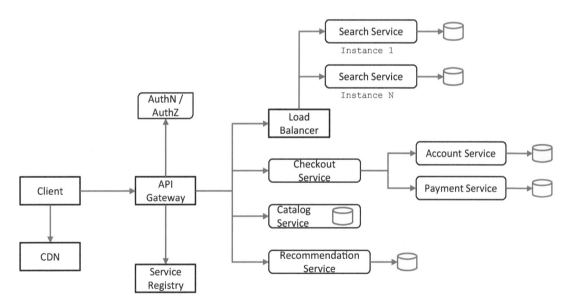

Figure 3-12. *Introduction of load balancer for Search Service*

---

[11] www.nginx.com/resources/glossary/load-balancing/

As an example let's suppose that Search Service from our ecommerce website is under huge load and needs to be horizontally scaled. In such a case, we would just introduce the load balancer as the entry point into the Search Service (Figure 3-12). Load balancers can be introduced on a per-needed basis, or be a part of standard architecture to be deployed for every microservice.

There are different ways how do load balancers make decisions where to send customer traffic; the most popular ones are

- **Round-robin** – Load is handled in a rotating sequential manner. The algorithm assumes that each host is able to process the same number of requests and each new request is sent to the next host in a loop.

- **Weighted round-robin** – Servers are rated based on the relative amount of requests each is able to process. Those having higher capacities are sent more requests.

- **Least connections** – Load balancer maintains the information on how many active connections each server has and sends requests to the server having the fewest number of active connections, assuming all connections generate an equal amount of server load.

- **Weighted least connections** – Servers are rated based on their processing capabilities. Load is distributed according to both the relative capacity of the servers and the number of active connections on each one.

- **Source IP hash** – Combines the source and destination IP address in a request to generate a hash key, which is then designated to a specific server. This lets a dropped connection be returned to the same server originally handling it.

Some algorithms are more sophisticated, like weighted least connections, which provides additional balancing by preferring the most available server, but it also requires maintaining additional information, or in some cases obtaining the information from servers.

No matter which the load balancer will be used, they provide numerous benefits to your application:

- **Increase scalability** – Application can react to increased customer load by adding additional servers behind load balancer.

- **Redundancy** – When you have all the servers behind the load balancer and one of them fails, the load balancer will just send subsequent requests to another server, mitigating impact to users from single host failure.

- **Reduced downtime** – Servers behind the load balancers can be under maintenance, replacement, or update process without any impact to users.

- **Increased flexibility** – Allows maintenance, traffic redirection, and other operations on servers fleet easily.

Load balancers are most commonly deployed when a site needs multiple servers because the volume of requests is too much for a single server to handle efficiently. Deploying multiple servers also eliminates a single point of failure, making the website more reliable. One useful function of some load balancers is session persistence, which means sending all requests from a particular client to the same server.

But there is another useful concept for serving customer traffic which is close to load balancers which is worth touching here, reverse proxy. A reverse proxy accepts requests from a client, forwards it to a server that can fulfill it, and returns the server's response to the client. It sounds close to what load balancers do but still different.

Deploying load balancers is usually useful when you have multiple servers, but reverse proxy is useful to deploy even with a single host. Reverse proxy acts as an interface to the server for client traffic and accepts requests from web browsers and mobile apps for the content hosted at the website, providing the following benefits:

- **Increased security** – Hiding information about internal networks, could include features to prevent DDoS attacks, for example, rejecting blocklisted IP addresses.

- **Increased scalability and flexibility** – Because clients see only the reverse proxy's IP address, you are free to change the configuration of your back-end infrastructure.

157

- **SSL termination** – Reverse proxy could be a common solution for your web servers, since decryption and encryption can be computationally expensive.

- **Caching and compression** – Reverse proxy can add additional layers of cache and perform compression of traffic for increased network through output.

API gateway, load balancer, and reverse proxy are closely related. Often these are functionalities within the same product. For example, nginx can be used for API gateway, load balancing, and reverse proxy.

Cache

Usually dev teams and product owners face the situations when the performance of the service needs to be optimized, response time to simple retrieval requests needs to be improved, or the load on the back-end system needs to be reduced. One of the most popular solutions to these types of problems is caching.

So what is a cache? A cache is a hardware or software component that stores data so that future requests for that data can be served faster; the data stored in a cache might be the result of an earlier computation or a copy of data stored elsewhere.

Motivation

Why do we need caching at all? What benefits does caching provide?

First, it reduces application latency a lot. Simply, due to the fact that it has all the frequently accessed data stored, it doesn't have to make a request to the data source when the user requests for the data, or does not need to compute the data which was previously computed and currently stored in cache. This makes the application response times faster.

Second, it intercepts all the user data requests before they go to the database. This averts the database bottleneck issue. The database is hit with a comparatively lesser number of requests reducing database contention making database access more performant.

Third, cache improves availability. When accessing a remote data source, caching the returned data allows our service to continue to function when there are temporary disconnect at the remote source.

And the last, cache usually helps with application costs. By using cache on different layers, we reduce compilation/processing costs, database requests, etc. Database read and write operations are expensive, or there are situations when too much write is happening to the service with short-lived data (e.g., online games), in which cases data can just be written to cache.

For example, in our ecommerce application, we might notice that requests to Catalogue service are highly repetitive, listing largely similar sets of data which require relatively costly queries to the database. By introducing a cache layer (Figure 3-13), we are reducing the cost of operations and improving application latency and availability. If the Catalogue service is down, the main service is not impacted.

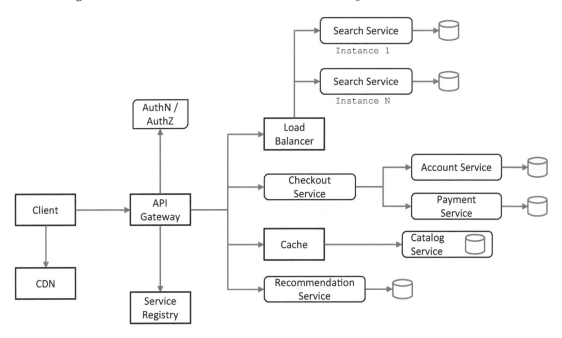

Figure 3-13. *Introduction of cache layer for Catalogue service*

Types of Caching (Client, Server, Distributed)

Let's discuss the types of caching out there. We know that the main purpose of caching is to store intermediate data which would be accessed when needed, speeding up execution of operations.

As an example we take a simple retrieval call in the user's web browser. The first and most basic type of cache on the requests path would be application or client-side cache. The Application Cache allows to specify which files the browser should cache, which saves the network time not having to redownload the data again. It will give an application several advantages such as

- **Speed** – Since resources come from local storage and there is no need for the network request.

- **Resilience** – If your site goes down for "maintenance" (as in, someone accidentally breaks everything), your users will get the offline experience.

The next type of caching is server-side caching, which is the temporary storing of web files and data on the origin server for reuse. When the server receives a request, it then checks the local cache on the host if the requested information is already present. If it is present (cache hit), the information returned in request saving computational and network resources. In case information is not present (cache miss), the usual computation, database calls, etc., are performed. The generated result is usually stored locally for potential future usage.

This process helps avoid repeatedly making expensive database operations to serve up the same content to many different clients. Server-side caching is often a good option, as it significantly reduces the operation on the server, especially for static content. Without it the server needs to recreate the entire content per user request, so it helps limit the cost of servers and resources during the process of a data request from the database and back to the browser.

There are obvious differences between client-side and server-side caching, and depending on use case, one or another solution could be proven better. But in a lot of cases, the product could benefit from implementing both.

And there is a third type of caching used in large-scale distributed systems. A distributed cache is a cache which has its data spread across several nodes in a cluster, across several clusters or across several data centers located around the world.

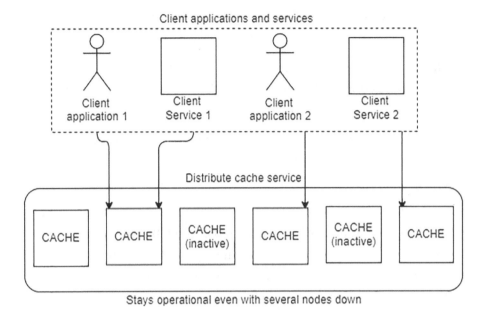

Figure 3-14. *Distributed cache*

Distributed caching is being widely used in the industry today. It has the potential to scale on demand and is highly available due to being deployed on multiple nodes.

Scalability, high availability, and fault tolerance all are crucial to large-scale services, and going offline is usually unacceptable, which would cause huge losses for business. Examples are stock markets, finance sector, payments, cloud providers, etc. They have no scope for going down. They are distributed across multiple nodes with a pretty solid amount of redundancy. This type of caching is preferred for cloud computing.

How is distributed cache different from simple server-side caching? The traditional cache is hosted on a few instances and is limited by it; that is why it's hard to scale it on the fly. It's not so much available and fault-tolerant in comparison to the distributed cache design.

There are several common use cases for distributed caching[12]:

- As with traditional server-side caching, the most important use case is the cache layer in-front of a database which saves frequently accessed data in-memory to cut down latency and load on it. It greatly helps with removing DB bottlenecks.

---

[12] Khan, Iqbal. "Distributed Caching On The Path To Scalability". MSDN (July 2009)

- **Storing user sessions** – They are stored in the cache to avoid losing the user state in case any of the instances go down.

- **Shared storage** – In-memory distributed caching could also be used for message communication between the different microservices running in conjunction with each other.

- **In-memory data stream processing and analytics** – In-memory data stream processing requires low latency and can use the data in a distributed cache during the processing of the data in the stream.

So how does distributed cache work? It is essentially an in-memory key-value database, implemented by a distributed hash table which has a responsibility of mapping object values to keys spread across multiple nodes. Distributed hash table allows easy horizontal scaling of the cache and helps manage node failures.

And what are the strategies of caching? There are several strategies for caches which are applicable to the corresponding use cases:

- **Cache aside** – The most common strategy. Cache works along with the data source. When a request comes in, data is first checked in a cache; if not found, it is fetched from the data source, returned to the user, and written to cache.

- **Read through** – In this strategy the cache is always consistent with the database. The information in this strategy is lazy loaded in the cache, only when the user requests it. The cache is sitting on the path of every request, and when a cache miss happens, the data is fetched using a registered factory or fallback function from the data source, gets written to cache, and only after that gets returned to the user.

- **Write through** – In this strategy, every information written to the database goes through the cache. Before the data is written to the DB, the cache is updated with it. Although it adds some latency, this works well for write-heavy systems.

- **Write back** – In this strategy the data is directly written to the cache instead of the database. And the cache after some delay as per the business logic writes data to the database. It is a fast strategy, but a risk in this approach is if the cache fails before the DB is updated, the data might get lost, so should be applicable to use cases when data loss is acceptable.

The popular distributed caches used in the industry are Ehcache, Memcached, Redis, and Riak. For example, Memcached is heavily used in Google Cloud.

Asynchronism

In the distributed systems, a single service can span a great number of hosts, all of them doing some computational tasks and need to collaborate to accomplish one or another process. And although some systems can be synchronized, where operations (instructions, calculations, logic, etc.) are coordinated by one, or more, centralized clock signal, usually it is complicated and/or too restrictive for a lot of use cases. And an asynchronous system, in contrast, has no global clock. Asynchronous systems do not depend on strict arrival times of signals or messages for reliable operation. Coordination is achieved using event-driven architecture triggered by network packet arrival, changes of signals, handshake protocols, and other methods.

In the event-driven architecture, hosts perform actions in the reaction to events. An event generally could be defined as a change in state. This architectural pattern may be applied by the design and implementation of applications and systems that transmit events among loosely coupled software components and services. Building systems around an event-driven architecture simplifies horizontal scalability in distributed computing models and makes them more resilient to failure. This is because application state can be copied across multiple parallel snapshots for high availability. Adding extra nodes becomes easy since you can simply take a copy of the application state, feed it a stream of events, and run with it.

In the event-driven architecture, application data is defined as a stream of events, usually distributed by a central system called event broker and consumed or published by other systems directly or via adapters. This streaming of data uses various mechanisms like message queues, enterprise service bus (ESB), or out-of-the-box solutions like Apache Kafka[13].

---

[13] K. Mani Chandy Event-Driven Applications: Costs, Benefits and Design Approaches, California Institute of Technology, 2006

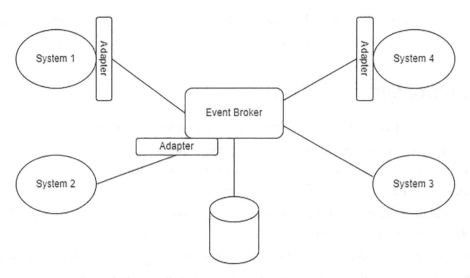

Figure 3-15. *Event-driven architecture*

The core of event-driven architecture is a notion of event – a significant change in state, which is triggered when a user takes an action. For example, a customer buys a product or books a ticket.

There are no specific rules for developing an event-driven application, but developers use solutions from different technology providers instead like RabbitMQ, ActiveMQ, Apache Storm, etc.

Advantages of event-driven architectures are

- Adding events, data producers, and consumers is very easy.

- Rolling back and rolling forward (preplaying) changes is relatively easy and helpful when issues occur.

- Can support transactional guarantees.

- Versatile, the functionality can run in parallel and be added, extended, upgraded, or replaced without taking the system down.

But there are some downsides to the event-driven architecture:

- **Complexity of the development** – It's hard to know which event is connected to which microservice and what is the dependency between them, so understanding the flow of events in the architecture can be hard.

- There's not much control on when events occur and how they are consumed.

- Certain events cannot be rolled back.

- Event broker is a single point of failure and single point of contention. Noisy neighbors and events backing up blocking the queue can cause major data latency and performance degradation.

So let's look back at our ecommerce microservices architecture. We can introduce event-driven architecture as a means of communication between payments and notification service as seen in Figure 3-16. After the payment is processed, the event is sent via the event broker which gets asynchronously consumed by the notification service. The event would trigger email notification to the corresponding user.

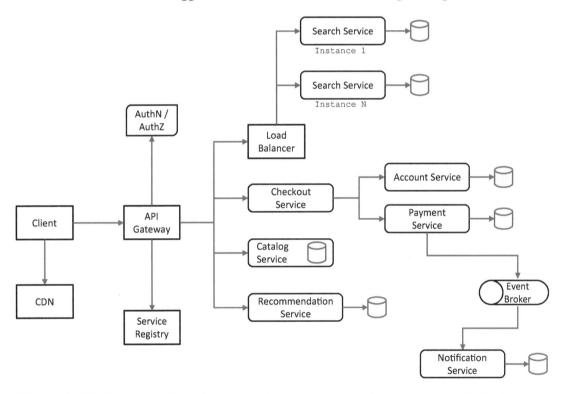

Figure 3-16. *Introduction of events into ecommerce microservices architecture*

Testing and Security

Finally we get to a very important aspect of every system – its security. Security is a complex issue related to infrastructure, software, people, and processes. There are threats against all of these dimensions. And most security issues happened because of people and processes rather than caused by machines.

And thus there are a lot of different threats to distributed systems, so it is important to implement countermeasures for expected threats for the purpose of the system to remain operational and cost-effective. Those threats are

- Threats which make your system nonaccessible like denial-of-service attacks. Unavailability of information from the system to the user would result in paralysis of the entire operation of an organization or part of activities depending on the attack. Mechanisms like timing responses, sizing responses, and connection control can help in solving the problem.

- **Information leakage** – Sensitive information can easily be revealed to unauthorized users that results in all types of consequences.

- **Unauthorized access** – Access control needs to be implemented involving models, access control policies, as well as mechanisms. Access control policies will provide a way to specify different roles and permissions that will lead to proper management of access to resources as well as information.

So what common mechanism should we implement when developing a distributed system to prevent the abovementioned threats? They are

- **Encryption** – There is a need of using a proper method of transforming sensitive data into unreadable formats (secret writing) through cryptography. The data needs to be encrypted in transit while transferred over the network as well as at rest when stored in one of the storing solutions like file system or database. Data in transit is encrypted via one of secured transfer protocols (i.e., TLS), and at rest via one or another encryption algorithms (i.e., AES).

- **Authentication** Usage of protocols which provide a series of communication procedures between users of the system and the server for the purpose of securing the communication process. The result of the process is validation by the system that the request is coming from the known user (i.e., logging in to the system).

- **Access control** – Would specify which users can access which resources in the system and can be done using access control list (ACL) that consists of permission lists related to resources. Or can be done by integrating a separate access management system which would validate access to the resources for each user request.

- **Change auditing** – A solid process with controls and auditing ensuring changes are reviewed, captured, and auditable.

Distributed system security is fundamentally more complex than stand-alone system security. This would be covered in more details in a separate chapter.

Wrap-Up

In this chapter we learned the main concepts on system design and how the systems evolved over time. A lot of companies started with monolithic design with now known and successful products, but they switched to service-oriented and microservices architectures over time due to the benefits they provide.

While building microservice-oriented systems, there are a lot to consider. Among the most important choices would be the communication style between services (REST, RPC, SOAP, or GraphQL). Do we need a speed of execution for internal services communication? RPC might be the right solution here. Are we looking to expose public API in alignment with other company's products and need to provide REST API along the company's policy guidelines? No matter the choice, good and comprehensive documentation is an almost mandatory part of any product.

Depending on the use cases, we might select either relational database or one of NoSQL solutions. For example, if a use case allows relational databases, such as MySQL could be a good choice, which would bring transactional guarantees and ease of use due to the massive ecosystem and a lot of knowledge in the developers' community. Or if data we want to store is fairly isolated and speed is the top priority? Then, one of the key-value stores might suit the use case.

API gateway in front of the service(s) would simplify authentication, authorization, rate limiting, and monitoring for the product. Content delivery networks will put the media resources closer to the user improving speed and reducing the load on the central infrastructure. And adding cashing solutions would further improve the availability of the system.

In the next chapter, we would learn about another important aspect of almost any product in the market, which is data. We would explore the aspects of data engineering, how data is modeled, organized, and used.

## CHAPTER 4

Data Engineering: The Supply Chain of Data

In 2006, British mathematician and Tesco marketing mastermind Clive Humby said, "Data is the new oil." This started a revolution where companies across industries started gathering more and more data of their customer usage patterns on digital and physical devices, data from machines, etc. and started to enrich them with other data sources both internal and external (to these companies) to understand what their customers like and dislike, improve customer experience through personalization, reduce waste, optimize operations, and eventually make more revenue.

With the digital experiences becoming more mainstream such as buying a coffee on the Starbucks app and advancement of Internet of things (IOT) – smart watches, smart thermostat, smart cars, etc. – the amount of data generated has increased exponentially and is only growing. As per an IDC whitepaper[1], the world's data is predicted to grow to 175 zettabytes by 2025; for reference, 1 zettabyte is equivalent to 1 trillion gigabytes. If you try to download 175 zettabytes over the average Internet connection speed of 25 Mb/s, then it will take you 1.8 billion years to do it.

To handle this humongous amount of raw data, data engineering was created which is the practice of designing, building, and operating data processing systems for collecting, storing, and analyzing data at scale. Two specialist roles were created as well, the first being "data scientist" – a role coined in 2008 by Dr. DJ Patil and Jeff Hammerbacher, heads of analytics and data at LinkedIn and Facebook – the second being "data engineer" – a role that started to crop up around 2011 in data-driven companies such as Facebook and Airbnb and eventually spread over to other companies.

---

[1] www.seagate.com/files/www-content/our-story/trends/files/idc-seagate-dataage-whitepaper.pdf

© Gaurav Sagar, Vitalii Syrovatskyi 2022
G. Sagar and V. Syrovatskyi, *Technical Building Blocks*, https://doi.org/10.1007/978-1-4842-8658-6_4

Existing tools and techniques weren't efficient or capable of handling this amount and diverse data, and a lot of innovation took place in the field of data storage, processing/transforming data, visualization, machine learning, etc. both by traditional software companies like Google, Amazon, Microsoft, and Facebook and a new wave of start-ups that tried to tackle some of these challenges. Some noteworthy start-ups in this space that you may have heard of are Tableau, a data visualization company that salesforce acquired in 2019 for $15.7 billion; Cloudera, a data management company that went private in an all cash transaction of $5.3 billion in 2021; Snowflake, a data warehousing company that reached a valuation of $70 billion on its first day of trading after its initial public offering (IPO), making it the biggest software IPO of all time; and Databricks, a company that offers an analytics platform for business, data science, and data engineering which raised $1.6 billion in August 2021 at a $38 billion valuation.

The data engineering team is very central to the functioning of any data-centric organization. Most often data engineering teams are nested within software engineering organizations, and most data engineers have education and skill sets that highly overlap with software engineers.

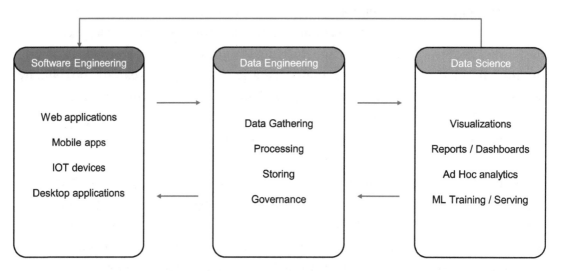

Figure 4-1. *Relationship between application software and system software products*

From a functional perspective, software engineering teams build the products end customers use such as web applications and mobile apps, and these **produce** the data from interactions of users with the product or the machine's telemetry data, etc. Data engineering teams collect this data and make it accessible and useful for the data science team, and finally, the data science teams generate ML models, do ad hoc analysis, and create visualizations to turn the data into information that the business executives "consume" to make data-driven decisions.

Refer to Figure 4-1 to see how data engineering fits between software engineering and data science and the movement of data. Data science teams can generate new data or enrich existing data to be used by the software engineering teams in the customer-facing product; an example is the data science team which generates a credit score for users that is saved in a data table by the data engineering team, which is accessed by the end-user application to make a decision to approve or deny the credit card application of an applicant.

You may still be wondering if data engineering is so new, how were companies making decisions before – was it all gut and intuition? Let's go into some history to find out.

Business Intelligence

Data engineering is the practice of collecting raw data from various sources, processing it, and storing it in formats to make it accessible to gain insights. Although data engineering gained a lot of attention since 2010, it was already practiced in finance, banking, and insurance industry verticals and was called "business intelligence" (BI). BI teams would enable business executives to make data-driven decisions and perform quantitative analysis to create predictive models for pricing, risks, trading, etc. For that they would get data from multiple sources and make it consumable for decision-making and analytics. Prior to 2010, data analysis required expensive products from the likes of SAS and Informatica, which were not affordable to other industries with less money; however, since 2010, the techniques utilized in above industries become more widely available and affordable. We will learn more of it, however, before that was BI looked like so we can understand in the later part of the chapter what has evolved from BI to data engineering.

Business intelligence (BI) is best understood with the relationship between two data processing systems called online transaction processing (OLTP) system and online analytical processing (OLAP) system. BI systems are focused on the OLAP side of this relationship. Let's understand the relationship between these systems and learn their architecture and the challenges that brought out the need to modernize the BI teams into data engineering teams.

OLTP Systems

Online transaction processing systems (OLTP) are a form of data processing system that are designed for real-time execution of large volumes of database transactions by many people, sometimes even at the same time, usually over the Internet, hence the word online. OLTP systems are designed and managed by software engineers and not generally by the members of business intelligence teams (or data engineers). Transaction here refers to the database transaction that signifies an atomic change of state for a business such as delivery of an order, salary received by an employee, adding a product to the online shopping cart, etc. Transaction atomicity ensures that either all "multiple changes of state" happen or none happens – to prevent issues like the debit happens in one account but the credit fails to happen.

Most applications we interact with on a day-to-day basis such as hotel reservation systems, airline booking systems, ATMs, etc. all use some flavor of OLTP systems. OLTP systems traditionally used a relational database for storage, to maintain data integrity and to support multitenancy. The transactions are either INSERT, UPDATE, or DELETE operations. To exemplify, if a user creates an account with a bank, the OLTP will do an INSERT of the customer details in a data table specific for storing the account details. If the user transfers money to another person, OLTP may do an UPDATE to reflect the right amount in her account, as well as UPDATE of the other account to deduct the amount transferred. Either both UPDATEs must occur or none. Now, let's say there wasn't an OLTP system; in that case, a couple can withdraw more amount of their joint bank account if they both made the request to withdraw the amount from two different ATMs but at the same time, or it may happen that a customer may get charged twice for a single purchase of the product.

Since this system is so business critical, these systems are made to process transactions fast (in milliseconds), and for that the database schema is designed to be highly normalized (generally 3NF) – that is, breaking data up into smaller reusable chunks to reduce redundancy. This increases efficiency as it makes it easy for the OLTP to process high volumes of transactions independently and it also saves from the extra processing required for maintaining data integrity if there is data redundancy. Data in OLTP systems is backed up religiously as this data is critical to run the business and any loss of data may result in significant loss of revenue as well as legal issues.

OLAP Systems

Businesses need insights into their operations over time to track and improve them. For example, the business executive of a large ecommerce company, say "Mythical Inc.," would like to track the number of orders made in a given quarter and compare it to the number of orders made in the previous quarter and the same quarter from the previous year. One may think, since the ecommerce company OLTP system's database has the transactions for all orders, it should be used to aggregate all transactions of orders for the given quarters. This approach has two challenges:

- **Limited resources** – This will require aggregation of data across millions of individual transactions that would be very resource intensive and, besides being slow to execute may slow down or block the real-time transactions being recorded in the system, which will have an adverse effect on the business and customer experience. Also, more complex queries will need more resources.

- **Missing data** – If the data required for aggregation was old, it may have been put in an archive and would not be available in the database of the OLTP for aggregation. Besides, the aggregation may need data from more than one of the OLTP sources, such as in case there is a dedicated OLTP by country to complete the ecommerce executive request.

To solve this, the second form of data processing systems were created called the online analytical processing (OLAP) systems which were aimed at people who need easy access to historical data to be able to analyze it and derive insights from it. The term OLAP was coined by E.F. Codd in a paper published by him in 1993, titled "Providing OLAP (On-line Analytical Processing) to User-Analysts: An IT Mandate." If you aren't already aware, E.F. Codd also invented the theory behind the relational databases and coined the term "relational databases" at IBM in 1970. At the core of the OLAP system lies a data storage system called "data warehouse." This is the bulk of work that the business intelligence teams would do, and even today most data engineers are primarily tasked with it. It wouldn't be wrong to say that the root of data engineering lies in OLAP.

While transactions from OLTP systems move to OLAP systems which are used to gain insights and make decisions, these decisions lead to the development of new business rules and strategy that changes in the OLTP systems. Hence, it's important to recognize that there is a two-way flow between OLAP and OLTP. The relationship between OLTP and OLAP is illustrated in Figure 4-2.

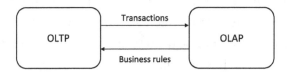

Figure 4-2. *Relationship between OLTP and OLAP systems*

Data Warehouse

A data warehouse is a central repository of data integrated from one or more data sources such as OLTP systems. Data warehouse stores current and historical data aggregated at various levels for analytical purposes in an enterprise. In simple words, it's another database that stores data from other data sources such as OLTP databases after processing that data and aggregating it to make it suitable for complex analytical (read SQL) queries. The concept of data warehouse dates to 1988 when Barry Devlin and Paul Murphy, researchers at IBM, introduced the term "business data warehouse" in their article "An architecture for a business and information system." The data in the data warehouse is added/updated periodically, usually every day but could be a shorter timeframe such as every 8 hours depending on the need of the business. There are four basic features of a data warehouse:

1. **Subject oriented** – Data warehouse only stores data around themes, i.e., subjects that are of interest to the enterprise such as finance, sales, inventory, etc. In simple words, this data should enable a subject matter expert to take business decisions.

2. **Integrated** – Data in the data warehouse is integrated from multiple data sources and shouldn't have any inconsistencies such as naming conventions of fields (columns), encoding scheme (such as referring to values of Male as "M" for the field "gender"), etc.

3. **Time variant** – Data in the data warehouse is historical and is timestamped. This means that unlike in OLTP systems where only the latest data is stored, the data warehouse stores all historical data. For example, an OLTP system used by an insurance company may store only the current address of the customer; however, a data warehouse will store all the addresses the customer had at different points in time.

4. **Nonvolatile** – Data in the data warehouse is read-only and can't be updated or deleted unless there is a legal or regulatory reason to do so.

Moving the data into data warehouse is done in a three-phase approach called extract, transform, and load (ETL) where data is first extracted from the data sources; then transformed with activities like joining data from multiple sources and aggregating it (e.g., summarizing data as total orders by region, by quarter, etc.) and deriving a new calculated field (e.g., final_price = discount_rt * product_price), etc.; and finally loaded into the data warehouse. We will learn of transformations in more detail later in this chapter.

Since data in the data warehouse is in an aggregated state, the business can now easily query data that helps in making data-driven decisions. The executive at Mythical Inc. can now get the number of orders made in a given quarter and compare it to the number of orders made in the previous quarter and the same quarter from the previous year and see if the business is growing or not through simple SQL query or using some business intelligence tools that offers a GUI to pull this data from the data warehouse.

Data Mart

A data mart is a subset of data from the data warehouse. This subset of data is specific to a subject such as finance and linked to the corresponding business team such as the finance team as end users in this case. In some cases, the subset can also be by region, or by both subject and region, etc. There are two ways of building data marts as shown in Figure 4-3:

1. **Independent data mart** – Data here is aggregated from OLTP systems based on subjects and saved into the data mart directly through the ETL process. The union of multiple data marts, either logical or physical, is what composes the data warehouse. This view was proposed by Ralph Kimball.

2. **Dependent data mart** – This is an actual subset of the data warehouse, which means this needs the data warehouse to exist first. The subset could be logical, where it could be a view on the data warehouse, or it could be a physical subset where data is extracted from the data warehouse and pushed into a separated data mart (a database again). This view was proposed by William H. Inmon.

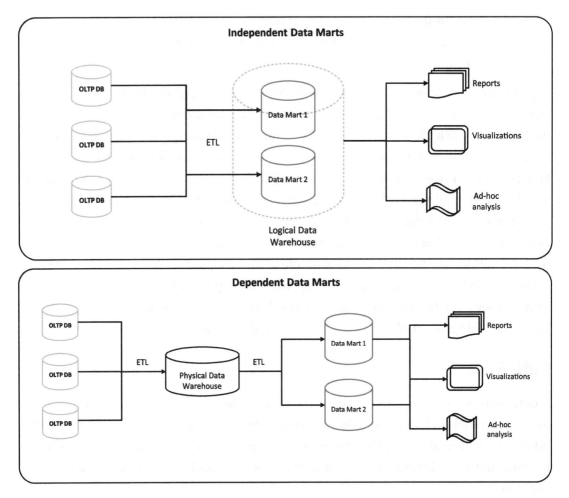

Figure 4-3. *Architectural difference between independent and dependent data marts*

Since data mart is a subset of data warehouse, it inherits all its features along with the fact that it is read-only. However, the biggest benefit lies in the fact that since data is now a subset, the queries are less complex and run faster; only data around a subject is available to the users. So, data marts bring some improvements over the data warehouses. However, queries can still be complex and, besides taking time to fetch data, may also require people with advanced SQL knowledge to be able to use them.

Data Cube

Data warehouse and data mart are at the end of the day still databases, and SQL queries would be executed to get data from them. Business reporting and executive decision-making require access to a lot of summarizations and numerical computation, something that is displayed in cross tabulations. Generating cross tabulations through SQL can get very complex and resource intensive. Let's understand that better through a hypothetical scenario. Let's say in 1994 the executives at the Honda car company wanted to see how the sales of their sedans were doing over the previous three years in the United States. They have the sales numbers (in thousands) by car and year recorded in a data mart (or data warehouse) as shown below in Figure 4-4.

Car	Year	Sales
Accord	1991	53
Civic	1992	65
City	1993	42
Civic	1991	75
City	1992	141
City	1991	127
Accord	1992	77
City	1993	128
Civic	1993	90
Civic	1992	33
City	1993	29
Civic	1992	23
Accord	1992	114
Accord	1993	69
City	1991	32

Figure 4-4. *Data in the OLAP table for Honda car sales in the United States; data is hypothetical*

And they would like to get a cross tabulation like shown in Figure 4-5. These cross tabulations are very popular, and reports generally have multiple of them.

Table: Car sales from 1991 - 1993				
Car	1991	1992	1993	Grand Total
Accord	53	191	69	313
City	159	141	199	499
Civic	75	121	90	286
Grand Total	287	453	358	1,098

Figure 4-5. Cross tabulation of Honda car sales data from the data in Figure 4-4

This request from the executive will likely come to a business analyst, and the business analyst will use SQL to get this data aggregated in the right format to create this crosstab. The SQL query to get data in this format is listed in Listing 4-1. The business analyst wrote two SQL queries that are union-ed together. The first SQL query creates the first three rows of cross tabulation in Figure 4-5, and the second SQL query creates the last "Grand Total" row. Each aggregation "SUM" creates the column for each year and the "Grand Total" for all years for a car.

Listing 4-1. Creating a cross tabulation through SQL

```
SELECT
  Car,
  SUM (CASE
    WHEN YEAR = '1991' THEN 1 ELSE 0
  END * Sales) AS '1991',
  SUM (CASE
    WHEN YEAR = '1992' THEN 1 ELSE 0
  END * Sales) AS '1992',
  SUM (CASE
    WHEN YEAR = '1993' THEN 1 ELSE 0
  END * Sales) AS '1993',
  SUM (Sales) AS 'Grand Total'
FROM sales
GROUP BY Car
```

```
UNION
SELECT
  'Grand Total',
  SUM (CASE
    WHEN YEAR = '1991' THEN 1 ELSE 0
  END * Sales) AS '1991',
  SUM (CASE
    WHEN YEAR = '1992' THEN 1 ELSE 0
  END * Sales) AS '1992',
  SUM (CASE
    WHEN YEAR = '1993' THEN 1 ELSE 0
  END * Sales) AS '1993',
  SUM (Sales) AS 'Grand Total'
FROM sales
```

I wouldn't be surprised if you are thinking that this looks too complex with SQL queries and you could have created this cross tabulation using something like Microsoft Pivot tables in Excel – however, don't forget this is 1994. Microsoft brought for the first time the "PivotTable" feature in Excel 5 in 1994, and Excel 5[2] could only have a maximum of 16,384 rows and 256 columns. All other spreadsheet software had similar limitations on size of rows and columns due to limited compute power (CPUs) and RAM size, so using SQL became a necessity.

What if I tell you that the "CASE" conditional expressions were launched in the third version of SQL called SQL-92 in November 1992, which means there is a high likelihood that the business analyst may have the OLAP data tables on a database that may not have support for SQL-92, i.e., no CASE expressions. Remember this is 1994 and software wasn't auto upgraded from the cloud; people would manually do upgrades of the software. The question is: How would the business analyst create this cross tabulation? Let's find out:

1. Write three SQL queries to get the sales by car for each year.

2. Write one SQL query to get the sales by car summed up for all the years.

---

[2] https://office-watch.com/2021/excel-a-history-of-rows-and-columns/

3. Join the output from these queries to get the first three rows of the crosstab.

4. Write three SQL queries to get the sales for each year (summed across the cars).

5. Write one SQL query to get the total sales across cars and years.

6. Join the output of these queries in 4 and 5 to get the last row of the crosstab.

7. Union (append) the first three rows with the last row to create the crosstab.

Eight SQL queries need to be executed first, and their output is joined or union-ed together to create a small crosstab, and I am sure you must have seen reports with far bigger and complex crosstabs. Since generating this kind of data in reports and for other ad hoc analysis required such complex SQL queries that would run over large data tables in the data warehouses or data marts, it would take long time (couple of minutes to hours) to get results of these queries as compute and storage resources were expensive. As a reference the price of 1 GB of RAM in 1995 was $32,000! This would impact the speed at which business can make decisions and executives wanted these insights fast.

So, a new data storage and analysis medium was introduced called data cube, also called the OLAP cube. A data cube aggregates and caches a subset of data from a data warehouse or a data mart in terms of facts and dimensions. A data cube is not another database but a completely new form of data storage that is used for reporting and analysis.

Caution   Don't confuse data cubes with cubes in mathematics as data cubes don't have equal sides and can also have more than three dimensions.

A simple data cube can be visualized as shown in Figure 4-6 which has three dimensions (categories), namely, region, day, and product, and each cell of the data cube has aggregated data around a fact (metric) like sales. Note that the dimensions may have a hierarchy. For example, Day dimension may have a higher hierarchy of Months, Quarters, and Years.

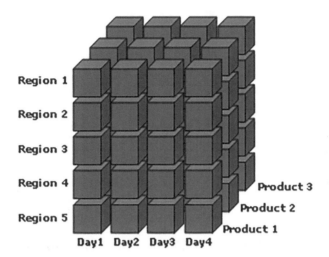

Figure 4-6. *A representation of a data cube with three dimensions. Source: Microsoft*

Data from data cubes is accessed not by SQL but through multidimensional queries (MDX); however, the most common form is to connect a spreadsheet such as Excel with the data cube and fetch data through drag and drop in a pivot table. Just imagine the productivity boost for the business analyst, who is now able to make the cross tabulation in Figure 4-3 within minutes and without having to write any SQL statement, all by dragging and dropping dimensions into rows and columns, and the facts into values of the pivot table. Even the business executives can do themselves now, and decisions backed by data can be made fast – isn't that what the executives wanted after all? So, it seems all the challenges have been solved now from access control all the way to speed of getting results of analysis. Figure 4-7 illustrates the conceptual relationship between a data warehouse, a data mart, and a data cube.

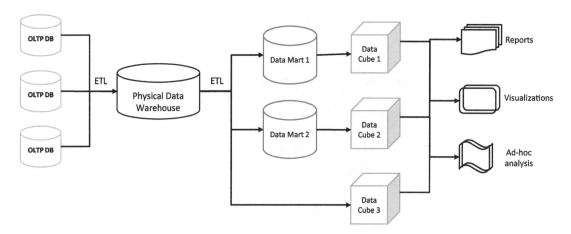

Figure 4-7. *Relationship between OLTP systems, data warehouses, data marts, and data cubes*

Need for Evolving Traditional BI

The teams continued with this traditional BI model of OLAP for some time until the mid-2000s, and then multiple things happened:

1. Big data came into existence which forced research and development of new forms of data storage and retrieval. This led to significant developments in open source space to process big data, reducing the reliance of enterprises on expensive solutions from traditional BI vendors.

2. Both compute and memory became very cheap allowing storage of huge amounts of data without the need for a lot of aggregation (summarization) and distributed computation on the data without preoptimization.

3. Advances in artificial intelligence and democratization of it brought in the need to be able to access any data collected if the data needed isn't available in the data warehouse. This need got further propelled for unstructured data (images, raw text, etc.) use cases such as natural language processing and computer vision, as data warehouse is only meant for structured data.

4. ELT pipelines started to become more and more complex, and there became a need for better scheduling and orchestration tools for it, along with the need to develop some other forms of data processing pipelines.

With the advent of big data, traditional OLAP storages were no longer enough to support the volume of data or need to constantly update the schema based on a new variety of data added from source or new business request. Also, there was significant advancement in processing data through distributed massively parallel systems that made getting insights from this big data affordable and feasible. These developments led to the evolution of business intelligence teams into data engineering teams and made data marts and data cubes from being popular in the BI era to nearly obsolete today. Let's go through some of the key aspects of modern data engineering and learn more about big data, new data storage systems, and details of data processing pipelines.

Data Engineering

To support the growing needs of the enterprises with the advent of big data, traditional BI teams started to evolve. They split up two teams, namely, data engineering and data science teams. We will learn data science in Chapter 5. The primary function of data engineering teams became data integration. Data integration is the process of combining multiple heterogeneous data sources and providing a unified view of that data often in terms of a data warehouse. You may wonder how this is different from ETL pipelines – the short answer is that ETL is one of the types of data pipelines used for data integration. We will learn about data integration and data pipeline in more detail shortly. But before that, let's build some foundational knowledge on some new types of data sources, storage mediums, and processing which are necessary to understand data integration better.

Big Data

Big data refers to data that is too large or complex and is growing exponentially with time making it hard and/or impossible to store in a traditional database or process in a traditional data processing application. Gartner gives a good definition of big data:

Big data is high-volume, high-velocity and/or high-variety information assets that demand cost-effective, innovative forms of information processing that enable enhanced insight, decision making, and process automation.

—Gartner Inc.

The above definition is based on the three characteristics of big data, introduced by Doug Laney, an analyst at Gartner Inc.:

1. **Volume** – This should be obvious as the word big data itself is about the sheer volume. Big data is at the very least in TBs but can be in petabytes (PBs) too for an enterprise. An example of big data set by volume would be all credit card transactions in the United States for a day.

2. **Variety** – Back in the days, data was only in the form of spreadsheets and databases, also called structured data as the data is stored in a tabular format. However, big data encompasses unstructured data like images, audio, ebooks, etc. and semistructured data like twitter tweets which have a JSON structure, but it's not structured enough to be used directly for analysis.

3. **Velocity** – Big data is produced more continually as compared to data saved in OLAP in the early 2000s. This brings two related forms of velocity; one is the rate at which big data is generated and the other at which big data is processed and made available for decision-making.

An important consideration of big data is its metadata, i.e., the data about big data. This is of significant value while processing big data and is usually of structured type. For example, a big data set of images may contain metadata of the location of the image, the timestamp of when the shot was taken, the focal length of the camera, camera name, etc.

Big Data Sources

In the traditional OLAP world, the sources of data were OLTP databases that were recording transactions, i.e., business activities. Today the scope has expanded on what transactions are being recorded and new sources introduced that have become critical to analytics for making business decisions. The three biggest sources of big data are

1. **Transactional data** – This is the data gathered from online and offline business activities. This data includes attributes of the activity such as transaction time, products purchased, payment method, payment amount, etc. This is what the traditional OLTP systems were capturing; however, in the current times, the volume of data and the different attributes of the business activity being captured have both increased making this big data.

2. **Social data** – This is the data gathered from media platforms like Facebook, Twitter, YouTube, etc. and comprises tweets, shares, uploads, comments, etc. This data is important for a business as it helps them learn of their customers' sentiment regarding their products and services besides helping with marketing their products and services to the right target audience through brand-customer initiatives.

3. **Machine data** – This is the data generated automatically by operations and activities of the machines, such as IoT devices, servers, industrial machinery, mobile phones, end-user applications, etc. Network logs, transaction records from an ATM, and heart rate log from a wearable device are examples of machine data. Metadata is an important category of machine data. Each time you click a picture from your phone, the metadata around the location, time, and camera's focal length, etc. are automatically recorded for that image.

Data Processing

Data processing is the collection and manipulation of data into usable information. It is interesting to note that unlike in traditional BI systems, where the urgency to make a data-driven decision could be a couple of days, which means data made available to the data warehouse from the sources every 24 hours would suffice the needs of the end customer, the modern needs have become more demanding. Not only do businesses need the most recent data fast to process it and make decisions quickly, but also there are specific use cases where lag in data gathering may make a huge impact, besides the fact that the decision-maker may not be a human but a machine (a software). We will learn of more of these decision-making applications in our chapter on machine learning.

An example could be a credit card transaction fraud detection ML system, where it needs data from the sources in a couple of seconds to either approve a transaction or mark it as "fraudulent" and decline it. Failure to meet this single digit second timeline may result in a huge impact to the business. Then, there are even more extreme cases like data coming from the pacemaker sensor of a human, and this information needs to be processed in milliseconds as it's about the life of a person. The most common forms of data processing are batch processing and streaming processing. Let's learn more about them.

Batch Data

This is the traditional way to gather data from a system that has recorded transactions and processes them through ETL pipelines and is still used today. In this model, a time interval is defined (say every 24 hours, every 6 hours, etc.), and data is collected from the data source as a set of records called a batch at each of this time interval. Batch is usually saved as a file and processed as a unit. Exemplifying it, the business may want to collect a batch of customer orders from an ordering system every three hours to be processed for packaging and shipping. Due to this periodic nature of data collection, by the time the data is made available for analysis, it is usually a few hours to a few days old. When the use of data is over a period of days, weeks, months, etc., batch data processing is used as it is most efficient and has a lower cost for this huge size of data.

Micro Batch Data

This is an improvement over the batch data processing where the time interval of processing the batch data is reduced further to a few minutes or even a few seconds. This results in a smaller batch called a micro batch, and the data freshness is near real time. An example use case would be web analytics on click stream data for an ecommerce company where the business would want to know any drop in customer purchases after a change to its user interface, soon enough to prevent a huge loss in revenue. Apache Spark streaming is a popular micro batch processing framework.

Streaming Data

In this form of data processing, the data is processed as soon as it is generated at the data source. The data size is much smaller than the micro batch, and the data processing rate needs to be faster than the data generation rate to prevent data loss. This data is continuously getting generated from either machines or user activity and hence is called a data stream, like a stream of data flowing from a data source. Streaming data processing is used when data freshness is mission critical like detecting fraudulent credit card transactions using machine learning, anomaly detection in network traffic in a data center to prevent a distributed denial-of-service (DDoS) attack, or showing videos to watch recommendation to customer on a video sharing site based on customer's real-time behavior on the site. Figure 4-8 shows how message processing differs in streaming and micro batch.

Apache Kafka is one of the most popular open source platforms for stream processing. Apache Flink and Storm are other popular open source platforms. Kafka was developed at LinkedIn and open sourced in 2011. All major cloud providers have their own products for streaming such as AWS Kinesis, Azure Events Hub, Google Cloud Pub/Sub, etc.:

1. **Producers** – These are the data sources that produce (or publish) the data stream in the form of events or messages. Messages are organized into topics, and each topic has a unique name.

2. **Consumers** – These are agents that subscribe to the topics of interest and only get the messages that are organized in that topic on a continuous real-time basis.

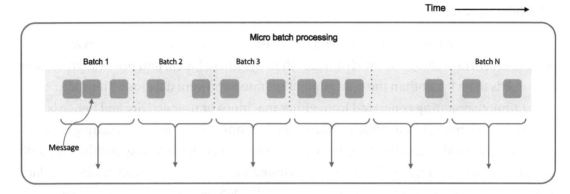

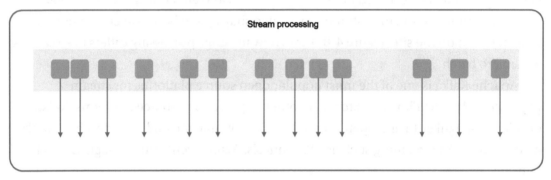

Figure 4-8. *Messages from a data stream are collected and processed in a batch in micro batch processing, but collected and processed right away in stream processing*

Big Data File Formats

Apache Hadoop is a collection of open source utilities, initially released in 2006, for distributed storage and processing of big data through a programming paradigm called map-reduce. We wouldn't dive into Hadoop's map-reduce framework as it isn't used that widely anymore and has been replaced by Apache Spark.

Hadoop Distributed File System (HDFS) was the primary storage medium for big data in the late 2000s, where big data was stored as a set of files. Most cloud providers today have replaced it with their own deep storage solutions like AWS S3 and Google Cloud Storage (GCS). There are few file formats that have gained popularity for storing big data. Each file format has its pros and cons, and choosing one over the other depends on the use case. Let's learn some details about them.

CSV

Comma-separated values (CSV) is a delimited text format with the delimiter being a comma. Delimited text format can have other delimiters like semicolon ";" or pipe "|"; however, CSV is one of the oldest data formats and predates personal computers. IBM Fortran supported CSV files in 1972. Each line of the CSV file represents a record (row), and each value separated by the comma the value corresponding to a field (column). CSV files are human readable and extensively used today across data analysis and integration use cases due to its simplicity. However, the data in CSV is flat and can't have complex data such as nested, hierarchical, or relational data. The CSV data is usually compressed when storing in a big data store to save on storage. The following is a sample of csv data:

```
petid,name,type,age
2335,Mini,dog,8
9349,Jambo,dog,6
124,Luna,cat,3
334,Snow,rabbit,1
```

JSON

JavaScript object notation (JSON) is a partially structured data format just like CSV and first introduced in the early 2000s. Data is represented as key-value pairs in a human-readable format. JSON does allow support for storing complex relationships such as nested data. JSON data is the most popular form of data exchange on the Web, primarily because of its support from REST APIs. JSON is a widely used format for NoSQL databases such as MongoDB. Also, it is the format most widely used for transferring data between systems of different implementations. Just like CSV, JSON-formatted data is usually compressed during network transmission and file storage; however, it isn't as compact as binary formats. The following is sample JSON data that has properties of a person such as name, age, etc., and nested data about friends:

```
[
  {
    "id": "2c26b5",
    "balance": "$2,130.05",
    "picture": "/images/2c26b5/32x32",
    "age": 35,
```

```
      "name": "Mckenzie Castro",
      "friends": [
        {
          "id": 92ec9b,
          "name": "Gilmore Gillespie"
        },
        {
          "id": b7294e,
          "name": "Woodard Bates"
        },
      ]
    },
    {
      "id": "e83bf7",
      "balance": "$3,614.29",
      "picture": "/images/e83bf7/32x32",
      "age": 40,
      "name": "Anita Hill",
      "friends": [
        {
          "id": "c96bf3",
          "name": "Whitehead Orr"
        }
      ]
    }
]
```

Parquet

Apache parquet is a binary file format that was developed jointly by Twitter and
Cloudera and released in 2013. It is a columnar data storage format, which means the
values of the columns are stored together in blocks with built-in compression on the disk
(memory) unlike row-oriented data storage where all values in a row are stored together
in the blocks. Parquet files contain metadata about their content; therefore, even without
parsing the content of the file, the big data engine can determine column names,
compression/encoding, data types, and even some basic statistical characteristics.

Data

	Car	Year	Sales
Row 1	Accord	1991	53
Row 2	Civic	1992	65
Row 3	City	1993	42

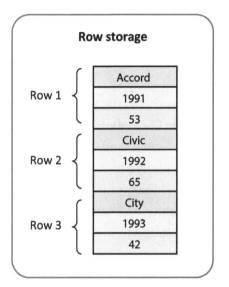
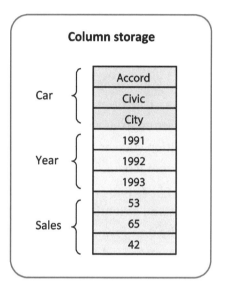

Figure 4-9. *Data stored in row-oriented storage and column-oriented storage*

Reads on this format are very fast especially with a subset of columns as it drastically reduces the overall disk I/O operations and the amount of data that needs to be loaded from disk for analytics-oriented use cases. For example, let's say we need the "total sales" of cars (refer to Figure 4-9); in columnar data format, only Sales column is fetched and summed up. In row storage, all rows need to be loaded and "Sales" extracted from them and then summing of "Sales" happens making it expensive to compute. Parquet can also store nested data and provides very good compression. This makes Parquet a great candidate for fast analytical workloads. Another popular columnar file format is *Optimized Row Columnar (ORC)*. Although very similar to Parquet, ORC also supports ACID properties and is more compression efficient. However, Parquet is better at storing nested data.

Note   It is expensive to add new data to Parquet (or any column-oriented storage) as the new data can't be just appended (as in the case of row-oriented storage). It needs to be placed at different positions on-disk for each of the columns; besides, multiple records of data need to be collected first such that they can form a batch and be compressed together into columnar blocks to achieve the efficiency of a Parquet file.

Avro

Apache Avro is a row-oriented data storage format released by the Hadoop group in 2009. Avro file consists of a file header that contains the file metadata including the schema definition such as field names stored in JSON format, and data blocks that consist of the actual data. This allows for humans to understand the fields present which is a drawback of Parquet. The data blocks can either be binary or JSON; however, binary is mostly preferred as it minimizes the file size. Compared to all other formats described here, Avro is the only format that supports schema evolution by managing added, missing, and changed fields. Avro allows for efficient compression and supports complex data structures. Since it is row based, it is the preferred format for data ingestion (data writes) especially with streaming data as the rate of writing new data is very high.

Data Storage

A data storage system is where the data is stored either as a source or as a sink or both when looked at in terms of data flows in data integration. We will learn of data flows when covering data integration. A very simple data storage system is a database; however, new forms of data storage systems have emerged with the rise in big data. This is the last foundational section before getting into data integration, the core of data engineering.

Data Lakes

A data lake is a highly scalable storage repository that is used to store raw (big) data in its original form until it is needed. Data in the data lake comes from multiple heterogeneous sources and can include a mix of structured, semistructured, and unstructured data.

You can imagine transaction data from business applications like CRM and ERP, device logs in text format, documents in CSV/JSON, big data files in Parquet and Avro, images, videos, etc. all present together in a data lake without altering their original structure. All deep storages are data lakes that include HDFS as well as the ones offered by cloud providers like AWS S3, Google Cloud Storage, Azure Data Lake, etc. A data lake typically stores petabytes of data.

There are two big advantages of data lakes. The first is unlike data warehouses, data lakes can store all forms of data. Since machine learning (ML) tasks like computer vision and natural language processing require nonstructured data such as images, raw text, audio files, etc., ML teams can fetch data they need and when they need from data lakes easily. The second is that since the data is stored in its raw form, it enables ad hoc exploration of the data without predefining an ETL pipeline. After an ad hoc process discovers the right use of the data, an ETL can then be created to standardize the use of the data through a data warehouse built on the data lake. Multiple new data warehouses based on the specific business use cases with their own schema can be created from the data lake.

Query Engines

Data lake is only a data repository and unlike a database or a data warehouse doesn't have any inbuilt means to query structured or semistructured data for analytical purposes. This is where query engines, also called compute engines, come into play. A query engine allows analytical queries expressed in high-level language (often SQL) to be executed across multiple data stores like data lakes, databases, data warehouses, etc. as if they are all part of a single virtual database. The query engine connects to multiple data stores with the help of **data connectors**. A data connector is a software component that translates between the target data store and the query engine.

When querying from the data lake, query engines need a schema for the data to be retrieved and processed, also called schema on read. Most of the query engines were initially developed for querying data from HDFS using SQL and therefore are also referred to as SQL-on-Hadoop engines. Query engines are not only used by data science team members to analyze data or create datasets for machine learning directly from data lakes but also by data engineers who want to build ETL pipelines that have data lakes as sources. Let's get a high-level overview of some popular query engines.

Hive

Hive was developed at Facebook and open sourced in 2010 as an Apache project. It can execute queries against HDFS as structured tables, other deep storages like AWS S3, and conventional databases. Hive contains a metastore that stores metadata of each table such as the schema and the location. There is also a compiler that translates the HiveQL query statements into map-reduce, Tez (a successor to map-reduce framework), or Spark jobs.

Data engineers can also use Hive to work with unstructured data (e.g., a log file), by parsing it and saving it into a structured table. For unstructured data, the data engineers can use SQL functions if the transformation is simple or write custom user-defined functions. In almost all cases, the unstructured data in the data lake are first ETL into a structured format before analytics.

Spark SQL

Spark is an open source analytics engine that was originally developed by the University of California, Berkeley's AMPLab in 2012, and was later donated to Apache foundation in 2014. Spark was developed in response to the limitations of the map-reduce computing paradigm which forces a linear data flow structure. Spark is ~100x faster than traditional map-reduce framework on Hadoop and hence has made map-reduce obsolete. Spark SQL is a component of Spark that allows making SQL queries to structured and semistructured data along with the ability to connect to other types of data stores.

Presto

Presto was originally developed in 2012 at Facebook for its data science team to run interactive SQL queries against its ~300 petabyte data warehouse[3] and get results fast as Hive had become slow on this data volume. Presto can query across multiple data sources like HDFS, AWS S3, MySQL, etc. through a single SQL query by means of its connectors. Presto can also connect to both Spark and Hive and execute queries on them.

---

[3] https://prestodb.io/

Data Warehouse

The foundation of a traditional OLAP system is a data warehouse. We know that since a traditional data warehouse is a database at its core, it couldn't scale up to the challenges with the volume of big data. Running analytical workloads on data lakes requires learning new concepts and tools, besides the complete domain expertise to be able to filter and process the right data. This skill set is available with data engineers, data scientists, and some data analysts, but not with most subject matter experts taking business decisions. They still like data warehouse as it has a schema and uses pure SQL to get insights required for decision-making. This need kept the data warehouses alive, and some major advances in technology enabled data warehouses to upgrade themselves to manage structured and semistructured big data well. These advancements are

- **Columnar storage** – Just like how column-oriented big data file formats like Parquet and ORC are more suited for analytical workloads as data reads are so much faster; similarly, if we start to store data in databases in a columnar format, the writes would be slow, but reads would become very fast. This idea was presented in 2005 in a research paper popularly called "C-Store paper"[4] and adopted by most modern data warehouses.

- **Compression** – Since the data is stored by columns and all the data in the column is of the same data type, data compression is easy and more efficient. Most modern data warehouses perform automatic compression, which also gives the user the choice to choose the compression encoding or apply no compression at all.

- **Massive parallel processing (MPP)** – In this architecture, there is a leader database that is connected via a network with multiple worker databases where each database machine has its own data storage and compute (CPU). Here data is partitioned across the workers, and the SQL query is sent to the leader, which splits it into a set of coordinated processes to be executed by the workers in parallel and then merges the results from the workers to return the query response. This parallelization makes query run faster than traditional

---

[4] https://people.brandeis.edu/~nga/papers/VLDB05.pdf

single machine databases along with the ability to store more data.
MPP isn't a new innovation; however, this ability to run queries fast
gave data warehouses a leg up against map-reduce implementations
like Hadoop and Spark RDD. Figure 4-10 illustrates the architecture
of a MPP system.

Note   MPP is set up as a finite cluster of compute nodes already live and
ready for work. Each node is set up to the same code and doesn't change per
query. As a result, the query startup time is very low compared to map-reduce
implementations like Hadoop and Spark RDD. This low latency to start enables
interactive queries where the human operator need not wait seconds or minutes
before their query starts to run.

- **Elastic parallel processing (EPP)** – This builds on top of MPP by
  using multiple MPP clusters, all connecting to the same storage.
  This allows for separation of storage and compute into separate
  layers of machines. This allows for scaling storage and compute
  independently and hence is elastic. The compute layer usually has
  a fast SSD for local storage to load data from the storage layer and
  process it to send it as a response back to the leader in the service
  layer. Figure 4-11 illustrates the architecture of an EPP system.

These advancements led to a wave of new data warehouses that were more
performant and better at handling structured and semistructured big data. Most
modern data warehouses are cloud based as it allows for easier scaling of compute and
storage, besides freeing the user from maintaining and managing infrastructure. Some
noteworthy modern data warehouses are Greenplum, AWS Redshift, Google Big Query,
Azure Synapse Analytics (previously called Azure SQL Data Warehouse), and Snowflake.
Modern data warehouses typically store terabytes of data. The key differences between
data lake and data warehouse are listed in Table 4-1.

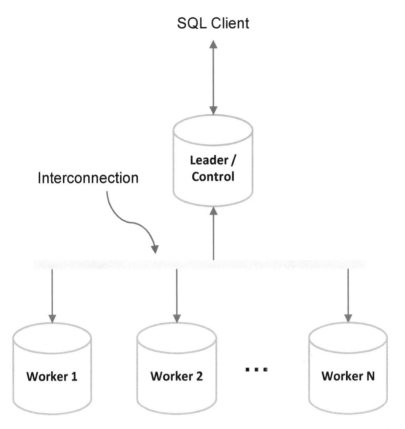

Figure 4-10. *Massive parallel processing architecture where each worker node has both storage and compute*

The modern data warehouses are what made data cubes obsolete as these new data warehouses could achieve almost the same speed as cubes without the need for preaggregation of data with dimensional reduction and caching it into another data structure, which would have management and maintenance overhead of its own. On top of it, data warehouses have more recent data than data cubes as data cubes need processing to aggregate data from data warehouses which would take time.

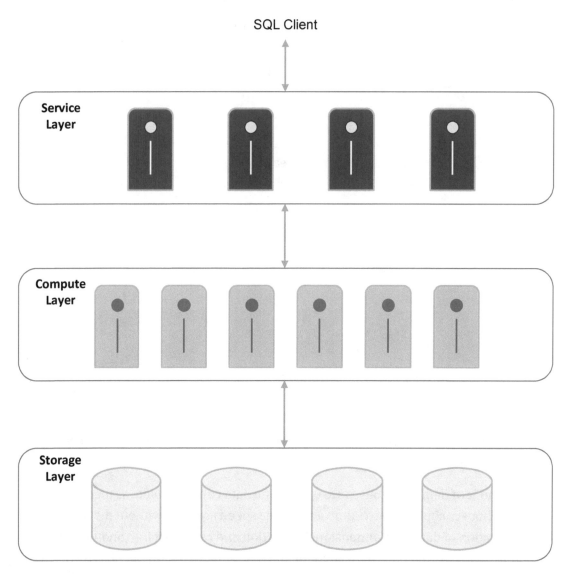

Figure 4-11. *Elastic parallel processing architecture where the compute and storage nodes are separated to enable independent scaling of compute and storage*

Table 4-1. *Key differences between data lake and data warehouse*

	Data Lake	Data Warehouse
Data	Structured, semistructured, and unstructured	Structured only
Schema	Schema on read, i.e., schema is written at the time of retrieval from data lake, or no schema (when retrieving images, text, etc.)	Schema on write, i.e., schema is designed prior to data warehouse implementation
Use cases	Machine learning, data exploration	Analytics, reporting, and machine learning
Users	Data scientists, data engineers, and some data analysts	Data scientists, data engineers, and data analysts
Cost	Cheap and fast to set up, but slow in running queries	Expensive and longer to set up, but runs queries fast

Data Lakehouse

Data lakes are a great low-cost storage solution, but they suffer from issues like lack of support for ACID transactions like in a data warehouse, no enforcement of data quality, and their inability to mix data appends and reads. Data warehouses can only handle structured, and semistructured data and some machine learning teams also need unstructured data (images, audio, text, video), which data warehouses aren't optimized to handle. Companies usually first store all data in a data lake and then create multiple systems like data warehouses, image databases, etc. from it to serve the needs of the diverse consumers of this data. Maintaining these many data systems is complex and introduces delay in moving data from the upstream data source to the downstream data source. This isn't the best experience for either the data system maintainers or the end consumers.

Data lakehouse is a new data storage system that implements the data structure and data management features as those in the data warehouse directly on top of the low-cost object stores like AWS S3 and Google Cloud Storage, although distributed file systems like HDFS can also be used. This brings the best of both data warehouse and data lakes; the data lakehouse supports all structured, semistructured, and unstructured data, has the storage separate from compute, supports ACID transactions like those in data warehouse, supports schemas' enforcement and governance, and provides support for a variety of tools and engines to efficiently access data directly for diverse workloads ranging from SQL analytics (OLAP) to machine learning. Databricks Lakehouse and AWS Redshift Spectrum are some examples of data lakehouses.

It's important to understand that while a data lakehouse brings system-level simplification by using the same system for both data lake and data warehouse needs, it does not simplify any of the work done by the data engineers. Unstructured data will still be slow to process; one will still need to do ELTL to get data and then convert them into structured format to make them ready to consume. While it benefits an enterprise's IT teams and developers to use a consistent set of tools, it doesn't remove the complexity of managing data ingestion, data cleaning, processing, and analysis. Figure 4-12 shows a high-level architecture of a data lake, a data warehouse, and a data lakehouse.

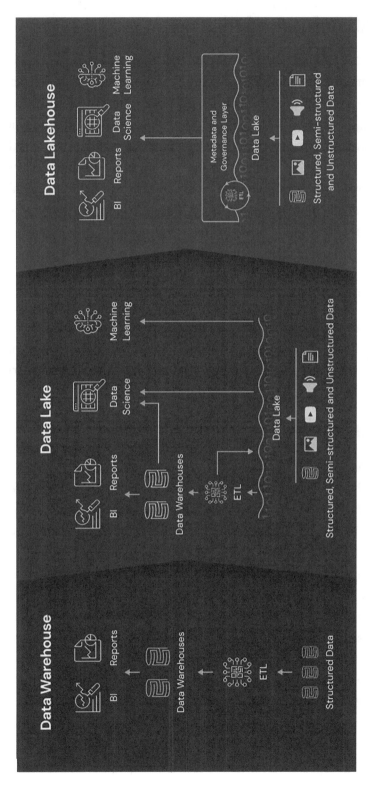

Figure 4-12. *A high-level architecture of data warehouse, data lake, and data lakehouse. Source: Databricks blog*

Data Integration for Analytics

So we are finally at the section which is the core of data engineering work. Data integration is the process of combining data from heterogeneous data sources into a unified view. In the past, OLTP sources and flat files were the data sources from where data was extracted, but with big data, the variety of data sources and data types grew considerably, making this process of integration of data across data sources the primary function of data engineering teams to ensure the business is able to make effective decisions in a timely manner through reports, visualizations, and ad hoc analysis, and the data is made available to machine learning and some software teams who may need it for building machine learning models or some product feature that may need data in a specific format.

Integration Approaches

There are multiple forms of data integration ranging from manual to completely automated. Interestingly, all of them are still in usage as some are driven to optimize on cost and others to reduce time to delivery of an analytical result. Let's learn of them below.

Manual Integration

This approach involved the data analyst to log into each data source individually and fetch and process the data from each source and save the output on disk. The analyst may then read the outputs from these different data sources using some programming language (like R or Python) or some tool for it like SPSS and merge them and further process them finally getting the resultant report, analysis, or visualization.

This approach has many issues such as the analyst needing to know what data can be found in the data source and how the data can be merged offline besides the analyst needing to have access to all these data sources. Also, since analytical queries are complex and usually expensive, if any of the data source isn't built for analytical loads (say it's an OLTP database), then these may start causing end customer impact as the processing of the whole system may become very slow or come to a halt. Even with the disadvantages, the approach is used by analysts for onetime analysis or creating a specific dataset for machine learning, data for which isn't available in a unified data storage system like a data warehouse.

Data Virtualization

In this approach multiple heterogeneous data sources are federated together, and a virtualization layer is provided to the customer which gives a "view" to the customer from where all these disparate data sources can be queried as a single data source. The schema of these sources and their access details are saved into this data virtualization solution, so the analyst now doesn't need to know what data lives where and need to have access to all these data sources. The analyst just executes the query against this virtualization layer, and it takes care of fetching the data from these different sources and combining them into a single result and returning it back to the analyst. TIBCO Data Virtualization is a popular product for this. Cloud companies also have their data virtualization solutions like AWS Glue. Apache Presto can also be thought of as a data virtualization product, as it can also integrate data from multiple data sources.

One of the major drawbacks of this approach is the one seen in manual integration too where if any of the federated data source isn't built for analytical loads, then the data source may become slow or unresponsive risking impact to end customers. However, this is a perfectly fine approach when the data sources are data marts. Nowadays, OLTP providers are also providing OLAP capabilities alongside it, which allows the use of these systems as data marts. Through data virtualization, a virtual data warehouse can be created by federating these data marts. Also, enterprises these days generally use multiple SaaS applications, where each SaaS provides its own analytical capabilities. By using a data virtualization layer spanning analytical capabilities of various SaaS applications, a federated data warehouse can be created without the need for another ETL. Hence, data virtualization is a great way to bring federated access across multiple domain-specific data warehouses and data marts.

Application Integration

In this approach, the different applications are connected through connectors enabling data to be moved from one application to another and process that data. The applications can be cloud-based and SaaS applications to custom on-premises and legacy applications to data storages like databases, etc. This form of integration is done and managed by software engineering teams and not by data engineers as the use case isn't usually integration of data that is huge in size but rather moving small data from one application to another. An example could be integrating Slack with Salesforce for providing customer quick notifications in Slack when there is a change in Salesforce case history.

Although data integration can be achieved through application integration, it is not well suited for it as it may not be able to handle large data volumes which may impact the functioning of the system impacting end customers. Application integration is commonly used for integrating small real-time data between applications. MuleSoft is a popular company that offers application integration.

Unified Destination

This is the most popular approach of data integration where data from multiple data sources are unified and saved in a centralized data storage system as a data warehouse or a data lake in an automated way. This creates a single source of truth for all consumers allowing faster data analysis as this centralized data storage system is optimized to handle complex analytical workloads. Unified data storage systems also improve security as the administrator can now determine what user should have access to what data.

The key building block of unified destination integration is the data pipeline that moves and processes data from one system to another. Extract-transform-load (ETL) is a type of data pipeline used for data warehouse destinations and extract-transform (EL) for data lake destinations. We will learn more on these types of data pipeline soon. Creating, managing, and maintaining data pipelines is what the bulk of data engineering is these days. Traditionally data engineers would build data pipelines manually using multiple tools and technologies; however, most cloud companies these days offer data pipeline products for data integration such as AWS Data Pipeline and Azure Data Factory which simplifies creating the data pipelines. Let's dive into a more formal understanding of what data pipelines and what are its key constituents.

Data Pipelines

In its most simple form, data pipelines are a set of processes that move and/or transform data from one system that acts as a source to another system that acts as a data storage destination as shown in Figure 4-13. The complexity of a data pipeline depends on the data volume, data structure, and data freshness.

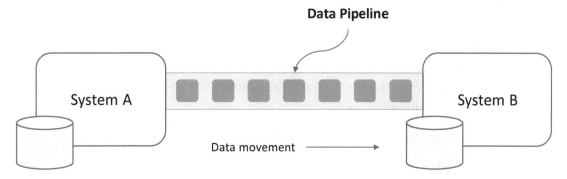

Figure 4-13. A simplistic representation of a data pipeline

Anatomy of a Data Pipeline

Data pipeline is a simple concept. Understanding what goes on inside the hood will help you have more thoughtful conversations with your data engineering team around the choice of their architectural design and reasons for delays or errors, and build an appreciation of the work they do.

Source(s)

This is the system from where the data is ingested into the data pipeline using connectors. The source system could be either on-premise or in the cloud. There can be multiple sources in a data pipeline too where a step in the data pipeline would then merge the data from these origins based on some logic. The common forms of data source system are

- Data warehouse, data mart, or an OLTP system (database)

- A shared network file system, or flat files (CSVs)

- More real-time systems like Kafka streams from IoT devices, social media, etc.

- A data lake like HDFS or AWS S3

Destination

This is the system where the data is delivered. Reports, data visualizations, and dashboards pull data from destination sources. The destination system could again either be on-premise or in the cloud. The destination differs based on the use case. The common forms of destinations are

- Data warehouse, data mart, or an OLAP database

- A shared network file system, or flat files (CSVs)

- Streaming data sources like Kafka streams

- A data lake like HDFS or AWS S3

Workflow

This is the sequence of stages that includes processes and data storage systems, through which data moves from the source to destination. Workflows are also called data flows. Workflows are always unidirectional, i.e., the data flow only from source to destination. The stages in the workflows are acyclic, i.e., a stage doesn't pass data into a previously completed stage as then it would become an infinite loop and data will never reach the destination from this stage.

Processing

There are the activities in the workflow for data ingestion (extraction), storing data into a data storage as staging data for transformation, transforming the data, and delivering it to the destination. The transformation step is where most of the logic in the data pipeline lives. Some of the common transformations are listed here:

- **Filtering** – Here a subset of data from the origin or any of the intermediate storage is filtered based on use case, e.g., filtering certain columns and rows from an OLTP database.

- **Deduplication** – Deduplication means to remove duplicate data records before processing them further. Very often duplication happens due to the same data coming from multiple sources into the data pipeline.

- **Mapping** – This is the data standardization step where the data is changed into a form that is best understood and used by the consumer, e.g., changing local timestamp to UTC, encoding fields such as changing "Male" to 0 and "Female" to 1 and "Other" to 2, binning customer age into age groups, etc.

- **Deriving variables** – This is where new variables are created based on data from existing variables like creating "Net income" as "Gross profit" – "Expenses." Another type is where data is parsed and split to get information usually in the case of unstructured and semistructured data (raw text, JSON, etc.), e.g., deriving "Country" field from a string "Address field" with values like "10 Downing St, London SW1A 2AA, United Kingdom."

- **Masking** – Data masking is the process to conceal the true contents of sensitive information such as Personal Identifiable Information (PII) data.

- **Joins** – This is the merging of data from multiple data sources based on some common attributes such as keys in a database.

- **Aggregating** – This is summarizing data based on some dimensions of interest, e.g., total sales by region and weeks.

You must have realized that a lot of the above transformations can be done by SQL, and yes, data engineers heavily use SQL in data pipelines, but also use scripting languages like Python for logic which is easier or better to write in it. Query engines are commonly used in these transformations.

Workflow Orchestration

This isn't a direct component of a data pipeline but is an intrinsic part of building data pipelines. The stages of the workflow need to happen in a specific order. A process step is called a "task" in the workflow lingo. Tasks have upstream that is where they get the data from and the downstream, i.e., where they pass the data after the task is complete. This presents dependencies within tasks and is represented as graphs. Since we know that workflows are always unidirectional and acyclic, the task dependency graphs are called directed acyclic graphs (DAG).

Since data pipelines are not simple and have layers of complexity due to the diverse set of data sources and the need to serve multiple end users, a workflow orchestration tool is used that tracks the dependencies for the tasks and starts a task when all its dependencies are met. Apache Airflow is the most popular open source framework for workflow orchestration that was developed at Airbnb and open sourced in 2015. The workflows in Airflow are written as Python scripts. Workflows can be run either on a set schedule such as every six hours or when an external event is generated.

Monitoring

This is not a component of the data pipeline but is used to monitor the success or failure of the data pipeline workflow and track the health of the pipeline during execution. Metrics like data loss, data availability, data flow traffic, errors, etc. are commonly tracked to take remediate actions if something isn't healthy. Most workflow orchestration products like Airflow have monitoring inbuilt; however, products like Prometheus and Grafana are also commonly used.

Data Pipeline Architectures

There are two popular forms of basic data pipeline building blocks based on how the data flows from the source to the destination, especially around if the transformation is done before loading the data into the destination or after loading the data into the destination. Let's explore these in a little more detail.

ETL

We have already learned some bit of the extract-transform-load (ETL) pipelines in our data warehouse section in traditional BI. They date back to 1970 and have existed even before the term "data pipeline" was coined. Refer to "Data Warehouse" part in Figure 4-12 to see how ETL pipelines are being used to extract data from multiple data sources and then transform it before being loaded into the data warehouse. This data warehouse now has "ready to use data" and is used to power dashboards, run complex analytical queries, and make reports/visualizations.

Since the data warehouse has a fixed schema, adding new data requires changing the schema of the data warehouse which can take up weeks if not months for the data engineering team as it's not a trivial process. The tools available for the ETL are very mature as this practice dates back many decades. ETL is mostly used with semistructured and structured data and supports batch mode of data gathering and processing.

ELT

Extract-load-transform is the more recent form of data pipeline architecture where data is extracted from the data sources and is stored (loaded) first in its raw form into a *staging data store*, like a data lake, although a data warehouse can also be used if the data isn't unstructured. Then, this data is transformed by leveraging query engines on a need basis to create data warehouses and power dashboards, create reports, or get data for machine learning tasks. In Figure 4-12 refer to the "data lake" part to see how the unstructured data is extracted and loaded into a data lake and then query engines are used on this data lake to do transformation steps and create data warehouses, generate reports, and fetch data for machine learning.

This form is used often when there are multiple heterogeneous data sources that have data in unstructured, semistructured, or structured formats. Most of the big data is processed through ELT as the data volume is high and it can be ingested significantly faster than in ETL due to the lack of transformation step which requires compute resources. Also, when we don't know what data we may need in the future for machine learning tasks or other ad hoc analysis, ELT is used to avoid reextracting from the data source when the destination needs changes.

Note   Staging data store is a data storage system where raw/unprocessed data is stored before being modified for downstream (further) usage.

EtLT

Extract-transform-load-transform is a hybrid of ETL and ELT and works in two stages. In the first stage, data from data sources is extracted, and only simple transformations are done such as masking PII, data cleansing, etc. Then, the data is loaded into a staging data store such as a data warehouse. In the second stage, complex transformations like joins, aggregation, reshaping data, etc., are performed to get "ready to use data."

Since the first stage only has simple data transformations, data ingestion can be fast, which is an issue with ETL pipelines. Also, since the transformations that are required for preserving data quality and satisfying data compliance requirements are performed in stage one before loading it into the data warehouse, the issues that ELT pipelines have around having data in raw form in a data lake which becomes a data compliance issue and lack of data quality are also solved. Figure 4-14 shows the different types of data pipelines.

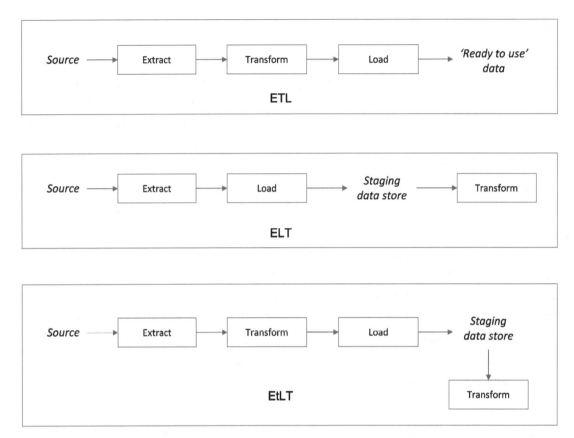

Figure 4-14. *Different architectural types in data pipelines*

Wrap-Up

OLAP needs are the prime driver of data engineering teams; however, these needs
have not changed. Just as before, data from various OLTP and other sources needs to
be captured, stored, and transformed for analysts, business decision-makers, and data
scientists to use them. There has always been a preference of declarative (no-code/low-
code) ways to access and manipulate data which has kept SQL popular for data retrieval
and analytics over writing code. Images/video/voice data has become more common
than before with the advent of big data for use cases like computer vision and natural
language processing, but most enterprises do not use this type of data.

Technologies have become more democratized with the open source developments.
New data storage systems were developed like data lakes and data lakehouses to be able
to process and store big data (structured and unstructured) and support diverse use

cases more affordably. Data warehouses have continued to be popular, some traditional data warehouse systems survived their lower cost (but less capable) competitors, as premium offerings in the OLAP world, while others died out as they didn't offer enough capabilities for the price charged. MPP came out of database and data warehouse and is being implemented by newer OLAP query systems. Although data cubes are no more common for data engineering teams to develop, specialized data cube implementations are still used, as they are built into popular analytics products like Microsoft Power BI and Tableau, to speed up human interaction with Pivots. Data pipelines can be of ETL, EL, and EtLT types, and their complexity has grown overtime requiring the data engineering teams to use specific tools for their scheduling, workflow orchestration, and error management.

Let's end this chapter by looking at how data engineering landscape evolved at Uber since 2014 with the arrival of big data in Figures 4-15, 4-16, and 4-17, so we can see how the various data engineering tools and techniques that we learned in this chapter were using during the evolution of BI/data engineering landscape at enterprises.

Generation 1 (2014-2015) - The beginning of Big Data at Uber

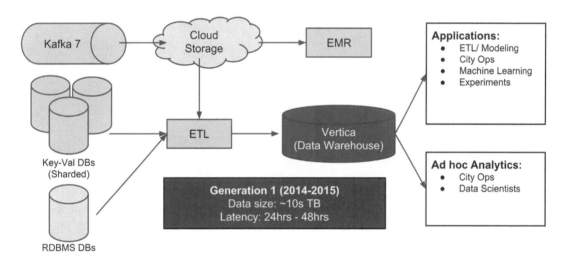

Figure 4-15. *Generation 1 of the big data platform at Uber used a commercial data warehouse to power all data use cases. Source: Uber engineering blog*

Generation 2 (2015-2016) - The arrival of Hadoop

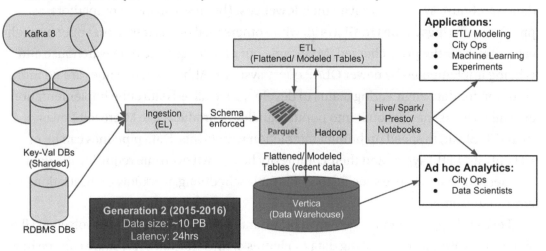

Figure 4-16. *Generation 2 of the big data platform at Uber saw the use of both EL and ETL data pipelines and big data engines like Hive and Presto to process big data. Source: Uber engineering blog*

Generation 3 (2017-present) - Let's rebuild for long term

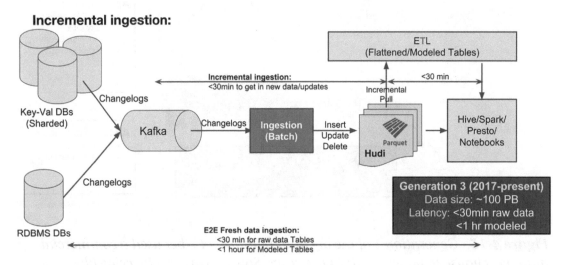

Figure 4-17. *Generation 3 of the big data platform at Uber focused on reducing the latency through incremental ingestion of data. Source: Uber engineering blog*

CHAPTER 5

Artificial Intelligence: Making Machines Learn

Artificial intelligence (AI) is the intelligence demonstrated by machines that allows them to learn, reason, and solve problems. Artificial intelligence has been one of the key driving forces in bringing about a lot of innovation in the technology world. However, more recently it has been hyped a lot, and there are many articles, videos, and telefilms that paint a picture that AI can do everything that humans can without much proof. As a person involved in building products and features using AI, it's important for you to separate the hype from the facts and understand what modern AI can and cannot do.

AI is *neither artificial nor intelligent*[1] – it is far away from how the human brain works. It's real people who develop and train these AI algorithms on vast amounts of curated data making it quite powerful as a tool to amplify, automate, and reflect tasks and decisions that humans do. As a result, AI also tends to repeat our biases and stereotypes. You will want to know if building an AI-powered feature would really be that big of a significant improvement to the user experience, company revenue, etc.; however, it may also be important to understand issues around AI ethics. If an AI model is made the sole decision-maker to identify if a person has cancer or not and it misclassifies a person, who would be responsible for the loss of life to bad diagnosis? Where lies the territory of overpromise that might adversely affect trust? Let's learn of this building block in more detail and separate the facts from fiction.

---

[1] www.wired.com/story/researcher-says-ai-not-artificial-intelligent/

G. Sagar and V. Syrovatskyi, *Technical Building Blocks*, https://doi.org/10.1007/978-1-4842-8658-6_5

213

Expert Systems

The field of AI isn't new. Soon after the modern computers came into being in the early 1950s, researchers took up the challenge of making a machine capable of thinking like humans, in particular making machines make decisions like humans do.[2] This led to the development of the first form of AI software in the later part of the 1960s, known as the "expert systems." These systems contained a knowledge base, essentially facts about a particular domain (say medicine), and an inference engine, which is an automated reasoning system that looks into the knowledge base, applies some rules, and arrives at a particular conclusion (answer to the question from the user). This approach was called "symbolic AI." Figure 5-1 illustrates symbolic AI.

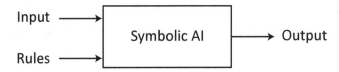

Figure 5-1. *Input = user question, rules = expert knowledge, and output = answer*

Though looking promising, these expert systems had major issues around getting the experts for knowledge acquisition, performance, and computational challenges with big data (knowledge base) and ensuring that the rules (over 100 million at times) are consistent with each other. Toward the end of the 1980s, expert systems started fading off, and mostly the rule engine was forked from the inference engine and included in many business applications to add business logic in the form of rules by business application suite vendors such as SAP and Siebel. Rules were no longer something that only an expert will define and use but for anything that is complex and is critical.

Machine Learning

The term machine learning was coined by Arthur Samuel in 1959, a prominent researcher at IBM in the field of computer gaming and artificial intelligence. Machine learning is a subset of AI that employs various approaches to teach machines (computers) to learn from data (or experiences) so that they can accomplish certain

---

[2] Yanase J, Triantaphyllou E (2019). "A Systematic Survey of Computer-Aided Diagnosis in Medicine: Past and Present Developments". Expert Systems with Applications. 138: 112821. doi:10.1016/j.eswa.2019.112821

tasks without being explicitly programmed to do so. This solves one key issue of expert systems where the expert knowledge was hard to acquire. In ML the knowledge (rules) is learned by the machine itself through the statistical structure of the data provided. This is illustrated in Figure 5-2.

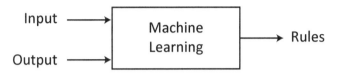

Figure 5-2. *Input = user question, rules = knowledge learned by machine, and output = answer*

With the advancement in computational power, cheaper memory, and availability of large datasets (big data), there came a big push in the development of ML algorithms. ML quickly became the most successful stream of AI, and much prominent research in this space has only been done after the 1990s. Modern machine learning is primarily focused on solving two categories of tasks; the first is to classify data, such as classifying emails into spam and nonspam. The second is to make predictions or forecast future outcomes, such as predicting the price of homes.

The efficiency of machine learning is heavily dependent on the feature extraction, feature generation, and feature selection, where a feature is an attribute of the data under analysis. For example, for predicting house prices, the input features of the house data could be ZIP code, number of rooms, area of the lot, year of built, etc., corresponding to the price of house as the output.

Deep Learning

Deep learning is a subset of machine learning that can perform feature learning or representation learning automatically. Deep learning algorithms seek to exploit the unknown structure in the input distribution to discover good representations, often at multiple levels, with higher-level learned features defined in terms of lower-level features.[3]

---

[3] Yoshua Bengio, (2012). "Deep Learning of Representations for Unsupervised and Transfer Learning". http://www.jmlr.org/proceedings/papers/v27/bengio12a/bengio12a.pdf.

In simpler words, as most deep learning algorithms are implemented through artificial neural networks, they can be visualized as layers stacked on top of each other, where the first layer takes in the input (data) and learns some features from it, and passes on those learned features to the next connected layer, which further learns some features from the features learned by the first layer and passes it on to the next layer and so on until it reaches the final layer. These interconnected "layers" represent the depth of deep learning, a concept missing from traditional machine learning; therefore, a lot of traditional machine learning algorithms are also called "shallow learners," as the feature extraction and learning are done manually by people (data scientists) and not machines themselves. Figure 5-3 shows an overview of a deep learning algorithm.

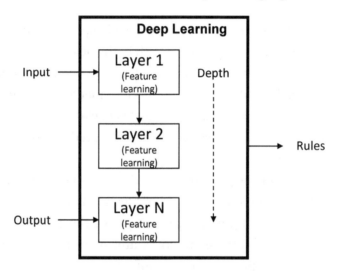

Figure 5-3. *A high-level view of a deep learning algorithm*

Because of the capability of deep learning to learn features automatically, they are heavily used in computer vision, language translation, image restoration, etc. If we want to estimate the house price from the photographs of a home, based on a dataset of home photographs and their corresponding prices, deep learning becomes a prime candidate to solve for this kind of problem as it can learn features automatically from the photographs as against machine learning where someone manually will have to generate features for the home. As we get into the application part in the upcoming sections, things will become clearer; however, keep in mind the relationship of deep learning, machine learning, and artificial intelligence as shown in Figure 5-4 where deep learning is a subset of machine learning which is a subset of AI.

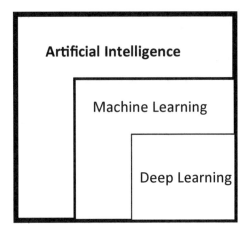

Figure 5-4. *Deep learning is a subset of machine learning which is a subset of artificial intelligence*

Before we proceed, I want you all to know or refresh on some basics:

1. A dataset is a collection of data points. It's usually represented in a tabular format as rows and columns. The input features and output are represented as columns, and each row contains values for a data object for the features and output. Rows are also called instances by some.

2. Features, attributes, and variables all mean the same for a dataset and are used interchangeably.

3. Variables can be continuous (numerical) such as age, area, and height, or they can be categorical (nonnumerical) such as color, sex, education level, etc.

4. Machine learning algorithms take in the input data and give out a model. This model has modeled the association of the features to the output and is used for inference and prediction.

"Learning" Approaches of Machine Learning

A lot of algorithms are available today for machine learning, and the choice of the algorithm is primarily dictated by the type of data and the problem at hand. The following are the three main approaches of machine learning.

1. Supervised Learning

This learning approach is used when the data has the inputs and the corresponding outputs, and the problem is to learn how the inputs map to the outputs. This form of data is also called "labeled data," where the output is the label to the set of inputs. The labeling of outputs is generally done by humans. Also, this is the most popular form of machine learning. Supervised learning is used to solve two kinds of problems, namely, regression and classification.

Regression

This is used to find out the relation between a continuous output variable and the corresponding input variables (features). As an example, if we have a dataset of house prices along with their corresponding features such as number of bedrooms, lot area, age of home, etc., and we want to predict house price of a home based on its features, regression can be used to predict the house price. Online real estate marketplace companies like Zillow and Redfin most likely use some form of regression to give house estimates.

Classification

This is used to find out the relation between a categorical output variable and the corresponding input variables (features). This could be used to solve binary classification problems such as classifying new emails into "spam" and "nonspam" (binary or two classes) based on a labeled dataset of emails which are labeled as spam and not with features such as "number of recipients," "email domain of sender," "number of words in email," "quality of grammar," etc. This is also used for multinomial classification problems where the problem is to classify an instance into one of the many classes available. An example could be to classify images of handwritten numbers into the corresponding digits from 0 to 9, i.e., into ten classes.

There are problems that may require both regression and classification, such as "object detection." For example, in most modern phone cameras, object detection is used – the human faces are recognized, and a circle or square is made around them before you click the photo. Identifying a face in the frame (picture) uses classification, and the coordinates of the circle or square shape around the face use regression.

2. Unsupervised Learning

This learning approach is used to learn patterns from unlabeled data, i.e., the dataset only has features and no output label. The following are the two kinds of problems solved through unsupervised learning.

Clustering

This is used to identify groups of objects such that the objects in the group are more similar than the objects in the other groups, based on a similarity criterion. If the dataset does not have labels and the goal is to identify if there are some hidden classes present, clustering is used to discover those groups (classes). Clustering is a hard problem as the clustering algorithm creates groupings that are mathematically valid but doesn't care about any real-world significance. Therefore, they often require subject matter experts to evaluate outputs and/or to make inferences.

Let's say the Internal Revenue Service (IRS) wants to identify people who filed false tax returns. Tax return attributes such as taxable income, number of dependents, ZIP code, etc. can be used for clustering, and groups can be formed. Then, a couple of tax returns in each of these groups can be investigated by experts to determine if they are false returns. Due to the similarity of objects in the groups, the group with false returns likely will have a lot of other false returns too and hence can be identified.

Association

This also comes under association rule mining in the field of data mining. The goal here is to learn associations among variables, i.e., frequently co-occurring events (variables) in a large dataset. These associations are then used commonly for making recommendations.

Let's say we have a dataset with the titles of movies watched by the users of a video streaming service in a given week (each row is movie titles watched by a unique user). Association learning can then be used on this dataset to discover associations among movie titles, for example, if a lot of users who watched the movies *'Superman'* and *'The Avengers,'* also watched the movie *'Wonder Woman,'* then there is an association among these movies. The users of who haven't watched the *'Wonder Woman'* movie, but have watched the movies *'Superman'* and *'The Avengers'* can be recommended to watch the *'Wonder Woman'* movie by the video streaming service. You must have seen similar recommendations on online retail sites as Amazon under "Frequently bought together" as seen in Figure 5-5.

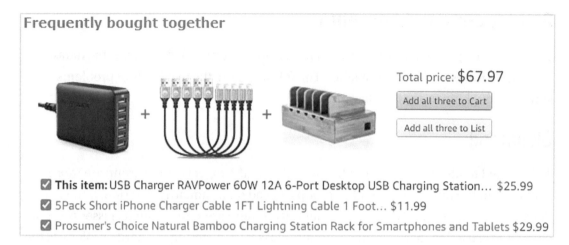

Frequently bought together

Total price: $67.97

[Add all three to Cart]

[Add all three to List]

☑ **This item:** USB Charger RAVPower 60W 12A 6-Port Desktop USB Charging Station... $25.99
☑ 5Pack Short iPhone Charger Cable 1FT Lightning Cable 1 Foot... $11.99
☑ Prosumer's Choice Natural Bamboo Charging Station Rack for Smartphones and Tablets $29.99

Figure 5-5. *Amazon using association to recommend charging cable and rack for a charger*

3. Reinforcement Learning

In this approach to machine learning, an intelligent agent (an autonomous computer program – bots – that carries out tasks on behalf of users) is given a delayed reward for its previous actions in a given environment. The goal of the agent is to maximize the cumulative reward. This form is done through artificial neural networks and isn't used much in practical applications. This form has little to no data, and everything is learned as it comes on the fly. Explaining this in more detail will be outside the scope of this book, but let's take an example to understand it a bit better.

Imagine we want the machine to learn how to play a video game (environment). We can create a bot that can interact (take actions) with the game based on the state (screenshot of the game at a given time) given to it by the game. After the agent takes an action (moves, jumps, etc.), the game can send the next state and the reward (say points/coins earned, fights won, etc.). Using reinforcement learning, this agent can learn how to maximize total reward (say points), and in essence learn to play the game and win it.

This is exactly what Google did. On January 1, 2013, Google's DeepMind published a paper where they demonstrated how it used reinforcement learning to teach an agent how to play seven Atari 2600 games and surpass humans on three of them.[4] In 2017

---

[4] https://deepmind.com/research/publications/playing-atari-deep-reinforcement-learning

another DeepMind's product called AlphaGo that uses reinforcement learning beat Ke Jie, the number one ranked player in the world in board game Go.[5] DeepMind retired AlphaGo after the match.

Steps to Solve a Machine Learning Problem

Machine learning is now an established field, and with that the process to develop ML models has got standardized across companies too. Here we will share the different steps of building a ML-based feature/product. Figure 5-6 shows the six steps of machine learning. Let's learn details of each of these steps.

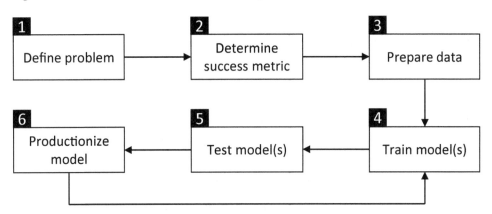

Figure 5-6.   *Overview of the steps to solve a machine learning problem*

1. Define the Problem

We need to have a clear understanding across stakeholders, as to what we are trying to solve as a business problem. This business problem is then translated into a specific machine learning problem in terms of a new feature or products. Let's get some clarity through an example business problem for a hypothetical online advertising company:

1. **Business problem** – Advertisers are frustrated with the lack of an understanding of what their advertising budget for a set of online ads can get them (clicks) in a timeframe.

---

[5] www.wired.com/2017/05/revamped-alphago-wins-first-game-chinese-go-grandmaster/

2. **Product feature** – Show advertisers the expected clicks on their ads for a given budget in a future timeframe, to help advertisers get an estimate of return of investment.

3. **ML problem** – Develop a ML model that uses historical ad performance data to predict the number of clicks a particular ad will get in a given timeframe.

Determine the type of machine learning problem – is it regression (as in the online advertising example), or is it classification, or is it identifying clusters – where the marketing team might want to segment the customer base to develop unique marketing strategies for each of those customer segments.

2. Determine the Success Metric

We define a ML model success metric that leads to an improvement in the business metric of the problem. Continuing with the online advertising example, the goal may be for the model to predict the number of clicks with high accuracy so that the customer satisfaction score (CSAT) increases to 80% for advertising campaign setup activity. Prediction accuracy is the model success metric and CSAT, the business success metric. It's important to understand that accuracy may be a vanity metric, and it's important for the stakeholders and cross-functional team to understand the true model metrics.

Popular Metrics for Regression Models

1. **R-squared or adjusted R-squared** – It's a measure of how successful the model has been to explain the output variability and is expressed as a percentage (0%–100%). The higher it is, the better. We have seen a lot of people calling this metric as accuracy, which it isn't – a proxy to it, maybe.

2. **Root mean squared error (RMSE)** – Error is the difference between actual and prediction value. RMSE is the standard deviation of the errors and helps quantify how spread out from the regression line are the errors. This metric is in the same units as the predicted and actual value. Say, if we were predicting house prices in US dollars, this value will also be in US dollars. The square of RMSE, mean squared error (MSE), is a popular regression metric for deep learning.

3. **Mean absolute error (MAE)** – This is like RMSE in a way that it is in the same units as the predicted and actual value. If there are many outliers (extremely high or low input or output values), then MAE is used over RMSE as RMSE is more sensitive to outliers. However, RMSE is a more popular metric in the industry.

Popular Metrics for Classification Models

To understand the popular metrics of classification models, we first need to understand the confusion matrix (refer Figure 5-7). Confusion matrix is a table where the rows represent the predicted class, and the columns represent the actual class. It shows how much the model is confusing one class for the other.

Exemplifying it, say we build a binary classification model to learn to predict if an email is spam or not. Our test data should already have emails labeled as "spam," called an actual positive event and "nonspam," called an actual negative event. Also, our classification model would have recorded for each email if it predicted it as "spam," called a predicted positive event or "nonspam," called predicted negative event. The aggregation of this information is captured in the confusion matrix in its four cells:

- **True positives** – Email instances which were predicted as spam and were spam. The count of these goes in the top-left cell.

- **False positives** – Email instances which were predicted as spam but were nonspam (class mismatch). The count of these goes in the top-right cell.

- **True negative** – Email instances which were predicted nonspam and were nonspam. The count of these goes in the bottom-right cell.

- **False negative** – Email instances which were predicted as nonspam but were spam. The count of these goes in the bottom-right cell.

		Actual	
		Positive	Negative
Predicted	Positive	(TP) True Positive	(FP) False Positive
	Negative	(FN) False Negative	(TN) True Negative

***Figure 5-7.** Confusion matrix for classification models*

The common metrics are

1. **Accuracy: (TP + TN) / (TP + TN + FP + FN)**

   This is the ratio of true predictions over the total predictions. It can be trusted when the classes are well balanced, i.e., all classes in the dataset have roughly the same number of instances. It is not to be trusted when there is a class imbalance. Say the number of actual spam email instances in our dataset is 10% and nonspam 90%. If our model predicts every instance as "nonspam," even then the accuracy will be 90% and hence is misleading.

2. **Precision: (TP) / (TP + FP)**

   The proportion of positive predictions that are positive. It tells us how valid the positive predictions are. If the precision of the spam detection model is 80%, then it means whenever the model predicts an email to be spam, there is a 20% chance it may be nonspam. You want to focus on high precision when a critical action is taken based on model positive prediction. If you cancel the accounts of customers if the model predicts the emails sent by them are spam, you will want the model to have very high precision to avoid any serious damage to your customer trust and revenue.

3. **Recall: (TP) / (TP + FN)**

   The proportion of actual positives that are predicted right. This deals with coverage and should be high for the model when we want to capture many actual positives. Say we have a model that predicts if a person has COVID-19 or not, we want the model to identify as many COVID-19 patients as possible. Generally, there is a precision-recall trade-off, i.e., if we increase precision, recall reduces and vice versa.

4. **F1 score: 2 x (Precision x Recall) / (Precision + Recall)**

    This is the harmonic mean of precision and recall and is useful if the model needs to have a good precision as well as recall – which is what most teams would want. This is also the most popular metric for models trained on a dataset with unbalanced classes. It has a range from 0 to 1, and the model is better the closer it is to 1. If we want our spam classifier to be able to detect as many spams as possible while ensuring that the spams identified are likely actual spams, the model with a high F1 score should be selected.

3. Prepare the Data

This step carries the highest weight (90%) of all the steps here. It constitutes identifying the data inputs, fetching them from the data warehouse, cleaning up the data, and split datasets for training, validation, and testing of models:

- **Data ideation** – The goal is to determine what factors would/may influence the ML model output and is done through brainstorming with the stakeholders from business, data science, product, and engineering.

- **Data collection** – The data engineering team then identifies how to (and if they can) get these factors from the data warehouse and other data repositories and save them in data tables or datasets (if to be used one time) or build data pipelines to continuously add/update datasets if the model needs to be refreshed frequently.

- **Data processing and feature extraction** – The data science team then prepares the input dataset for machine learning (clean data, treat missing data, normalize and/or transform data, feature engineering, etc.) from the data provided by the data engineering team. After this the data science team generally does an exploratory data analysis to understand more about the data and infer some properties of the data variables (univariate/bivariate analysis, correlation analysis, etc.).

Most modern data science teams store these datasets in a "feature store," a platform that automates the process of data extraction, processing, and feature extraction for future experiments and reproducibility. Before the model is built, there is a strong assumption made based on the analysis of data – the relationship between the output data and input data can be learned (for supervised learning) or the data has enough statistical structure to identify patterns in it (for unsupervised learning). Special attention must be paid to understand biases in the data. Biased data can lead to ML models that reinforce gender, racial, and other stereotypes, which damages a company's reputation and trust with the customers.

4. Train the Model(s)

This step is solely owned by the data science team who trains multiple models and then chooses the best performing model.

Split Input Dataset

The data science team splits the input dataset into three parts, namely, training data, data used to train the ML model; test data, data used to test the trained model to improve the model further; and evaluation data, data that is taken as the representation of real world and not used to train or improve the model, only to get an estimate of model's performance. 5%–10% of the input dataset is randomly picked up and saved as evaluation data. The remaining data is split up again with training taking around 70% of the data and test data (also called validation data) the remaining 30%. It's made sure that the test data is large enough to represent the input data.

Another popular technique to create test and validation data is called "K-fold cross-validation." Here the data is split (also called folded) into K equal parts, such that each part has a near equal number of instances. Then, one part is held for testing the ML model, and the other k - 1 parts are used for training. This is repeated K times, with each K part used exactly once as validation data. The performance of all the K times the model was tested is averaged and presented as the performance of the model. Figure 5-8 illustrates this technique.

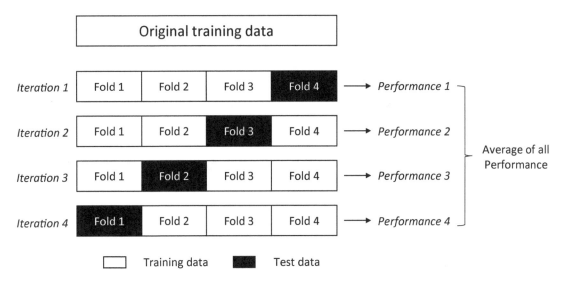

Figure 5-8. *K-fold cross validation (K = 4)*

If the data is temporal (has a time component to it as stock prices, vol. of rainfall, etc.), the test data should be events that come after the training data, to avoid training models on the future data (called temporal leak).

Train Model

The data science team generally trains multiple machine learning models on the training data and compares their performance through the success metrics and chooses the fittest model, i.e., a model that is neither underfitting nor overfitting. An underfit model is one that can't train well on the training data and has poor performance. An overfit model has learned patterns specific to the training data and has great performance on training data but poor performance on new data. Overfitting is usually a bigger challenge and is commonly handled by cross-validation and regularization. Getting in the details of regularization is beyond the scope of this book. Figure 5-9 shows what overfit, underfit, and good fit look like for a classification model where the task for the model is to create a separation boundary between two classes of data represented by circles and triangles. Similar is the task for regression where the model is supposed to fit a line to the data points represented by black dots.

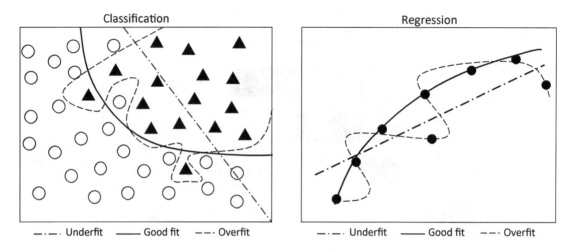

Figure 5-9. *Underfitting and overfitting in classification and regression*

5. Evaluate the Model

The model with the best performance at training is tested against our test dataset to get an estimate of how the model will perform on new data based on the success metric of the model. If it performs well, then the model is stored in a "model store," a repository that helps with versioning of models to allow easy rollbacks and to track history of models. This is the time when the team shares the results of the model and its limitations with the stakeholders. This is a crucial step as a lot of stakeholders feel machine learning to be a magic box that can do anything, and they get dissatisfied if their expectation isn't met.

6. Productionize Model

The chosen model is then put into production where it is applied to new data (real time or offline) and is used for prediction purposes. Most data science teams build models in Python due to the wide availability of ML libraries in it. However, sometimes the choice of programming language for the model deployed in the production environment is dependent on the platform it is deployed. For example, models built for high-frequency algorithm trading are usually developed in C++ because of the speed requirement. There are two popular ways of model deployment as follows:

- **Models as web services** – Here the model is deployed as a web API (generally REST), and the input data for prediction is sent to the API and the output received back in the response. This is the most common way of productionizing models for most web and mobile applications; however, they need to be connected to the Internet to make this work. Software engineering teams are asked to build these web APIs if there are business requirements to meet strict service-level objectives (SLOs).

- **Models embedded in the platform** – In this case the model is deployed directly on the platform where it will be used. It could be deployed and run from the client's web browser, an embedded device, or an edge device such as mobile and IoT device, which may require the model to be made lightweight to work with limited device resources. For example, Apple started using deep learning for face detection in iOS 10, to allow iPhone users to unlock their phones by simply looking into it.[6] The model used is deployed on the iPhone, and the phone can be unlocked with the face even when not connected to the Internet.

The model in production is evaluated periodically or in real time (through dashboards) to ensure there isn't any degradation of performance. If there is a drop in performance, a decision is made by the business stakeholders and the data science team, if the model needs to be retrained or if the team should wait for some time in case there was a known short-term impactful event which may have resulted in this performance drop.

Lastly, the team generally checks in with the business stakeholders from time to time to make sure they are seeing a positive change toward the business problem this model is solving for (in whole or as a small part) or if something additional or altogether new needs to be done. There are multiple products in the market now that support most parts of this machine learning pipeline as Databricks, AWS Sagemaker, Google Cloud ML, etc.

---

[6] https://machinelearning.apple.com/research/face-detection

Overview of ML Algorithms

Due to significant advancement in the field of machine learning in the last decade, several machine learning algorithms are out there which may get overwhelming to know them all. To further improve the performance of ML algo, researchers came up with the idea of ensemble models, which combines multiple ML algorithms to achieve far greater performance than any of the individual ML algorithms in the ensemble. Though ensembles are generally formed of shallow learners, of late, ensembles of deep learning models and shallow learning models grouped together are getting traction (especially in ML competitions). Before we get into specific ML algorithms you may have heard of, let's discuss the three common ways to create an ensemble:

1. **Bagging (bootstrap aggregating)** – Here multiple ML algorithms are connected in parallel and each trained on a random sample of training data (called bootstrapping). For regression, the average (aggregation) of the prediction made by each algorithm is taken, and for classification the class that is predicted by most of the algorithms is taken. Bagging helps with overcoming the overfitting issue. Figure 5-10 illustrates how aggregated prediction is done in bagging.

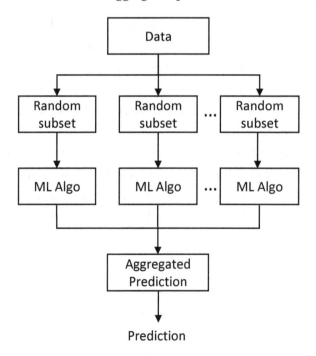

Figure 5-10. *Structure of a bagging ensemble learner*

2. **Boosting** – Here multiple "weak" ML algorithms like linear
    regression algorithm or a single-node decision tree – called
    decision stump – are connected in a sequence. The first model
    gets trained on the training data, and then the second model
    takes in the prediction made by the first model and tries to better
    classify the misclassified training instances by the first model
    by assigning higher weights to them. The next model does the
    same to better classify the misclassified training instances of the
    second model and so on. Boosting helps to reduce underfitting.
    Figure 5-11 illustrates how multiple ML algorithms are used in
    boosting.

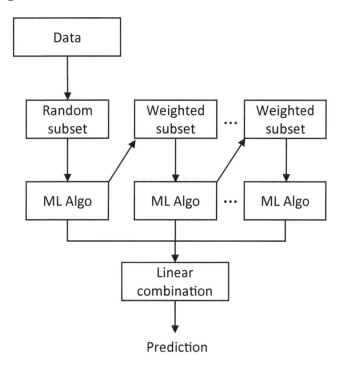

Figure 5-11. *Structure of a boosting ensemble*

3. **Stacking** – Here multiple ML algorithms (called base
    algorithms) are trained on random samples of training data,
    and the predictions of all these algorithms are combined into
    a dataset which is fed as input data to another classifier (called
    metaclassifier, usually logistic regression) to give the final output

prediction which is better than any of the base ML algorithm. Staking can have heterogeneous ML algorithms (decision tree, logistic regression, KNN, etc. in the base), whereas bagging and boosting can only have homogeneous algorithms. Figure 5-12 shows how the ML algorithms are stacked in a stacking ensemble.

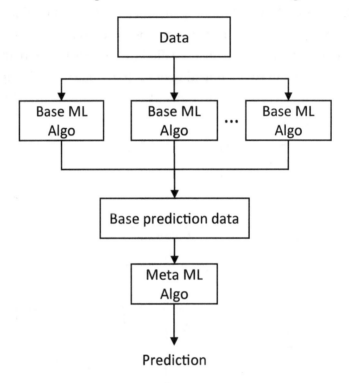

Figure 5-12. *Structure of a stacking ensemble*

We will pick some popular shallow ML algorithms which you might have heard (or may hear) your data science team speaking of and discuss them. Our focus here will be to give the practical approach to using the ML algorithms rather than going in the mathematical rigor of each.

Popular (Shallow) ML Algorithms

Let's get into some (shallow) machine learning algorithms that you may have heard your team speak of – what they are and what makes them so popular:

1. **Linear regression** – This is one of the oldest ML algos on this list and takes its roots from statistics. The goal of the algorithm is to come up with a linear mathematical relationship between the output and the input features. In statistics, a method called "ordinary least squared" and its variations are used; in machine learning, "stochastic gradient descent" (SGD) is used. It's interesting to note that SGD powers most modern machine learning algorithms including deep learning ones.

2. **Logistic regression** – This algorithm is again derived from statistics, and unlike what the name suggests, it's not used for regression but rather for classification. It uses a mathematical transformation called sigmoid that outputs the probability an instance is of a given class. The data science team generally comes up with the right probability threshold for the output probability value to call an instance of a specific class. For example, if probability > 0.72, then classify as "spam email," else classify "nonspam" email.

3. **Decision tree** – The goal of this algorithm is to come up with a flowchart that determines the prediction value. This algorithm can be used for both classification and regression. It's important to note that all decision trees (and all tree-based ML algos) are good at interpolation but not extrapolation. Linear and logistic regression are good with both interpolation and extrapolation.

4. **K-means** – This is the most popular unsupervised learning algorithm and used for clustering. It is simple to implement and works well on large datasets. It partitions the instances of the dataset into k clusters based on the distance an instance has from the mean of the cluster (also called centroid). Figure 5-13 shows how K-means can generate multiple clusters on the same data based on user input of "K," i.e., number of clusters.

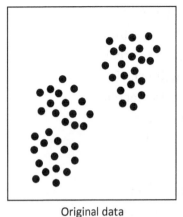 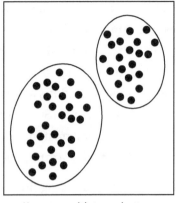 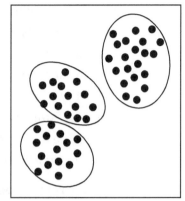

| Original data | K-means with two clusters | K-means with three clusters |

Figure 5-13. A view of the clusters k-mean can identify

These four models are one of the oldest ML algorithms and simple enough that they are taught in most beginner ML courses, yet they have been around and continue to find their spot in most modern companies. You may ask why? The short answer is interpretability, and we will discuss in an upcoming section on why interpretability and explainability of models are becoming so crucial. Coming back, the following are some of the popular ensemble models:

1. **Random forests** – They are the most popular bagging ensemble. They are composed of decision trees and can do both regression and classification. They are widely used in the industry as they need little configuration to set up and have good performance.

2. **XGboost machine (XGBM)** – It is short for "Extreme gradient boosting machine." It is a decision tree–based boosting ensemble machine learning algorithm. It can also do both regression and classification. It is the most popular ensemble today primarily due to its immense success in winning various machine learning competitions on sites like Kaggle.

3. **Light gradient boosting machine (LGBM)** – They are another form of tree-based boosting ensemble machine learning algorithm originally developed by Microsoft in 2106 and can do both regression

and classification[7]. LGBMs are becoming increasingly popular as they are much faster to train and have comparable performance to XGboost. XGboost algorithms take a long time to train.

Note   You are not expected to run any coding examples in this chapter; these are only meant to give you a sense of how the data science teams build models which isn't that intimidating and very logical.

Tip   You can download the IPython notebook containing all the code examples in this chapter from the book's code repository on your local machine and upload it to Google Colab at `https://colab.research.google.com/notebooks/`. From there execute the code blocks right from your browser for free. We recommend this approach as it will save you from having to set up the environment on your local machine, and since we build these examples on Google Colab, they will work there without any issue.

Shallow ML in Action

```
USE CASE 1: SHALLOW ML ALGORITHM FOR CLASSIFICATION
```

Objective: Using the Wine Quality Dataset, predict if the quality of a white wine on a scale given chemical measures of each wine is 6 or not.

There are 4,898 observations with 11 input variables and one output variable. The variable names in the dataset are as follows:

1. Fixed acidity

2. Volatile acidity

3. Citric acid

4. Residual sugar

5. Chlorides

---

[7]`https://github.com/microsoft/LightGBM`

6.   Free sulfur dioxide

7.   Total sulfur dioxide

8.   Density

9.   pH

10.   Sulfates

11.   Alcohol

12.   Quality (score between 0 and 10)

Solution: For building all ML and deep learning models, we will use Python as the programming language. We will create a new column called "is_med_quality" – a binary variable to suggest if the wine is of medium quality based on if the wine has the quality of 6 or not. Let's dive into the various steps to build this ML model.

Listing 5-1. Download and load the wine dataset

```
import pandas as pd
import numpy as np

# Loading the dataset as Pandas Dataframe and printing the last 5
rows of data
dataset = pd.read_csv('https://archive.ics.uci.edu/ml/machine-learning-
databases/wine-quality/winequality-white.csv', sep = ';')
print(dataset.tail())
```

Let's start by importing the packages "pandas" and "numpy" which are one of the most used packages for data analysis in Python. We load the data in a csv file (columns are delimited by semicolon ";") from an online archive to a pandas dataframe called "dataset." The output of the last print statement in Listing 5-1 gives us the last five rows of the dataset which are shown in Table 5-1.

Getting to see a few rows of the dataset helps to get some familiarity with the dataset. We would learn a bit more of the dataset and see if we need to do something else before we build the ML models. There are quite a few tasks that the data scientists would do which include cleaning data, imputing missing data, normalizing/scaling data, creating new variables (feature engineering), and transforming data. There are some other special tasks such as balancing classes that they will do as well. We wouldn't do those tasks as this toy dataset is already clean and the intent is to give a general understanding of building ML models.

Table 5-1. *Last five rows of the wine dataset*

fixed acidity	volatile acidity	citric acid	residual sugar	chlorides	free sulfur dioxide	total sulfur dioxide	density	pH	sulphates	alcohol	quality
6.2	0.21	0.29	1.6	0.039	24.0	92.0	0.99114	3.27	0.50	11.2	6
6.6	0.32	0.36	8.0	0.047	57.0	168.0	0.99490	3.15	0.46	9.6	5
6.5	0.24	0.19	1.2	0.041	30.0	111.0	0.99254	2.99	0.46	9.4	6
5.5	0.29	0.30	1.1	0.022	20.0	110.0	0.98869	3.34	0.38	12.8	7
6.0	0.21	0.38	0.8	0.020	22.0	98.0	0.98941	3.26	0.32	11.8	6

Let's create a new variable called "is_med_quality" to signify if the wine is of medium quality based on if the value of quality for a wine has the value of "6" or not. We then split the dataset into two parts, one to use for training and validation and the other smaller part to evaluate the ML model on data not used in training to get a sense of how the model will work on new (unseen) data. This is shown in Listing 5-2.

Listing 5-2. Create new "medium" quality variable and split data

```
# Using a simple if-else logic to create a binary variable 'medium quality'
dataset['is_med_quality'] = np.where(dataset['quality'] == 6, 1, 0)

dataset = dataset.drop('quality', axis=1) # Drop quality variable

# Split the dataset into two parts: 90% data for training and 10% for
# evaluation of model
data = dataset.sample(frac=0.9, random_state=123).reset_index(drop=True)
data_unseen = dataset.drop(data.index).reset_index(drop=True)

print('Data for Modeling: ' + str(data.shape))
print('Unseen Data For Predictions: ' + str(data_unseen.shape))
print(dataset.tail())
```

```
is_med_quality  group_size
       5    2700
       5    2198
```

```
Data for Modeling: (4408, 12)
Unseen Data For Predictions: (490, 12)
```

The output of the first print statement of Listing 5-2 is given in Table 5-2, and we can see how the is_med_quality variable has 1 for instances which had a quality of 6 and 0 for all others (as compared to Table 5-1). The number of instances in the class of medium quality wine (is_med_quality = 1) and the number of instances in the class of nonmedium quality wine (is_med_quality = 0) are roughly the same, so the classes are balanced, and we wouldn't have to do anything to balance them. Synthetic Minority Oversampling Technique (SMOTE) is a popular oversampling technique where the synthetic samples are generated for the minority class.

We have kept 90% of the dataset for training and held the remaining 10% for evaluation of the ML model, which can be seen from the output of data.shape() which shows that it has 4,408 rows and 12 columns and the output of data_unseen.shape() which shows that it has 490 rows and 12 columns. You can compare Table 5-1 and Table 5-2 for the bottom few rows and see wherever the quality of wine was 6, the is_med_quality has the value 1 and 0 otherwise.

Table 5-2. *Last five rows of the updated wine dataset with our binary variable "is_med_quality"*

fixed acidity	volatile acidity	citric acid	residual sugar	chlorides	free sulfur dioxide	total sulfur dioxide	density	pH	sulphates	alcohol	is_med_quality
6.2	0.21	0.29	1.6	0.039	24.0	92.0	0.99114	3.27	0.50	11.2	1
6.6	0.32	0.36	8.0	0.047	57.0	168.0	0.99490	3.15	0.46	9.6	0
6.5	0.24	0.19	1.2	0.041	30.0	111.0	0.99254	2.99	0.46	9.4	1
5.5	0.29	0.30	1.1	0.022	20.0	110.0	0.98869	3.34	0.38	12.8	0
6.0	0.21	0.38	0.8	0.020	22.0	98.0	0.98941	3.26	0.32	11.8	1

We will build the model next as seen in Listing 5-3. We will use a Python ML library called "pycaret" which allows us to build and test several ML models with very less code. Since we are doing classification, we will import the classification module. Pycaret uses the concept of experiment which is a ML task in simple words, and we define our target (output variable to predict) and the data used for training. By default, 70% of the data is used for training using K-fold cross-validation and 30% saved for testing (not to be confused with unseen data). It also has a session_id field whose value is passed as seed to all functions to isolate the effect of randomization. This ensures that the models can be reproduced accurately given the same dataset later in the same or different environment.

Listing 5-3. Train and test the model

```
from pycaret.classification import *

# Compare the performance of multiple ML classification models
experiment_1 = setup(data = data, target = 'is_med_quality',
session_id=123)
compare_models(fold = 4, sort = 'Accuracy', include = ['rf', 'lightgbm',
'dt', 'lr'])

# Build random forest ML model and tune it
rf = create_model('rf', fold = 4)
tuned_rf = tune_model(rf, choose_better = True, optimize =
'Accuracy', fold=4)
```

Pycaret's compare_models function automatically creates many ML models; however, we pass in a list of ML algorithms that we would like to build sorted by our chosen performance metric "Accuracy." The parameter "fold = 4" refers to K-fold cross-validation with K=4. From the result of the compare_models, we can see that random forest has the highest accuracy but also took the longest to train (1.44 seconds). The output from the compare_models function is shown in Table 5-3 where we can see that ensemble models (random forest and gradient boosting machine) have higher accuracy than singleton models like decision tree and logistic regression. We use the create_model function to create the same random forest model that was built automatically by the compare_models function earlier and fine-tune it.

Table 5-3. *Result from the compare models showing the performance metrics of different ML models*

	Model	Accuracy	AUC	Recall	Prec.	F1	Kappa	MCC	TT (Sec)
rf	Random Forest Classifier	0.6820	0.7717	0.5872	0.6599	0.6212	0.3489	0.3507	1.4425
lightgbm	Light Gradient Boosting Machine	0.6807	0.7364	0.6178	0.6478	0.6322	0.3505	0.3510	0.2250
dt	Decision Tree Classifier	0.6480	0.6461	0.6295	0.5994	0.6139	0.2908	0.2912	0.0375
lr	Logistic Regression	0.5569	0.5916	0.2706	0.5034	0.3514	0.0592	0.0660	0.0875

The next step is to visualize the model performance, and plots like "Feature importance plot" can be of great interest to see what features influence the model the most. After which we check the tuned model performance on the 30% test data and then create a final model by training the model on all the training data (including the 30% test data). All these steps are shown in Listing 5-4, and the feature importance graph is shown in Figure 5-14.

Listing 5-4. Predict tuned model performance on test data

```
# Generate various plots to visualize model performance such as
# feature importance by clicking the Plot type
evaluate_model(tuned_rf)

# Use the model to predict the class of the 30% data saved from
training data
predict_model(tuned_rf)

# Train the model on 100% of training data (including the 30% of the data
saved earlier)
final_rf = finalize_model(tuned_rf)
```

The output from the predict_model function is shown in Table 5-4, where we can see that the model's performance on the test data has an accuracy of close to 70% which is pretty good. We can see from the feature importance graph that both features of "Sulfur dioxide" and "volatile acidity" have the most influence on the model prediction. This graph is usually of interest to the business stakeholders as it provides some insight into the model's working and serves as a good means to earn trust.

Table 5-4. *Tuned model performance on test data (30% of training data held in experiment)*

Model	Accuracy	AUC	Recall	Prec.	F1	Kappa	MCC
Random Forest Classifier	0.6984	0.7966	0.6419	0.6922	0.6661	0.3918	0.3928

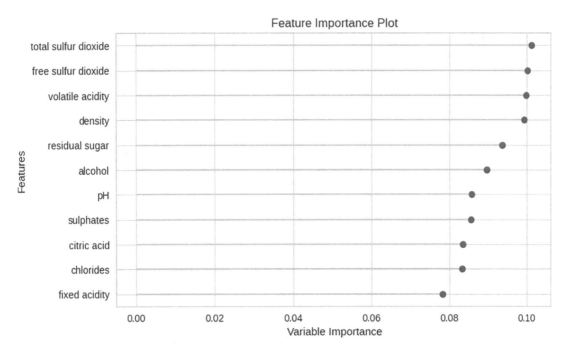

Figure 5-14. *Feature importance of the tuned random forest model*

With our model now final, the last step is to make predictions on unseen data (which can be seen as the proxy for the model's performance when it will be deployed in a production environment) and see its performance. We do that in Listing 5-5.

Listing 5-5. Predict class of unseen data

```
# Making predictions on the unseen data and seeing the last 5 rows
unseen_predictions = predict_model(final_rf, data=data_unseen)
unseen_predictions.tail()

from pycaret.utils import check_metric
check_metric(unseen_predictions.is_med_quality, unseen_predictions.Label,
'Accuracy')
```

Output:

0.9714

We can see from the unseen_predictions (refer to Table 5-5) that the *Label* matches with the is_med_quality for the few instances we printed. We also have a "Score" variable in the dataset, which is the probability of the instance being in a particular class. The check_metric function computes the accuracy of the model on the unseen data, and it comes out to be 97% which is great considering the fact that we didn't do any feature engineering.

Table 5-5. *Predicted label on the unseen data*

fixed acidity	volatile acidity	citric acid	residual sugar	chlorides	free sulfur dioxide	total sulfur dioxide	density	pH	sulphates	alcohol	is_med_quality	Label	Score
6.2	0.21	0.29	1.6	0.039	24.0	92.0	0.99114	3.27	0.50	11.2	1	1	0.90
6.6	0.32	0.36	8.0	0.047	57.0	168.0	0.99490	3.15	0.46	9.6	0	0	0.82
6.5	0.24	0.19	1.2	0.041	30.0	111.0	0.99254	2.99	0.46	9.4	1	1	0.59
5.5	0.29	0.30	1.1	0.022	20.0	110.0	0.98869	3.34	0.38	12.8	0	0	0.91
6.0	0.21	0.38	0.8	0.020	22.0	98.0	0.98941	3.26	0.32	11.8	1	1	0.82

USE CASE 2: SHALLOW ML ALGORITHM FOR REGRESSION

Building a regression model is very similar to classification, just that the target (output variable) will be a continuous value and our performance metrics will be things like MSE, R-squared (represented by R2 in pycaret).

Objective: Predict the price of a diamond based on its attributes using ML. The dataset used here is called diamonds and contains 54,000 records (instances) of diamonds. The dataset was prepared by Greg Mills (MBA '07) at the University of Virginia Darden School Foundation and is used as a classic dataset for regression and data visualization. A short description of each column is as follows, and some rows of the dataset can be seen in Table 5-6:

1. **carat** – The weight of the diamond. 1 carat is 200 mg.

2. **cut** – Quality of cut, perceived as sparkle (signature – ideal, ideal, very good, good, fair).

3. **color** – Diamond's color (D, E, F, colorless; G, H, I, near colorless).

4. **clarity** – Diamond's clarity code (F, flawless; IF, internally flawless; VVS1 or VVS2, very, very slightly included; or VS1 or VS2, very slightly included; SI1, slightly included).

5. **depth** – Total depth percentage.

6. **table** – Width of top of diamond relative to widest point.

7. **price** – The amount in USD that the diamond is valued.

8. **x** – Length in mm.

9. **y** – Width in mm.

10. **z** – Depth in mm.

Table 5-6. *Few instances of the diamond dataset*

carat	cut	color	clarity	depth	table	price	x	y	z
0.23	Ideal	E	SI2	61.5	55.0	326	3.95	3.98	2.43
0.21	Premium	E	SI1	59.8	61.0	326	3.89	3.84	2.31
0.23	Good	E	VS1	56.9	65.0	327	4.05	4.07	2.31
0.29	Premium	I	VS2	62.4	58.0	334	4.20	4.23	2.63
0.31	Good	J	SI2	63.3	58.0	335	4.34	4.35	2.75

Solution: Due to the high similarity in the process of building a regression model through pycaret, we wouldn't get into a very detailed approach. Have a look at the code in Listing 5-6, and you will find it very similar to the classification example above.

Listing 5-6. Predicting the price of diamond

```
import pandas as pd
import numpy as np

# Loading the datasets as Pandas Dataframe
dataset = pd.read_csv('https://raw.githubusercontent.com/tidyverse/ggplot2/
master/data-raw/diamonds.csv')

# Splitting the dataset into seen and unseen data
data = dataset.sample(frac=0.9, random_state=123).reset_index(drop=True)
```

```
data_unseen = dataset.drop(data.index).reset_index(drop=True)

print('Data for Modeling: ' + str(data.shape))
print('Unseen Data For Predictions: ' + str(data_unseen.shape))

from pycaret.regression import *

# Compare the performance of multiple regression models
experiment_2 = setup(data = data,  target = 'price', session_id=123)
compare_models(sort = 'R2', include = ['lr', 'lightgbm', 'rf', 'dt'])

# Develop and fine-tune the light GBM model
lightgbm = create_model('lightgbm')
tuned_lightgbm = tune_model(lightgbm)
evaluate_model(tuned_lightgbm)

# Use the model to predict the class of the 30% data saved from
training data
predict_model(tuned_lightgbm)

# Train the model on 100% of training data (including the 30% of the data
saved earlier)
final_lightgbm = finalize_model(tuned_lightgbm)
unseen_predictions = predict_model(final_lightgbm, data=data_unseen)
print(unseen_predictions.head())

from pycaret.utils import check_metric
check_metric(unseen_predictions.price, unseen_predictions.Label, 'R2')
```

Let's have a look at the output from the code from Listing 5-6. The dataset was first split for training and for evaluation. The following output shows the number of rows and columns in each of the data splits:

```
data for Modeling: (48546, 10)
Unseen Data For Predictions: (5394, 10)
```

Then, the experiment is set up with price being the target (or output) variable to be predicted based on all other features in the data. We compared the performance (with focus on R-squared metric) of some models of interest and found that light GBM has the highest R-squared (R2) and the lowest RMSE as seen in Table 5-7. This shows again how ensemble methods are so much better than the nonensemble (singleton) ML algorithms.

Table 5-7. *Result from the compare models showing the performance metrics of different ML models*

	Model	MAE	MSE	RMSE	R2	RMSLE	MAPE	TT (Sec)
lightgbm	Light Gradient Boosting Machine	294.4985	3.172773e+05	562.8601	0.9802	0.1113	0.0856	0.310
rf	Random Forest Regressor	283.4676	3.272881e+05	571.1140	0.9796	0.0960	0.0687	14.246
dt	Decision Tree Regressor	377.3960	6.080199e+05	779.5280	0.9621	0.1307	0.0899	0.249
lr	Linear Regression	743.4296	1.286633e+06	1134.1055	0.9197	0.5737	0.3899	0.040

We create and fine-tune the model and look at some graphs as feature importance. Width, depth, and carat (i.e., shape and weight) seem to be the most important features as seen in Figure 5-15.

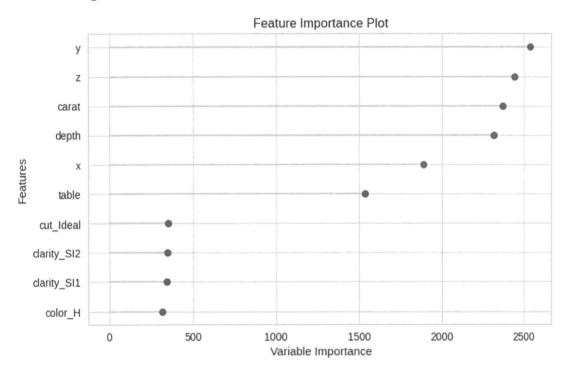

Figure 5-15. *Feature importance of the tuned light gradient boosted model (light GBM)*

We use the tune model to test its performance on the 30% data held from the data used for training and see that R-squared drops a bit and RMSE increases slightly as seen in Table 5-8.

Table 5-8. *Tuned model performance on test data (30% of training data held in experiment)*

Model	MAE	MSE	RMSE	R2	RMSLE	MAPE
Light Gradient Boosting Machine	304.5302	348781.1696	590.577	0.978	0.1264	0.0883

In the end, we train the model on the whole of training data to create a model called "final_lightgbm" and use it to predict prices of diamonds on the unseen data (our evaluation dataset) as seen in the Label Value of Table 5-9. The R-squared value on the unseen data is 84% (0.8428) which is good given the fact that there was no feature engineering or any custom hyperparameter training done to improve the performance of the model.

Table 5-9. *Predicted label on the unseen data*

carat	cut	color	clarity	depth	table	price	x	y	z	Label
0.61	Very Good	F	VS2	61.8	56.0	1989	5.42	5.46	3.36	1952.151757
0.72	Very Good	J	SI1	63.0	58.0	1989	5.67	5.70	3.58	1748.455453
0.74	Good	H	VS2	59.2	64.0	1989	5.79	5.66	3.40	2138.917103
0.65	Ideal	E	SI1	62.7	54.0	1989	5.58	5.56	3.49	2073.322465
0.54	Premium	F	VS2	62.0	59.0	1989	5.22	5.16	3.22	1705.712407

Overview of Deep Learning Algorithms

Deep learning algorithms are powered by artificial neural networks (ANNs) which are inspired by the biological neural networks of brains. Let's first understand the core components of a deep learning algorithm based on a feedforward ANN. Figure 5-16 shows the structure of an artificial neural network:

1. **Nodes –** ANNs are composed of nodes (as it is a graph), also called neuron or perceptron at the most fundamental level. Nodes are the computational units of ANN and aggregated into layers. These are based on biological neurons and take inputs and produce an output, also called signal, which can be sent to all the other connected nodes. The inputs can be features from data or the output of other nodes.

2. **Edges –** These are the connections representing the output from one node to another. The edge has a weight associated that represents its relative importance. A node can have multiple incoming edges and outgoing edges.

3. **Input layer –** This is the first layer of the ANN and accepts the input data. The number of nodes in this layer is the same as the features (e.g., columns for structured data) of the input data.

4. **Hidden layers –** These layers are stacked between the input layer and the output layer. They take input from the input layer (or another hidden layer) and provide output to the output layer (or another hidden layer). These layers are where most of the learning happens in an ANN. The more the number of these layers, the deeper is the ANN. Although an ANN can work without a hidden layer, it likely wouldn't be performant enough.

5. **Output layer –** This is the last layer of the network, and the output of its nodes accomplishes the task as predicting the price of a home (regression) or identifying faces in an image (object detection). The number of nodes is determined by the ML approach. For regression, it usually has a single node, and for classification, the number of nodes is usually equal to the number of output classes.

6. **Loss metric –** This is the ML success metric that we specify in the ANN based on the machine learning problem we want to solve (regression or classification). As in any ML algorithm, the goal is to minimize the loss, e.g., cross-entropy, mean absolute error (MAE), mean squared error (MSE), etc.

7. **Optimizer –** This is an algorithm that computes updates in weights of the layers in the ANN to minimize the loss computed from the loss function.

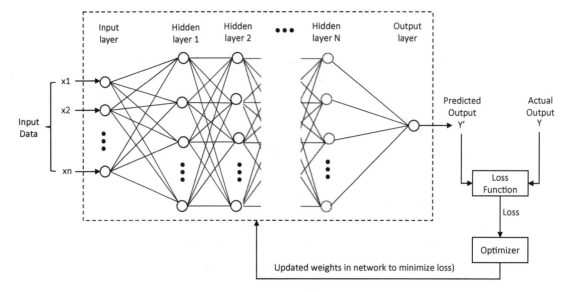

Figure 5-16. *Structure of a hypothetical artificial neural network*

8. **Activation function** – This helps the network to learn complex patterns. This function determines how the weighted sum of the inputs to a node is transformed into the output of the node. All nodes in a layer have the same activation function. The activation function in the nodes of the output layer is dependent on the machine learning problem type. Figure 5-17 illustrates the activation function inside a node. The most common activation functions are

a. **Rectified linear unit** – It is the most popular activation unit for hidden layer nodes due to its simplicity to implement and ability to learn complex patterns in data. For hidden layers, rectified linear unit (ReLu), a type of nonlinear activation function, has become the popular choice due to its simplicity. Given an input number, it returns 0 if input is less than 0 or the input number itself if it is greater than 0.

b. **Sigmoid** – It is the same mathematical function that is used in logistic regression, and it bounds the output between 0 and 1, which is used as a probability of an instance being in a particular class or not. It is used for performing binary classification tasks where the network has a single node in the output layer.

c. **SoftMax** – It can be seen as a combination of multiple sigmoids and used for multiclass classification (e.g., predict if the image is of a car, boat, or airplane). It returns the probability of an instance belonging to each individual class. The number of nodes in the output layer will be equal to the number of classes if SoftMax is used.

d. **Linear** – There is no activation function here. It simply takes in the input and passes it as the output. This is used for regression tasks.

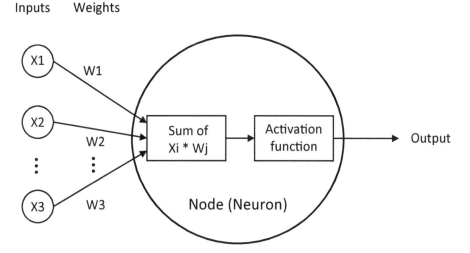

Figure 5-17. *Structure of a node in an artificial neural network*

Popular Deep Learning Algorithms

1. **Convolution neural networks (CNNs)** – Also known as "convets," they are a kind of ANN that are particularly useful for image-processing applications. They are used for supervised ML, and the first CNN was developed by Yann LeCun with the goal to recognize handwritten digits. CNN introduces two kinds of layers to ANN, namely, the convolution layer and the pooling layer. The first few convolution layers in CNN extract features from the input layers such as edges of a shape in an image, and the later layers combine these features into higher-level features. Between two convolution layers lies the pooling layer, which summarizes the features learned by the convolution layer by reducing the

dimensionality of the extracted features. This reduces the number of parameters to learn and the amount of computation to perform in the network. A high-level view of a CNN can be seen in Figure 5-18.

Applications – Image classification, video analysis, and natural language processing

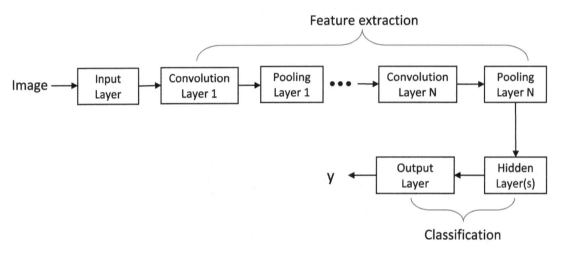

Figure 5-18. *A high-level view of a CNN used as image classifier*

2. **Recurrent neural network (RNN)** – CNNs fail at interpreting data that is a part of a sequence, where the different parts of the data affect each other. Common examples are blocks of text (such as sentences), audio, video (sequence of frames), etc. RNNs come to the rescue here and are effective at modeling sequence data. Unlike ANN and CNN, the input data to RNN is not fed all at once, but rather the sequence is fed one by one. For example, the sentence (sequence of words) "When is my meeting?" will be fed into RNN word by word, starting with "When." The RNN will process it, then it will take in the next word "is," and it is processed along with the result from "When," and so on. You see there is an order of the sequence of words, and if the order changes, the sequence will change and hence the RNN will learn it differently. In Figure 5-19, the image on the left is the simplified view of RNN, and the one on the right is how it processes input over time (to show order) called unfolding.

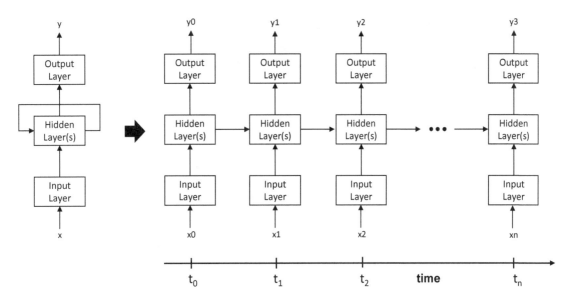

Figure 5-19. *Recurrent neural network unfolded in time*

RNNs are computationally very expensive and suffer from vanishing gradient, a problem where, as the length of sequence increases, the network learning reduces or may stop in the worst case. Still, they were a breakthrough and had major success in sequence data.

Applications – Time-series analysis, speech recognition, language translation, etc.

3. **Long short-term memory network (LSTM)** – These are a type of RNN that can learn from long sequences, a problem faced by RNN. The learning is done by means of "memory cells"; each cell has three gates that control how learning is performed. The forget gate controls when a certain memory of the cell is forgotten to allow the cell to remember new data and forget any irrelevant part from the previous state. The input gate controls which value from input should be used to modify memory and the output gate controls when the memory of the cell is sent out of the cell. Since the memory cell can retain its value for as long as it seems the information is important, it solves the issue of long sequences with RNN.

251

A simplified form of LSTM was introduced in 2014 called "gated recurrent unit" (GRU), which has only two gates, an update gate that controls what parts of the previous cell contents to store and a reset gate that controls how to add new input with previous cell contents. GRUs can be trained faster; however, LSTMs have better performance with more data. Besides doing what RNN does, LSTMs have also been used along with CNNs for developing image captioning applications, where the CNN processes the image, and the output of CNN is fed into LSTM to give a natural language caption.

Applications – Sentence completion or autocompletion, image captioning system, language translation, etc.

4. **Autoencoders** – These are a type of neural network where the objective is to replicate data from the input layer and therefore have the input and output are identical. Here, first an encoder transforms an input (say an image) into a different and smaller representation, and then a decoder takes that as an input and reconstructs the image which is sent as output. These are semisupervised deep learning algorithms. Figure 5-20 shows an autoencoder.

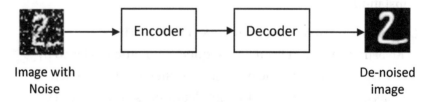

Image with Noise   De-noised image

Figure 5-20. *Autoencoder for removing noise from image*

Applications: Anomaly detection, image processing, dimensionality reduction, etc.

5. **Generative adversarial networks (GANs)** – They are a class of deep learning algorithms developed by Ian Goodfellow and his colleagues in 2014 that generates new data that resembles the

training data.[8] It has two components, a generator that learns to generate the data and a discriminator that distinguishes the output generated by the generator from the true data distribution. Both the generator and discriminator are neural networks. The objective of the generator is to generate data that the discriminator fails to tell it as fake data (synthesized data) and starts to classify it as real (part of true data distribution). Figure 5-21 shows a GAN that learns from real images to generate realistic fake images.

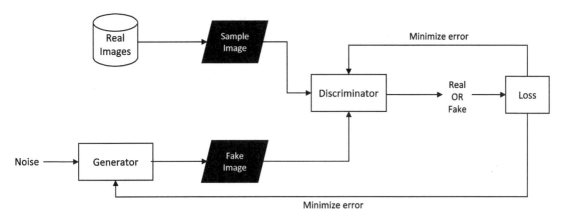

Figure 5-21. *A visual representation of a GAN to generate fake images*

GANs have been greatly improved over time, and a couple of variations have been developed for various applications. StyleGAN is worth special credit here as it is a type of GAN that can create fake realistic images of human faces by learning features of the human face. It was developed by the researchers at Nvidia in 2019.[9] An engineer at Uber used StyleGAN to create a website https://thispersondoesnotexist.com/, where the website shows a fake human face on each reload (some sample images in Figure 5-22).

[8] Goodfellow, Ian; Pouget-Abadie, Jean; Mirza, Mehdi; Xu, Bing; Warde-Farley, David; Ozair, Sherjil; Courville, Aaron; Bengio, Yoshua (2014). Generative Adversarial Networks (PDF). Proceedings of the International Conference on Neural Information Processing Systems (NIPS 2014). pp. 2672–2680.

[9] https://arxiv.org/pdf/1812.04948.pdf

Figure 5-22. *Fake human face images generated through StyleGAN. Source: thispersondoesnotexist.com*

GANs have been used along with autoencoders to generate "deep fake" videos in which a person in an existing image or video is replaced with someone else. Deepfakes have become quite infamous for their use in celebrity pornography, revenge porn, etc.

Applications – Text-to-image generation, image processing (increasing resolution of images), realistic image generation, 3D modeling of objects from images, etc.

6. **Transformers –** These were introduced in the deep learning world in 2017 and are primarily used in the field of natural language processing (NLP). These utilize the concept of attention, which focuses on the important parts of the input data and fades the rest, just like cognitive attention. A transformer consists of an encoding stack which contains a set of encoder layers and a decoding stack which contains a set of decoder layers. Encoders process the input to form encodings that contain information on what parts of input are relevant, and each decoder takes the embedding from the last encoder of the encoding stack and processes it to generate the output. The number of decoders is equal to the number of encoders. Figure 5-23 shows a high-level architecture of a transformer used to translate English to Spanish.

Output: *Hace calor hoy*

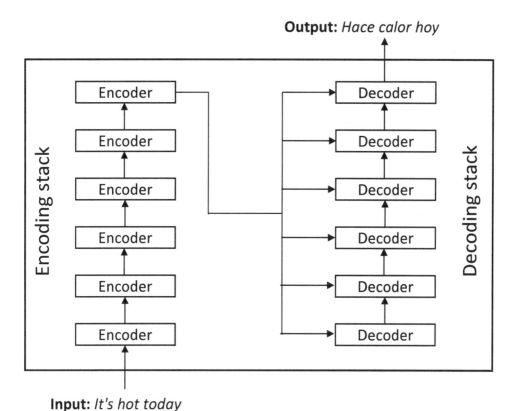

Input: *It's hot today*

Figure 5-23. *Architecture of a transformer that translates English to Spanish*

It is worth mentioning two transformers that have made transformers very famous. The first is BERT which stands for Bidirectional Encoder Representations from Transformers and is developed by Google and is used in Google Search in almost every single English-based query[10]. It was open sourced, and anyone can train their own state-of-art question answering system (or question answering system (or a variety of other models) in a few hours using a single GPU.[11] The other transformer is GPT that stands for Generative Pretraining Transformer and was developed by OpenAI. Its latest version is GPT-3 which contains 175 billion parameters. It wasn't immediately

---

[10] "Understanding searches better than ever before". Google. 2019-10-25. Retrieved 2019-11-27.

[11] https://ai.googleblog.com/2018/11/open-sourcing-bert-state-of-art-pre.html

released to the public over concerns of its misuse such as writing fake news. It was licensed to Microsoft in September 2020.[12]

Applications – Text summarization, natural language understanding, text generation, question answering, etc.

Before we move into building a deep learning algorithm, we would like to introduce you to two more topics so that you have a better understanding of what tools/techniques your ML teams might be using to solve the business problems quickly and effectively. Most of the ML (shallow as well as deep learning) is done through the Python interfaces of ML frameworks, and Jupyter (or similar) is the most common integrated development environment for ML algorithm development, which allows its users to save text, code, and plots together enabling easier future reference and faster development:

1. **Transfer learning** – It is the process through which an already trained model is applied to a different but related problem. It is commonly used in computer vision and natural language processing as deep learning models are expensive to train in terms of time and compute resources or if the new data size isn't enough to train the model effectively. For example, in image classification through transfer learning, the feature extraction layers along with their weights of an already trained deep learning model are taken and attached to the feature extraction and classification layers of a new deep learning model. The new model may fine-tune the feature extraction layers of the already trained model or freeze (make no change) them and use them to learn generic features and through its own layers learn more specific features to its problem from those generic features. A lot of third-party pretrained models are available for a variety of platforms and tasks. Some notable ones are MobileNetV2, VGG, InceptionV3, ResNet, and YOLO.

2. **Deep learning frameworks** – Building deep learning models from scratch for practical use can be very daunting and will require specific skill sets that are not easy to acquire in a short span of

---

[12] "Microsoft gets exclusive license for OpenAI's GPT-3 language model". VentureBeat. 2020-09-22. Retrieved 2020-09-24.

time. Most businesses don't have this expertise in-house and to solve this skill shortage and to speed up the ML lifecycle use deep learning frameworks. Deep learning frameworks are generally open source libraries that provide interfaces which can be used to build deep learning models without needing to know the intrinsic details (e.g., mathematics) of the model and also greatly reduce the time to build models. The popular deep learning frameworks are TensorFlow by Google, PyTorch by Facebook, CNTK by Microsoft, and MXNET by Apache software foundation, and they support a variety of programming languages (most commonly Python). In the example we provide in the following for image classification through deep learning, we will use Keras, which is a deep learning framework that is now a part of TensorFlow.

Deep Learning in Action

USE CASE 3: DEEP LEARNING ALGORITHM FOR MULTI-CLASS IMAGE CLASSIFICATION

To get a better sense of how deep learning algorithms work, let's build a simple deep learning algorithm for classification of images. To build the model, we will use Keras, an open source neural network API that provides a Python interface to the TensorFlow library. It makes building deep learning models easy and intuitive.

Objective: Predict the fashion product from the image of the product. To train the deep learning model, we will use the Fashion-MNIST dataset which is a collection of 70,000 low-resolution (28 by 28 pixels) grayscale images in 10 fashion categories.[13] It has 7,000 images in each category. This dataset is created from the pictures of the products on Zalando's website. Zalando is a fashion and lifestyle products ecommerce company based in Berlin, Germany. Sample images from this dataset are shown in Figure 5-24.

---

[13] https://arxiv.org/pdf/1708.07747.pdf

Class	Product	Product Image examples
0	T-Shirt/Top	
1	Trouser	
2	Pullover	
3	Dress	
4	Coat	
5	Sandals	
6	Shirt	
7	Sneaker	
8	Bag	
9	Ankle boots	

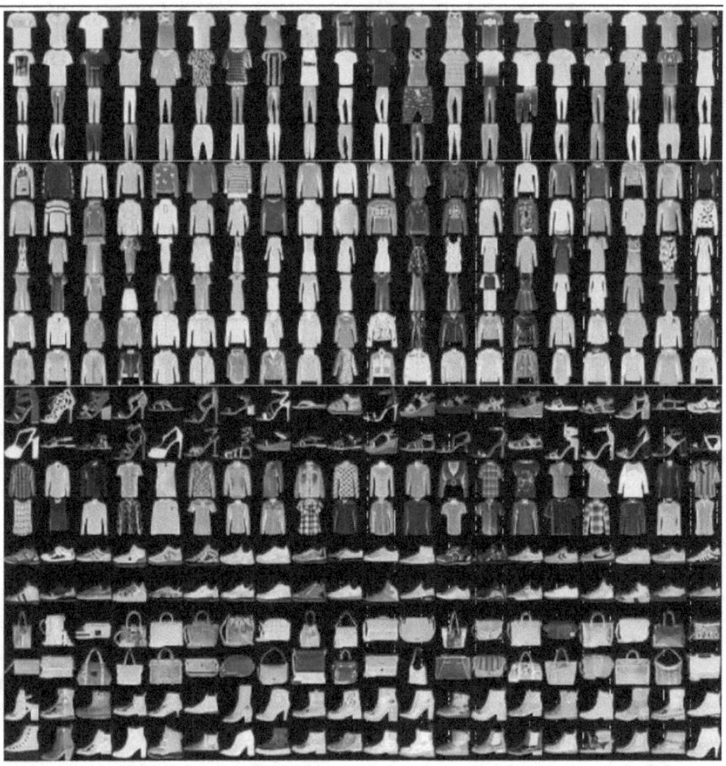

Figure 5-24. *Sample images from the Fashion-MNIST dataset*

Solution: Let us train a simple artificial neural network (ANN) for this task. Listing 5-7 shows the steps to load the data. We will first import the necessary deep learning library which is TensorFlow (Keras is available as a submodule of this library) and a plotting library (matplotlib) to plot images of the products. The Fashion-MNIST dataset is downloaded and loaded through the Keras datasets. The load_data() returns two datasets, one for training with 60,000 images and their corresponding labels and another for testing the model with 10,000 images and their corresponding labels. It's important to note that the image is not present as jpg or png but is rather coded as a numpy array (with rows and columns) of size 28x28 representing the pixels. The value of each cell of this array presents the pixel density on a scale of 0–255. The shape of the image datasets represents the number of images, weight, and height.

Listing 5-7. Load the Fashion-MNIST dataset

```
# TensorFlow and tf.keras
import tensorflow as tf
import numpy as np
import matplotlib.pyplot as plt

# Load the dataset
(train_images, train_labels), (test_images, test_labels) = tf.keras.
datasets.fashion_mnist.load_data()

print(train_images.shape)
print(test_images.shape)
```

Output:

```
(60000, 28, 28)
(10000, 28, 28)
```

As we know already that the labels in the dataset aren't names of the product class but a numeric coded value ranging from 0 to 9, so we will create a mapping of product class names to labels for easier understanding. This mapping is saved in the list "class_names" in Listing 5-8.

Listing 5-8. Load the Fashion-MNIST dataset

```
print(train_labels[:10])
# Create a mapping of labels (0-9) and their corresponding product
class names
class_names = ['T-shirt/top', 'Trouser', 'Pullover', 'Dress', 'Coat',
'Sandal', 'Shirt', 'Sneaker', 'Bag', 'Ankle boot']

plt.imshow(train_images[10], cmap=plt.cm.binary)
plt.colorbar()

train_images = train_images / 255.0
test_images = test_images / 255.0
```

Output:

```
[9 0 0 3 0 2 7 2 5 5]
```

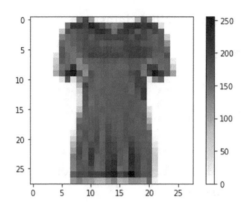

Figure 5-25. *Plot of the tenth training data image*

We plot the 10th image (stored as a numpy array) in Figure 5-25 from the training data using the functions from the matplotlib library in the listing above, and it shows on the grid the size (28 x 28) and the scale shows the range of pixel density (0–255). We will scale the pixel density (between 0.0 and 1.0) for both training and test images as it improves the accuracy and speed of training.

Listing 5-9. Build a function to plot multiple images and their labels

```python
def plot(images, labels, predictions = None):
  """ Plot 14 images from the training data or test data

     Parameters
     ----------
     images: list
         This is the list of fashion product images of which a subset of
         14 images are to be plotted (displayed)
     labels: list
         This is a list of labels (0-9) of the fashion products
         corresponding to the images.
     flag: Boolean
         This is set to True for showing training images and False for
         showing predicted labels on test images
  """
  plt.figure(figsize=(12, 16))
  for i in range(14):
    plt.subplot(7, 7, i+1)
```

```
    plt.xticks([])
    plt.yticks([])
    plt.imshow(images[i], cmap=plt.cm.binary)
    if predictions is None:
      plt.xlabel(class_names[labels[i]])
    else:                           # Set label color to red if prediction
                                      doesn't match actual
      plt.xlabel("{:2.1f}% {}".format(100 * np.max(predictions[i]),
                          class_names[np.argmax(predictions[i])]),
                          color = 'red' if np.argmax(predictions[i]) !=
                          labels[i] else 'black')
  return plt

# Plot the first fourteen training images and their corresponding labels
plot(train_images, train_labels).show()
```

We create a function to plot images and their corresponding labels. It takes in three parameters (one optional), the list of images, the list of actual labels, and the optional predictions input, which is to be provided for only when the predictions from the model are plotted. The function plots 14 images in a grid of 2 x 7 spaces. The label (on the x-axis) of the image plot is the name of the class if there are no predictions sent. The label and the corresponding probability of prediction are printed if predictions are sent. Also, if the actual label doesn't match the predicted label, then the color of the label is changed to red, else it is kept as black.

Another thing to note here is that each prediction of an image (generated by our model that will be defined next) is a list of ten values that sum up to 1. Each of the ten values represents the probability of the image of being in the ten product classes. We choose the product class with the highest probability as the label of the image. This is done using the argmax function in numpy. Before we move to building our model, let's see a sample run of the plot function with training images and their corresponding labels to see the plot of the first 14 images and their labels. The output of the plot function on training data is shown in Figure 5-26.

Figure 5-26. *First 14 images from the training data*

Let's build a simple artificial neural network of three layers – an input layer, a hidden layer, and an output layer. We can make the network deep by adding in more hidden layers; however, this network will suffice for our task and will be fast to train. There is no specific rule for selecting the number of hidden layers – generally, one to two layers should suffice for datasets that are not very complex and have few dimensions. For complex datasets that have a lot of dimensions (for tasks such as computer vision), more than two layers are generally needed. For the number of nodes in the hidden layers, choose a value between the number of nodes in input layer and the nodes in output layer, say

$$\sqrt{input\ nodes\ X\ output\ nodes}$$

Have a look at Listing 5-10 on the first few lines where the model is built. The input layer is a "Flatten" type of layer which transforms the two-dimensional array of 28x28 pixel values to a one-dimensional array of 784 pixels (28 * 28 = 784) and hence has 784 nodes. This layer isn't used in learning; its only purpose is to flatten the data. The next layer is the hidden layer with 32 nodes (neurons) and learning happens here. It is dense which means it's fully connected to all the nodes of the input layer. The last layer is the output layer and is dense as well, which means it's fully connected to all the 32 nodes of the hidden layer. Since we are dealing with a multiclass classification plot with ten classes, we have "softmax" as the activation function of this layer. Also, it has ten nodes where each node returns the probability of an instance belonging to each of the individual ten fashion product classes.

If you pay attention to the model compile part, we are using a kind of categorical cross-entropy as our loss that we want to minimize and function and accuracy (percentage of images classified correctly) as the metric to monitor the training and test steps. The model.fit function trains the neural network model on the whole training data (training images and their corresponding labels). This training is done ten times as represented by epochs.

Listing 5-10. Build the model and train it

```
model = tf.keras.Sequential([
    tf.keras.layers.Flatten(input_shape=(28, 28)),
    tf.keras.layers.Dense(32, activation='relu'),
    tf.keras.layers.Dense(10, activation='softmax')
])

model.compile(optimizer='adam',
              loss = tf.keras.losses.SparseCategoricalCrossentropy(),
              metrics = ['accuracy'])

model.fit(train_images, train_labels, epochs=10)

# Test the accuracy of model on test data
test_loss, test_acc = model.evaluate(test_images, test_labels, verbose=2)
print('\nTest data accuracy:', test_acc)
```

Output:

```
Epoch 1/10
1875/1875 [==============================] - 4s 2ms/step - loss: 0.7182 -
accuracy: 0.7573
Epoch 2/10
1875/1875 [==============================] - 3s 2ms/step - loss: 0.4187 -
accuracy: 0.8529
Epoch 3/10
1875/1875 [==============================] - 3s 2ms/step - loss: 0.3773 -
accuracy: 0.8665
Epoch 4/10
1875/1875 [==============================] - 3s 2ms/step - loss: 0.3603 -
accuracy: 0.8707
```

```
Epoch 5/10
1875/1875 [==============================] - 3s 2ms/step - loss: 0.3481 -
accuracy: 0.8739
Epoch 6/10
1875/1875 [==============================] - 3s 2ms/step - loss: 0.3303 -
accuracy: 0.8812
Epoch 7/10
1875/1875 [==============================] - 3s 2ms/step - loss: 0.3197 -
accuracy: 0.8821
Epoch 8/10
1875/1875 [==============================] - 3s 2ms/step - loss: 0.3133 -
accuracy: 0.8848
Epoch 9/10
1875/1875 [==============================] - 3s 2ms/step - loss: 0.3027 -
accuracy: 0.8894
Epoch 10/10
1875/1875 [==============================] - 3s 2ms/step - loss: 0.2995 -
accuracy: 0.8906
313/313 - 0s - loss: 0.3524 - accuracy: 0.8755
```

```
Test data accuracy: 0.8755000233650208
```

We can see from the output of the model training above how with each increasing epoch the cross-entropy loss is reduced, and the accuracy increased. The model shows an accuracy of 89% on the training data. When the model is evaluated (run) against the test data, the accuracy comes at 87.5% again. This is good accuracy considering the fact how simple our network is in the number of nodes and layers. Let's see some sample test images and what our model predicted them as.

Listing 5-11. Make predictions

```
predictions = model.predict(test_images)

print(">> Prediction for first test image", predictions[0], "\n")
print(">> Rounding the prediction values:", (np.
around(predictions[0],2)), "\n")
```

```
# Probability of image being each product class
print(">> Probability of the image being each product class:")
for i in range(10):
  print("Label:",i, "\tprobability:", np.around(predictions[0][i],2),"\
  tproduct name:",class_names[i])

# Class corresponding to the label with the highest probability is chosen
print("\n>> Label with the highest probability:",
np.argmax(predictions[0]),
      "| Predicted class:", class_names[np.argmax(predictions[0])],
      "| Actual class:", class_names[test_labels[0]])

# Plot the first fourteen test images and their corresponding labels
plot(test_images, test_labels, predictions).show()
```

   Output:

```
>> Prediction for first test image
[5.2205351e-06 1.0227712e-08 2.7468314e-08 6.2290461e-08 5.6611061e-08
 2.1482972e-02 5.2731643e-06 3.0313255e-02 4.3123856e-04 9.4776183e-01]

>> Rounding the prediction values: [0.   0.   0.   0.   0.   0.02 0.   0.03
0.   0.95]

>> Probability of the image being each product class:
Label: 0     probability: 0.0    product name: T-shirt/top
Label: 1     probability: 0.0    product name: Trouser
Label: 2     probability: 0.0    product name: Pullover
Label: 3     probability: 0.0    product name: Dress
Label: 4     probability: 0.0    product name: Coat
Label: 5     probability: 0.02   product name: Sandal
Label: 6     probability: 0.0    product name: Shirt
Label: 7     probability: 0.03   product name: Sneaker
Label: 8     probability: 0.0    product name: Bag
Label: 9     probability: 0.95   product name: Ankle boot

>> Label with the highest probability: 9 | Predicted class: Ankle boot |
Actual class: Ankle boot
```

As our output layer has a softmax activation function with ten nodes, there are ten prediction values for each image, as can be seen in the prediction output for the first test image. We have rounded the values so that they are easier to understand. From the prediction output of the first test image, we can see it has a 95% probability of being class 9 (the position of the value donates the class label), 3% probability of being a sneaker, and 2% probability of being a sandal. The model predicts it right as the image is indeed of an ankle boot.

However, we know that with our deep learning model's test accuracy of 87.5%, it did misclassify some 12.5% of the test images. Looking at the model's prediction for the first few test images as seen in Figure 5-27, we can see how the model misclassified the sneaker for a sandal (76.3% sandal).

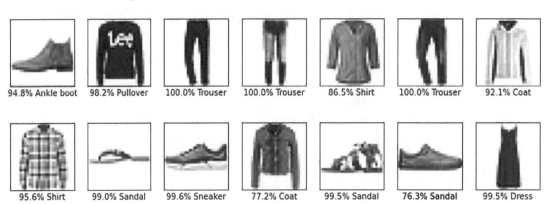

Figure 5-27. *Model prediction on the first 14 images from the test data*

If we want to further improve the accuracy of this ANN model, there are a couple of ways:

- Increase the number of epochs

- Increase the size of training data

- Increase the number of hidden layers

- Increase the number of nodes in the hidden layers

We also know that CNNs are great for image processing (classification here) due to their ability to learn abstract features and have much higher performance than ANN. Let us build a simple CNN and see how its performance compares to our ANN model.

Listing 5-12. Train CNN model and make predictions

```
# reshape image to add channel information
train_images = train_images.reshape(60000, 28, 28, 1)
test_images = test_images.reshape(10000, 28, 28, 1)
# Build and train CNN model
model_CNN = tf.keras.Sequential([
    tf.keras.layers.Conv2D(filters = 64, kernel_size = (3,3), activation =
    'relu', input_shape = (28, 28, 1)),
    tf.keras.layers.MaxPool2D(pool_size=(2,2)),
    tf.keras.layers.Flatten(),
    tf.keras.layers.Dense(64, activation='relu'),
    tf.keras.layers.Dense(10, activation='softmax')
])

model_CNN.compile(optimizer='adam',
            loss = tf.keras.losses.SparseCategoricalCrossentropy(),
            metrics = ['accuracy'])

# Train the CNN on training images
model_CNN.fit(train_images, train_labels, epochs=10)

# Get model accuracy on test images
test_loss, test_acc = model_CNN.evaluate(test_images, test_labels,
verbose=2)
print('\nTest data accuracy:', test_acc)
```

   Output:

```
Epoch 1/10
1875/1875 [==============================] - 5s 2ms/step - loss: 0.5207 -
accuracy: 0.8180
Epoch 2/10
1875/1875 [==============================] - 4s 2ms/step - loss: 0.2674 -
accuracy: 0.9029
Epoch 3/10
1875/1875 [==============================] - 4s 2ms/step - loss: 0.2253 -
accuracy: 0.9185
```

```
Epoch 4/10
1875/1875 [==============================] - 4s 2ms/step - loss: 0.1914 -
accuracy: 0.9294
Epoch 5/10
1875/1875 [==============================] - 4s 2ms/step - loss: 0.1635 -
accuracy: 0.9394
Epoch 6/10
1875/1875 [==============================] - 4s 2ms/step - loss: 0.1399 -
accuracy: 0.9490
Epoch 7/10
1875/1875 [==============================] - 4s 2ms/step - loss: 0.1185 -
accuracy: 0.9554
Epoch 8/10
1875/1875 [==============================] - 4s 2ms/step - loss: 0.1057 -
accuracy: 0.9615
Epoch 9/10
1875/1875 [==============================] - 4s 2ms/step - loss: 0.0944 -
accuracy: 0.9670
Epoch 10/10
1875/1875 [==============================] - 4s 2ms/step - loss: 0.0797 -
accuracy: 0.9717
313/313 - 1s - loss: 0.3340 - accuracy: 0.9087

Test data accuracy: 0.9086999893188477
```

We built a simple five-layer CNN in Listing 5-12. It can be viewed as a simple ANN with a convolution layer and a pooling layer. The convolution layer takes as an input the (length, width, channels) of the images. You may think of channels as the number of colors in the image. Grayscale images have one channel, and color images have three channels for red, green, and blue (RGB). We reshaped our images to add channel information. This will let the input convolution layer know that it should expect 1 grid (channel) of 28x28 pixels for each image. You might notice that the convolution layer has a parameter called filter and another called kernel size. Filters perform feature extraction such as detecting edges in images by evaluating intensity value changes in the image. The kernel size is the size of the filter. It is a matrix that scans through the image to filter.

The model was trained on a GPU to train faster, and hence the training time seems comparable to the ANN trained before which was trained on a CPU. In terms of performance, CNN's accuracy in the last epoch is 97%, which is way more than the 89% accuracy achieved by ANN during training. However, on the test data, CNN's accuracy drops to 91%. This shows that CNN got overfit on the training data.

When Not to Use Deep Learning

Deep learning algorithms are very powerful compared to shallow ML algorithms and with the democratization of AI have become easy to use. The question that arises is: Why not to use them for every machine learning problem? The following could be some reasons why you may still want to use shallow ML learners:

1. **Small dataset –** Deep learning algorithms take in an extremely large amount of data to train effectively (many thousands to millions of instances and features). You may not have that much data in the first place, and training a deep learning model on a small dataset will likely result in bad performance as it likely will overfit the data.

2. **Data is tabular –** If your data is not audio, images, unstructured text, etc., it may be better to use a shallow learner as you can bring in feature engineering there and get a high performance and interpretability. For image, audio, etc., the data is low level and feature engineering is hard; therefore, using deep learning makes more sense for them due to their capability of automated feature extraction.

3. **Need for interpretation –** If interpretability of a model is a necessity to establish causality or it's important to know what drives the model to predict in a certain way. Deep learning comes in the far end of black-box models and has the least interpretability.

4. **Limited data and/or compute –** If you have limited infrastructure (CPU, GPU, memory, etc.), it may not be possible to have a deep learning model trained. Even if you try to do it, it may take a lot of time while consuming most of your resources reducing your productivity. Getting better infrastructure will be an added expense. The other thing is, if you have limited data (say labeled image data for image classification), however you have a way to increase the size of the labeled data by hiring people to manually annotate the data, it may come at a high cost.

5. **Unavailability of ML scientists –** If you don't have some ML researchers (they are called by different names sometimes – data scientists, applied scientists, ML researchers/engineers) who have a good understanding of how to optimize the deep learning model parameters to get the best performance, it may not be worth building and maintaining a deep learning model primarily due to the complexity it has compared to the shallow learners.

Rise of AI Ethics

The use of AI has been on the rise across industries, and we (humans) are getting more and more exposed to the innovations brought in by AI. Critical functions impacting humans such as medical diagnosis, law enforcement, and transportation are seeing big strides by AI and with the benefits can come negative impacts unless there is a sense of responsibility associated with AI as, there is a gradual transition from AI being a tool to aid humans make decisions to make decisions now independently for humans. The following are some challenges with AI being so widely used.

1. Interpretability

An interpretable AI model can be understood by humans through the parameters of the model itself, without any other aid. We should be able to understand why it made certain predictions/decisions of an interpretable model. However, there is a trade-off between accuracy and interpretability. The simplest models like linear regression and decision trees are interpretable; however, more complex models like random forest and even more complex algorithms like convolution neural networks achieve far more accuracy but at the cost of losing interpretability. These models which don't have good interpretability are also called "black-box" models.

There are certain consequences to this lack of interpretability. You may have noticed that when you apply for a credit card online, you get an approval or denial within a couple of minutes. Well, you're thinking right, no human, but an AI model made that approval or denial decision. However, all loans in the United States are under the purview of "Fair lending laws," which ensure that financial institutions provide fair and uniform services and credit decisions (irrespective of age, sex, color, race, etc.).[14] How can a financial institution justify itself as fair, if it is using a non-interpretable AI to make loan decisions? Well, those institutions most likely aren't using the noninterpretable AI models and sticking with simple ML shallow models (like logistic regression, decision trees, etc.) while also doing human auditing to ensure fairness and transparency.

Does that mean advanced AI models aren't of any use? There have been model explainability techniques developed recently, namely, Local Interpretable Model-agnostic Explanations (LIME) and Shapley values (SHAP), that can help generate the explanations of how a prediction or decision is generated, essentially getting a sense of what features contributed positively and which ones negatively and by how much[15]. However, these techniques are only providing approximations of how the model is working and can't be trusted 100%.

2. Bias

The AI model (choice of algorithm, structure, etc.) and the data on which the AI model is trained are both developed by humans. Humans may have a conscious or unconscious bias while building these models or mining this data, and that may reflect in these AI models when they are used for prediction/decision-making.

Caution   AI models reflect, amplify, and automate the bias in the training data. AI is not intelligent to make any decisions outside of the bounds of the training data or correct the errors or bias in the training data.

---

[14]www.chase.com/personal/mortgage/fair-lending/fair-lending-overview
[15]https://github.com/slundberg/shap

These biases can bring in discrimination that can impact humans severely; also this problem will become more critical, as AI is more widely used across industries primarily due to the growing ease to build AI software, called by some as "democratization of AI." An experiment done at Carnegie Mellon University in 2015 found that women are shown significantly fewer online ads for jobs paying more than $200,000. A report from Reuters states that Amazon stopped using an AI algorithm for hiring and recruitment as it favored male candidates over female ones. This was because the AI algorithm was trained with data collected over a 10-year period that came mostly from male candidates. These examples show how bias has already starting impacting humans based on race, sex, color, etc.

3. Liability

When a human makes a mistake, then the person is made liable, but what do we do when decisions are made by AI algorithms? What kind of repercussions can an AI algorithm face? This is a question that has become very prominent primarily since the launch of initiatives around self-driving cars.

On March 19, 2018, Elaine Herzberg, aged 49, was hit and killed by a self-driving Uber as she was wheeling a bicycle across the road in Tempe, Arizona. The AI of the car failed to identify the person as an imminent collision danger. Since there was also a person inside on the steering wheels of the car, called the "safety driver," tasked to take over AI if required, the question becomes: Who should be held liable – Uber (the company that developed the AI), the person (driver) inside the car, the person who got hit and killed, or the government? In this case, it was found after investigation that the fatal incident could have been avoided if the driver in the car was not distracted as seen from the car's camera footage.[16] Also records from the streaming service Hulu show that the driver's personal cell phone was streaming a television show at the time of the accident. The driver is awaiting a trial of negligent homicide.

This incident alone has put a dent in the self-driving ambitions of a lot of companies, and for the time being, only semiautonomous driving is permitted where the liability lies on the driver of the car. Even with a more mature AI technology for self-driving cars, unless this liability dilemma is solved, it's unlikely they will be hitting the roads. This same liability issue also lingers with the prospect of using AI for warfare and if a mishap happens.

---

[16] www.bbc.com/news/technology-54175359

Outlook

These AI challenges may seem daunting at first to solve, but there is hope. For one, all the major corporations that are advancing and developing AI systems such as Amazon, Google, Facebook, Microsoft, IBM, and Apple have formed a nonprofit to establish best practices for the development of AI technology in partnership with academics and ethics experts.[17] Second, there have been many efforts from the governments around the world to ensure that AI is ethically applied, and it is observed through legislation and policing. The European Commission has a High-Level Expert Group on Artificial Intelligence. On April 8, 2019, this published its "Ethics Guidelines for Trustworthy Artificial Intelligence."[18] In January 2020, in the United States, the Trump Administration released a draft executive order issued by the Office of Management and Budget (OMB) on "Guidance for Regulation of Artificial Intelligence Applications" ("OMB AI Memorandum"). The order emphasizes the need to invest in AI applications, boost public trust in AI, reduce barriers for usage of AI, and keep American AI technology competitive in a global market. There is a nod to the need for privacy concerns, but no further detail on enforcement.[19]

Wrap-Up

In this chapter we started with learning that deep learning is a subset of ML, which is a subset of AI. In the field of machine learning, there are two main types of tasks: supervised and unsupervised. Supervised ML is done where the training data has labeled input and output variables, and unsupervised ML is done where the training dataset doesn't have these input and output labels. Supervised ML is of two types, namely, regression and classification. Clustering and association are two types of unsupervised ML. There are six steps to solve a machine learning problem. It starts with defining the problem and then determining the success metric which differs between classification and regression models. Then, the data is prepared for training

[17] https://money.cnn.com/2016/09/28/technology/partnership-on-ai/

[18] "Ethics guidelines for trustworthy AI". *Shaping Europe's digital future – European Commission*. European Commission. 2019-04-08

[19] "Request for Comments on a Draft Memorandum to the Heads of Executive Departments and Agencies, "Guidance for Regulation of Artificial Intelligence Applications"". *Federal Register*. 2020-01-13.

and evaluating the ML model. Finally training of a ML model is done, followed by its evaluation. If the success metric looks good, the model is put in production.

ML algorithms like decision tree, logistic regression, and their ensembles are called shallow ML models. Ensemble models have higher performance than a single ML model. Deep learning models use artificial neural networks and have a structure that is composed of nodes organized within layers. Deep learning models are generally used for tasks such as image classification and language translation. Each ANN has one input and output layer and one or more hidden layers. CNNs, RNNs, and transformers are some popular deep learning models used today. However, we do realize that AI can have bias and extreme care should be taken to ensure the models are free of biases inherited from the training data as otherwise they can impact customer trust and the company reputation.

CHAPTER 6

Information Security: Safeguarding Resources and Building Trust

Security is a complex issue which is related to infrastructure, software, people, and processes. There are threats against all of these dimensions. In this chapter we will talk about security aspects of building modern applications and understand which most common solutions are applied to protect software from common threats.

Need for Securing Digital Assets

Throughout history there was always the need for confidentiality, military, and government to facilitate secret communication or protecting information within many kinds of civilian systems. And encryption usually serves as such a mechanism. One of the earliest forms of encryption is symbol replacement, which was first found in Ancient Egypt and then was used throughout Ancient Greece and Rome for military purposes. One of the most famous military encryption developments was the Caesar Cipher, which was a system in which a letter in normal text is shifted down a fixed number of positions down the alphabet to get the encoded letter. A message encoded with this type of encryption could be decoded with the fixed number on the Caesar Cipher.

In World War II, the Axis powers used an advanced version of an encryption device called the Enigma machine, which each day was switching the combination of letters which was only known by the Axis, so many thought the only way to break the code would be to try over 17,000 combinations within 24 hours. The Allies used computing power to severely limit the number of reasonable combinations they needed to check every day, leading to the breaking of the Enigma machine.

© Gaurav Sagar, Vitalii Syrovatskyi 2022
G. Sagar and V. Syrovatskyi, *Technical Building Blocks*, https://doi.org/10.1007/978-1-4842-8658-6_6

Today, encryption is used in the transfer of communication over the Internet for security and commerce. As computing power continues to increase, computer encryption is constantly evolving to prevent attacks.

There are a wide variety of attacks that exist. Let's take a look at top common types of attacks which can be targeting users, applications, and different digital assets:

- **Malware** – Uses a vulnerability to breach a network when a user clicks a specially placed dangerous link or email attachment, which is used to install malicious software inside the system. This malware can deny access to the critical components of the network, obtain information by retrieving data from the hard drive, or disrupt the system or even render it inoperable. Malware is very common and itself has multiple types:

  - **Viruses** – Infect applications, inject themselves to executable code, or associate themselves with a file by creating a virus file with the same name but with an .exe extension, thus creating a decoy which carries the virus.

  - **Trojans** – A program which is planted inside a useful program with malicious goals. Unlike viruses, a Trojan doesn't replicate itself but is commonly used to create a backdoor to be exploited by attackers.

  - **Worms** – Also behave differently to viruses, they are self-contained programs that propagate across networks and computers without infecting other programs. Worms are often installed through email attachments, sending a copy of themselves to every contact in the infected computer email list. They are commonly used to overload an email server and achieve a denial-of-service attack.

  - **Ransomware** – A type of malware that denies access to the user's data, making different threats for ransoms. Advanced ransomware uses cryptoviral extortion, encrypting the user's data so that it is impossible to decrypt without the decryption key.

- **Spyware** – Collecting information about users, their personal data, their systems, and browsing habits. Collected data is sent to a remote attacker, who will use the information for blackmailing purposes or download and install other malicious programs from the Web.

- **Phishing** – Extremely common type of attack which involves sending emails to the targeted users, trying to disguise they came from a reliable source. They appear to be legitimate, but link the recipient to a malicious file, or website to lure individuals to disclose their personal information and passwords for later attacks, or script designed to grant attackers access to your device or data. Phishing attacks can also be made via social networks and other online communities, via direct messages from other users with a malicious intent. Attacks can also happen via phone call (voice phishing) and via text message (SMS phishing). Some types of phishing attacks include

  - **Spear phishing** – Targeted attacks directed at specific companies and/or individuals.

  - **Whaling** – Attacks targeting senior executives and stakeholders within an organization.

  - **Pharming** – Using DNS cache poisoning to capture user credentials through a fake login landing page.

- **Man-in-the-middle (MitM) attacks** – Attacker intercepts communication between two parties, inserting themselves in the middle. Then, the attacker can steal and manipulate traffic.

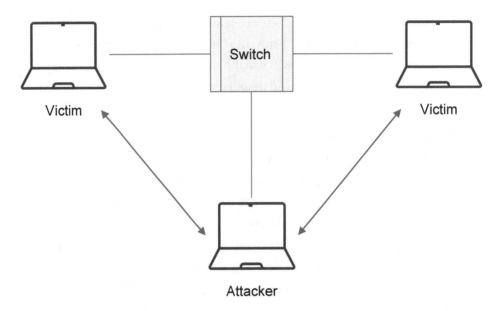

Figure 6-1. *Man-in-the-middle attack*

This type of attack usually exploits security vulnerabilities in a network, such as an unsecured public Wi-Fi, to insert themselves between a visitor's device and the network. These attacks are very difficult to detect, and phishing or malware attacks are often used to set up a MitM attack.

- **Denial-of-Service (DOS) attack** – Work by flooding and overloading systems, servers, and/or networks with traffic. As a result the legitimate calls from users of the targeting systems will not be processed, and users will be denied service since the server is busy responding to the attack requests. The most common types of DoS attacks are the TCP SYN flood attack, teardrop attack, smurf attack, ping-of-death attack, and botnets.

- **SQL injections** - Attacker injects SQL into a server that uses structured query language to retrieve data from a database. Modern development processes promote secure coding practices such as using prepared statements with parameterized queries, which is an effective way to prevent SQL injections.

- **Zero-day exploit** – It describes the attacks on the networks or systems when a vulnerability is new and/or recently announced, before the patch is released and the vulnerability is fixed. Preventing zero-day attacks requires constant monitoring, proactive detection, and agile threat management practices.

- **Password attack** – Since passwords are the most common methods of authenticating to a secure information system, they are an attractive target for cyberattackers. If an attacker gains access to the user's password, he can access all the information or steal the account. Password attackers use different methods to get a password; among them are using social engineering, gaining access to a password database, testing the network connection to obtain unencrypted passwords, and simply guessing or dictionary attack, when the attacker uses a list of common passwords to attempt to gain access to a user's computer and network. Common practice to prevent such attacks is two-factor authentication.

- **Cross-site scripting** – Such an attack injects malicious scripts into content from reliable websites. The malicious code joins the dynamic content that is sent to the user's browser. Usually, this malicious code consists of JavaScript code executed by the victim's browser, but can include Flash, HTML, and XSS.

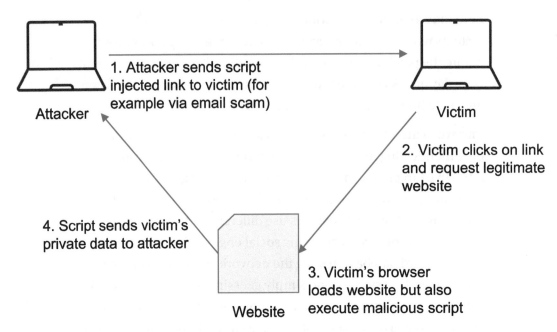

1. Attacker sends script injected link to victim (for example via email scam)

Attacker

Victim

2. Victim clicks on link and request legitimate website

4. Script sends victim's private data to attacker

3. Victim's browser loads website but also execute malicious script

Website

Figure 6-2. *Cross-site scripting attack*

- **Rootkits** – Installed inside legitimate software, where they can gain remote control and administration-level access over a system. The attacker then uses the rootkit to steal passwords, keys, and credentials and retrieve critical data. They install themselves in the system (host, computer, server, etc.) and remain dormant until the attacker activates it or it's triggered, and often distributed via email attachments and downloads from websites.

- **Internet of things (IoT) attacks** – Internet connectivity between multitude of devices presents a growing number of access points for attackers to exploit. It makes it possible for attackers to breach an entry point and use it as a gate to exploit other devices in the network. Best practices to help prevent an IoT attack include updating the OS and keeping a strong password for every IoT device on your network and changing passwords often.

So now let's look into the mechanisms of how to protect ourselves and our systems from these multitude of threats.

Encryption and Hashing

Applications and systems operate with some data, almost all of them. The data can vary from user-specific information like location or activity logs, user credentials, and product information which have been sold at Internet stores to publicly available data. In the majority of cases, it is important that only authorized parties can read and understand the corresponding data, which is achieved by scrambling the data via encryption.

So what is encryption? It is the process of converting human-readable plain text to incomprehensible text, also known as ciphertext. In other words encryption takes readable data and alters it so that it appears random and unreadable.

Figure 6-3. *Text encryption*

It looks like encrypted data is random, but the encryption process is logical and predictable. It allows a party that reads the encrypted data and has the right key to decrypt it, turning it back into plain text. Encryption process uses complex keys with the purpose that a third party is highly unlikely to break or decrypt the text without possessing such a key.

When we talk about encrypting the data, there are usually two types of encryption:

- **Encryption at rest** – Usually longer-term encryption of data that is persisted in some way, for example, data in a database or files on disk.

- **Encryption in transit** – Usually short-term encryption which is used to encrypt the request or response transmitted over the network. The message got encrypted at the sender and decrypted at the receiver's machine.

So why do we need data encryption? Is it necessary? Let's list the benefits data encryption provides:

- **Privacy** – When using encryption you make sure that no one can read data in transit or at rest except the intended party. This helps to prevent different types of attackers from intercepting and reading sensitive data.

- **Security** – Encryption helps in preventing data breaches. For example, if a company asset (i.e., laptop) is lost or stolen but the hard drive is encrypted, the data on the device will still be secure, value of which is usually way more higher than the cost of the device itself.

- **Data integrity** – Encryption ensures the consistency of data; it guaranties that the same data that left the sender will arrive to the recipient without being altered by a malicious third party on the way.

- **Regulations** – Due to all these benefits listed before, many industry and government regulations require companies to use encryption in handling business and user data. Examples of such regulatory standards are HIPAA, PCI-DSS, and the GDPR.

We mentioned that the encryption (and decryption) process requires a key, so what is a key in this context? A cryptographic key is a string of characters used within an encryption algorithm for altering data so that it appears random. Like a physical key, it locks (encrypts) data so that only someone with the right key can unlock (decrypt) it. The original data is known as the plain text, and the data after the key encrypts it is known as the ciphertext (Figure 6-1).

There are two main types of encryption:

- **Symmetric encryption** – There is one key which is used by all communicating parties. This key is used for both encrypting and decrypting the data.

- **Asymmetric encryption, which is also known as public key encryption** – There are two keys used in asymmetric encryption. One key, called a private key, is kept in secret and used to decrypt the data. The second key, called a public key, is shared openly and used for encrypting data.

The key is used in the encryption algorithm, which is the method used to transform data into ciphertext. An algorithm will use the encryption key to convert the data in a predictable way so it can be turned back into plain text by using the decryption key. The most common encryption algorithms are

- AES (symmetric encryption algorithm)

- 3-DES (symmetric encryption algorithm)

- SNOW (symmetric encryption algorithm)

- RSA (asymmetric encryption algorithm)

- Elliptic curve cryptography (asymmetric encryption algorithm)

For example, the public key for cloudflare.com is (copied from the cloudflare.com SSL certificate):

```
04 CE D7 61 49 49 FD 4B 35 8B 1B 86 BC A3 C5 BC D8 20 6E 31 17 2D 92 8A B7
34 F4 DB 11 70 4E 49 16 61 FC AE FA 7F BA 6F 0C 05 53 74 C6 79 7F 81 12 8A
F7 E2 5E 6C F5 FA 10 69 6B 67 D9 D5 96 51 B0
```

The key should be reasonably long and hard to guess as well as the algorithm which is used for encryption should be well known and trusted. When encryption is properly done, by using the correct encryption algorithm, the malicious third party, which does not know the decryption key, to a large extent is limited to only trying to brute force attack on the encrypted data. A brute force attack is when an attacker attempts to determine the key by making millions or billions of guesses. As computers evolve, brute force attacks become faster, and that is why encryption should be complex and strong, and most modern encryption methods, coupled with high-quality passwords, are resistant to brute force attacks.

Encryption also is very important in keeping the Internet secure. It is used for authenticating website servers via the protocol called HTTPS (Hypertext Transfer Protocol Secure). And HTTPS in turn uses the encryption protocol called Transport Layer Security (TLS).

Public Key Infrastructure

We have talked about the usage of public keys in encryption and certificate management. So let's learn more on what public key encryption is. It is a method of encrypting data with two different keys (public and private), called asymmetric, which is widely used, especially for TLS/SSL, which makes HTTPS possible. Data encrypted with the public key can only be decrypted with the private key, and data encrypted with the private key can only be decrypted with the public key.

So how does public key encryption work? We can use some form of analogy here. Imagine a box with a lock that two users, user A and user B, use to transfer information back and forth. This lock has locked and unlocked states. A lock can be opened with a key, and anyone with a copy of that key can unlock or lock the box. When user A puts information into the box, locks it, and sends it to user A, he knows that user A can use her copy of the key to unlock the box. It is how symmetric cryptography works since it uses the same single key for both encrypting and decrypting.

Now imagine we have a special lock[1], which instead of two states has three (Figure 6-2):

- **State 1** – Box is locked, key turned all the way to the left.

- **State 2** – Box is unlocked, key is in the middle.

- **State 3** – Box is locked, key turned all the way to the right.

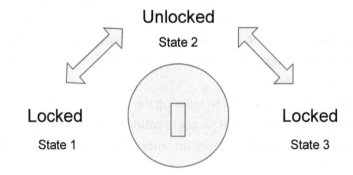

Figure 6-4. *Asymmetric key analogy*

---

[1]www.cloudflare.com/learning/ssl/how-does-public-key-encryption-work/

And instead of one key, we now have two keys:

- Key 1 can only turn to the left.

- Key 2 can only turn to the right.

This in practice means that once the box is locked by Key 1, it goes into State 1 and only Key 2 can now unlock it. And in the opposite case when the box is locked by Key 2 (State 3), only Key 1 can unlock it. So each key can lock the box, but once it is locked, another key is required to unlock it.

Now imagine User 1 makes a box and two keys. He takes Key 1 and makes multiple copies of it and then sends them to anyone who needs or wants them, which technically makes it a public key. But the Key 2 User 1 keeps to themselves, thus making it a private key. What situation do we get as a result?

1. User 2 can send the data using the box knowing that only User 1 can access it. This is because when User 2 locks the box with the public key (Key 1), they turn the lock to State 1, and now only the private key (Key 2) can unlock it, which is kept by User 1.

2. User 2 can be sure that box is from User 1 and not from some malicious third party. Why? Because only one key (private key – Key 2) can lock the box, so it is in State 3, so by unlocking the box with his public key (Key 1), User 2 can validate that the box is actually from User 1.

Now you can replace the box with the plain text information and keys with cryptographic keys and can see how the public key works:

- Only the private key owner can encrypt data that can be decrypted with the public key, so anyone can verify that data received from the owner of the private key and not from a malicious third party.

- Anyone can encrypt with the public key, but only the private key owner can decrypt, so anyone can send data securely to the private key owner.

Therefore, anyone can send data securely to the private key owner. Also, anyone can verify that data they receive from the owner of the private key is actually from that source, and not from an impersonator.

Certificate Authority

Another application of security is a certificate authority, which can help you to prove that you own a digital entity like a website or an email address. Sometimes certificate authorities are used for human verification, but in the majority of cases, they are used to help prove digital ownership and protect critical assets.

So what is a certificate authority? A certificate authority is a company which issues certificates to users and organizations. And every time you visit a protected website, certificate authority helps you to validate it. It is a trusted organization which can certify ownership, and in the example with a website, it can certify that the website is true to who it claims to be.

What things are provided by certificate authority:

- **Digital certificates** – Files which contain identity credentials.

- **Cryptographic keys**– For current use cases, these keys are used to encrypt and protect data in transit.

A certificate authority provides a digital certificate which is signed by their cryptographic keys. While visiting a website, your browser tries to ensure that the site is valid and looks for the keys as a proof. If the browser validates that the site is secure, the website and browser establish a secure connection by trading cryptographic keys (more on these later in the chapter). But if the browser cannot validate the site, the user will see a warning that proceeding to the website might be dangerous.

So how do certificate authorities work? When building a web product, the company may connect with a certificate authority organization to provide to users the proof that the website can be trusted. After picking certificate authority partner, you follow these steps:

- **Validation** – Certificate authority company will verify identity first. This is provided in the form of administrative contact to start the process. Some certificate authority companies will take additional steps to validate that there are trusted companies that own the site.

- **Generation** – You will generate a pair of cryptographic keys (private and public) and send them only the public key plus other information (but not the private key) along with a certificate signing request form to your certificate authority partner.

- **Verification** – Certificate authority partner will validate your data and, in case everything is correct, will use certificate authority's own private key to sign your certificate, and then will return to you your signed certificate.

- **Stored** – You will add your keys and certificate to your website.

There are a number of certificate authorities exists, but most certificate authorities' requests are handled by these seven companies (in alphabetic order):

- DigiCert

- Entrust

- GlobalSign

- GoDaddy

- Network Solutions

- Sectigo

- Trustwave

When picking your certificate authority partner, it is better to proceed with a known company, since dealing with imposter can create security risk both for your product and your users. And unless you have a very special use case, it is always a good idea to protect your website. Did you know that without a certificate, Google might devalue your site in search?

Certificate Management (TLS)

We have mentioned already that asymmetric encryption is used to secure the Internet, namely, in TLS (Transport Layer Security protocol), previously known as SSL (Secure Sockets Layer). So what is TLS? It is a protocol that authenticates the server in a client-server connection and encrypts communications between client and server so that external parties cannot spy on the communications.

To understand TLS let's look in its three logical parts:

- Public key and private key, which we discussed previously.

- TLS certificate, which is issued by certificate authority.

- **TLS handshake** – The process to verify the TLS certificate of the server and the server's possession of the private key. The TLS handshake also specifies what encryption will be put in place for communication between server and client once the handshake is finished.

Let's learn more on how TLS handshake works (Figure 6-3). When a user navigates to a website using HTTPS or when connection is established via other means (i.e., API call), TLS handshake takes place. During the handshake the client and server will perform several steps:

- Both client and server inform each other on the version of secure protocol they use (TLS v1.0, v1.1, v1.2, etc.) and decide on it.

- Decide on the cipher which would be used for communication.

- Client will validate the authority of the server by using the server's public key or SSL certificate authority's digital signature.

- Generate session keys to use in encryption after the handshake.

Now, we can walk over the steps in TLS handshake[2]; sometimes steps in the handshake process are different, but here is the most common flow of steps:

1. Establishing a connection starts with a TCP three-way handshake. It is a process which is used in a TCP/IP network to make a connection between the server and client. It is a three-step process that requires both the client and server to exchange synchronization and acknowledgment packets (**SYN**, **SYN ACK**, and **ACK**) before the real data communication process starts.

2. After the TCP connection is established, the client sends a "Client Hello" message. The message will include which TLS version the client supports, the cipher suites supported, and a string of random bytes known as the "client random."

---

[2] www.cloudflare.com/learning/ssl/what-happens-in-a-tls-handshake/

3. Server responds with a "Server Hello" message in the reply to "Client Hello" message. It contains SSL certificate, the server's chosen cipher suite, and the "server random" (another random string of bytes that's generated by the server).

4. **Authentication** – Client verifies first server's certificate with certificate authority. This step determines if the server is who it says it is, so the client interacts with the actual intended server.

5. The client sends the "premaster secret" (again, random string of bytes). It is encrypted with the public key, which the client gets from the server's certificate, and can only be decrypted with the private key by the server.

6. The server decrypts the premaster secret using a private **key**.

7. Client and server both **generate session keys** from the client random, the server random, and the premaster secret, and they both create the same results due to the process being deterministic.

8. The client sends a "finished" message to the server that is encrypted with a session key which indicates that the **client is ready**.

9. The server sends a "finished" message to the client that is encrypted with a session key which indicates that the **server is ready**.

10. The handshake is completed, and communication continues using the session keys. **Secure symmetric encryption** is established.

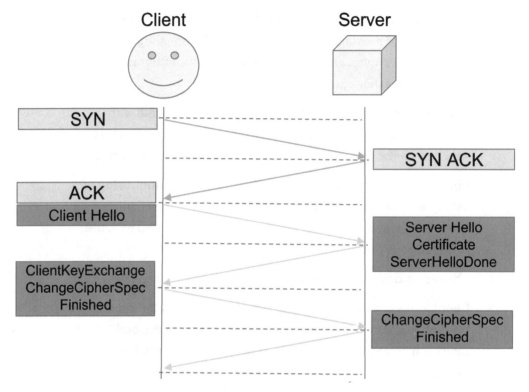

Figure 6-5. *TLS handshake*

Normally in TLS only, the server has a TLS certificate and a public/private key pair, but the client does not have. But sometimes the server also needs to validate the client who connects to it (often in service-to-service communications within the same enterprise), and so in such cases, Mutual TLS (mTLS) is used, where both the client and server have a certificate, and both of them authenticate using their public/private key pair. Additional steps in the handshake are performed in such cases:

- Client presents its TLS certificate.

- Server verifies the client's certificate.

- Server grants access to the client.

Another difference is that in mTLS organizations (sides in communication) usually implement their own certificate authority (compared to standard TLS where certificate authority is an external organization). The key concept here is a "root" TLS certificate, which is self-signed and enables an organization to be their own certificate authority.

mTLS ensures that the traffic is secured and trusted in both client and server preventing different types of attack because it validates the client system making the server calls:

- **On-path attacks** – When an attacker sits in between client and server and listens to their communication.

- **Spoofing attacks** – When an attacker tries to imitate a web server to a user, or vice versa.

- **Credential stuffing** – When an attacker uses licked credentials and tries to log in as a legitimate user.

- **Brute force attacks** – When an attacker tries to guess via trial and error credentials. mTLS ensures that password is not enough.

- **Phishing attacks** – When an attacker steals credentials, but it is still not enough in mTLS case.

- **Malicious API requests** – Since mTLS ensures that API requests come from legitimate, authenticated users only.

For general use on the Internet, TLS provides sufficient protection, since it makes sure users do not visit spoofed websites and keep private data secure in transit. But in specific applications mTLS is very useful for organizations, especially for the zero trust approach, where systems do not trust any user, device, or request by default.

Firewall

Another useful security concept is the firewall. A firewall is a security system that monitors and controls network traffic based on a set of security rules. Firewalls usually sit between a trusted network and an untrusted network; oftentimes the untrusted network is the Internet. For example, office networks often use a firewall to protect their network from online threats.

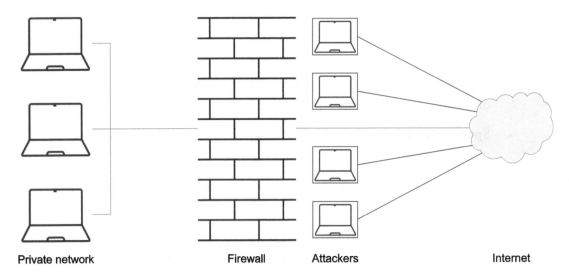

Private network   Firewall   Attackers   Internet

Figure 6-6. *How firewall works*

Firewalls filter incoming and outgoing traffic; they decide which traffic goes through and which is blocked. They can be built into hardware, be a software product, or both. The term "firewall" was borrowed from a construction practice of building walls in between or through the middle of buildings designed to contain a fire. Similarly, network firewalls work to contain online threats.

Why do we need to use firewalls?

Firewalls can block the bad traffic before it reaches the private network, i.e., intercepting malicious requests. They also prevent sensitive information from leaving the network. Firewalls also can be configured to block certain content (i.e., adult materials). Or even on a larger scale in some countries, firewalls are used to prevent people inside that country from accessing certain parts of the Internet.

Firewalls were developed back in the late 1980s, and first firewalls allowed or blocked individual data packets. They filtered packets and allowed or blocked them by inspecting their network layer and transport layer headers to see their source and destination IP address and port. While firewalls were evolving, the new capabilities were developed like stateful capabilities and the ability to inspect traffic at the application layer. Firewalls also evolved in ways they are deployed. Originally, firewalls were physical hardware appliances that plugged into a company's networking infrastructure. Firewalls today can also run in software or virtually in the cloud.

There are different types of firewalls that exist:

- Proxy-based firewalls

- Stateful firewalls

- Next-generation firewalls (NGFW)

- Web application firewalls (WAF)

- Firewall-as-a-service (FWaaS)

Proxy-based firewalls are located between the server and client. Clients connect to the firewall, and the firewall inspects the outgoing packets, after which it will create a connection to the intended target (the web server). In the same way when the web server attempts to send a response to the client, the firewall will intercept that request, inspect the packets, and then deliver that response in a separate connection between the firewall and the client. A proxy-based firewall effectively prevents a direct connection between the client and server. And a major drawback of a proxy-based firewall is that it can cause latency, particularly during times of heavy traffic.

Stateful firewalls save information regarding open connections and use this information to analyze incoming and outgoing traffic, rather than inspecting each packet. Stateful firewalls rely on a lot of context when making decisions, and they also protect ports by keeping them all closed unless incoming packets request access to a specific port which can mitigate an attack known as port scanning. A known vulnerability of stateful firewalls is that they can be manipulated by a client into requesting a certain kind of information. Once the client requests that response, the attacker can then send malicious packets that match those criteria through the firewall. For example, unsecure websites can use JavaScript code to create these kinds of forged requests from a web browser.

NGFW (next-generation firewalls) have a set of added features in addition to traditional firewalls. Those features are mostly to address threats on other layers of the OSI model. Some of the features are

- **Deep packet inspection (DPI)** – More in-depth inspection of packets than traditional firewalls, which checks packet payloads and which application is being accessed by the packets.

- **Application awareness** – This feature makes the firewall aware of which applications are running and which ports those applications are using, which protect against certain types of malware that aim to terminate a running process and then take over its port.

- **Identity awareness** – Enforcing rules based on identity, such as which computer is being used, which user is logged in, and others.

- **Sandboxing** – Isolating pieces of code associated with incoming packets and executing them in a "sandbox" environment to ensure they are not behaving maliciously.

WAF (web application firewalls) protect web applications from malicious users. It is filtering and monitoring HTTP traffic between a web application and the Internet. It typically protects web applications from attacks like cross-site forgery, cross-site scripting (XSS), file inclusion, SQL injection, and others. A WAF operates through a set of rules often called policies whose goal is to protect against vulnerabilities in the application by filtering out malicious traffic. The WAF is attractive in part from the speed and ease with which policy modification can be implemented, allowing for faster response to varying attack vectors; during a DDoS attack, rate limiting can be quickly implemented by modifying WAF policies.

FWaaS (Firewall-as-a-Service) is a model for delivering firewall capabilities via the cloud, also called "cloud firewall." FWaaS creates a virtual barrier around cloud platforms, infrastructure, and applications, just as traditional firewalls form a barrier around an organization's internal network. FWaaS is often better suited for protecting cloud and multicloud assets than traditional firewalls.

Identity Management

The concept of identity existed since very long ago, before the computer was invented. Identity existed (and still exists) in the form of names, titles, prefixes/suffixes, and photos. For example, someone was identified as Henry Smith, or Henry Smith Jr., or Baron Henry Smith, which in total was associated with the specific person and represented their identity.

In modern times the concept of identity has not changed much. We have logins/emails as primary identities; we associate users with groups, and assign roles (like titles) which allow users to access certain resources.

Identity and access management is the core process which is required to secure digital assets. It consists of the main two parts, which are to identify who is accessing resources (authentication) and to verify that the resource can be accessed (authorization). You can think of it as a framework of policies and technologies for ensuring that the right users (in an enterprise) have the appropriate access to technology resources.

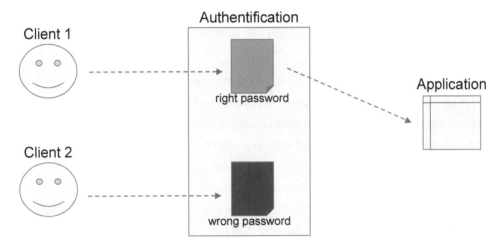

Figure 6-7. *Access to application is given based on the right password*

To verify identity, a computer system will assess a user for characteristics that are specific to them. If they match, the user's identity is confirmed. These characteristics are also known as "authentication factors," because they help authenticate that a user is who they say they are.

The three most widely used authentication factors are

- **Something the user knows** – A piece of knowledge that only one user should have, like a username and password combination. For example, a user wants to check their work email from home. First to establish their identity, they need to log in to their account. And the user enters their email, user@company.com, and the password that only they know – for example, "tjs)df!fk56." And we suppose that no one else besides the user knows this password, so the email system recognizes and lets them access their email account.

- **Something the user has** – Usually a physical token that is given to the authorized users. A real-life example of this authentication factor could be a physical house key to enter one's home. The assumption is that only someone who owns, rents, or otherwise is allowed into the house will have a key. And in a computing context, the physical object could be a key fob, a USB device, or a smartphone.

- **Something the user is** – Usually the physical property of the user's body. The most common examples are faceId or touchId on smartphones.

One of the first identity and access management systems was ACLs (access control lists). The server contained tables of access control records, which specified what user (username/password) can access which resource. When a user tried to access the resource and a corresponding record was found in the ACL, the access was granted, otherwise denied.

The systems evolved over time and new protocols for more complicated authentication and authorization use cases were invented, such as SAML, Oauth, and OpenId (more on them later). With the growing number of websites grew the pain of remembering logins which led to single sign-on. In order to secure the login and password of users even more, the industry adopted different schemes of multifactor authentication which validates additional user information.

On the access management site, the attribute-based authentication (ABAC) and role-based authentication (RBAC) were created. For thousands of users and resources, the management of raw ACLs was not a scalable solution. RBAC and ABAC utilized the concepts of grouping both on user and resource sides and assigned classes of permissions, which led to more transparent and easier management of access.

Securing digital assets is the top priority for leaders of large corporations as well as small businesses. Companies experience regulatory pressure to secure resources, protect, and regionalize the data. Unauthorized access to the critical information often results in catastrophic consequences such as loss of consumer trust and legal issues.

Due to the increased complexities of the systems and business use cases, companies could no longer rely fully on manual security processes and had to adopt automation of identity and access management.

Single Sign-On (SSO)

Single sign-on started with Active Directory (AD), a solution which was created to manage on perm networks with Windows-based systems. AD was introduced in 1999, and back then the majority of companies were running their on premise networks so AD gained a wide adoption.

With the rise of Internet and cloud services, the things have changed since AD was not designed to manage such environments. To address the challenges, a single sign-on was created via extending AD identities for web applications. This was done via add-on approach which soon faced its scaling limitations which made an approach no longer sustainable. The need has raised for architecturally different approaches for single sign-on.

So what is a single sign-on? Single sign-on works like an identity provider; the central identity system provides your identity identifier to the other system you try to log in to which validates your identity. In other words, it is an authentication method which allows users with a single login/password to authenticate into several related but independent websites/systems.

Why do we need a single sign-on? Single sign-on provides a set of benefits to the end users and big enterprises:

- It mitigates risk of exposing password to the third-party website or system, which means one less security concern of exposing customer data.

- Increases convenience for the user and reduces time to log in. When a user is already authenticated in identity provider, the single sign-on allows login with a single click.

- Reduce the password chaos for the user. The user does not need to keep reinventing passwords running into problems either having a big password mess or keep reusing passwords between the systems exposing additional threats.

- Every time a user logs to the new system, using login/password is a security risk to expose the credentials to man-in-the-middle attack and other third parties. Also managing a login/password for every website is quickly becoming unscalable for users to manage as the number of sites users use grows.

How does a single sign-on work? Single sign-on often operates on the trusting relationship between two systems, the identity provider and the system where the user tries to log in. The trusting relationship is established between systems based on security protocols and certificates.

What happens when a user logs in with an SSO to the website?

1. Site checks if you already logged in? If yes, you just proceed to the resource or page you wanted.

2. If you are not logged in, you will see an ordinary login page which would normally have login/pass and SSO options using popular customer identity providers like Google and Facebook.

3. Upon proceeding with the SSO option, you are redirected to the identity provider which checks whether you are logged in already or not.

4. If you are the identity, provider immediately redirect you to the intended resource/website with some sort of a token.

5. If you are not yet logged in at identity provider (i.e., Google), you put in credentials (login/password), got authenticated to the identity provider, and got redirected to the intended resource along with the generated token.

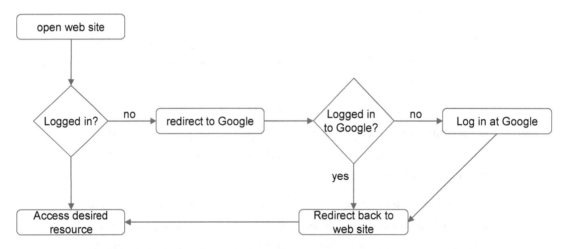

Figure 6-8. *Single sign-on flow*

How to implement single sign-on? Single sign-on is a well-established and tested technology which utilizes popular protocols such as Security Assertion Markup Language (SAML) and Web Services Federation (WS-Fed). When you decide to implement SSO for your application, you must consider:

1. Who are your users? What systems can they use or use the most? Which popular identity providers will be used the most?

2. What protocol do identified providers use? Do they use SAML2?

3. Do you want automatic provisioning? For example, on the first SSO login, the profile for the user will be autopopulated.

4. Realize the potential hidden costs of SSO. Some of identity providers allow SSO support only for higher-tier paid accounts (i.e., Dropbox).

Once you decide to implement SSO with identified provider(s), usually there are established processes and provided libraries for the integration.

SAML, OAuth, and OpenId

Single sign-on is powered by several technologies and frameworks. Among them are SAML, an xml markup language; OAuth, an open standard to access delegation; and OpenId, and authentication standard. Usually large organizations would use all of them in order to implement a comprehensive single sign-on solution.

What is SAML?

SAML is an xml-based markup language and is used to exchange authentication and authorization information between systems, often between identity and service provider. SAML v1 was developed by OASIS (Organization for the Advancement of Structured Information Standards) in 2002 to define an XML framework for exchanging authentication and authorization information.

After a series of modifications and improvements, SAML v2 was introduced in 2005 and quickly became the standard in the industry. Primary use case for SAML currently is in single sign-on.

What is OAuth?

OAuth is an open standard to access delegation. It is widely used in the use cases when users grant websites access to their information located on other websites. It is a way for the resource owners (users) to authorize access to their resources without granting credentials to third-party websites.

The OAuth protocol was originally published in 2010, and the OAuth v2 was standardized in 2012.

What is OpenId?

OpenId is a standard which organizations use to authenticate users. It is a decentralized authentication protocol which was originally developed in 2005. The final version of OpenId v2 was finalized and published in 2007.

Open Id is used for federated identity and widely adopted by a wide range of companies, including Google, Amazon, and Microsoft:

OpenId Connect, the next generation of OpenId technology, was developed in 2014 and it is an authentication layer which is using the OAuth 2.0 authorization framework.

So how do SAML, OpenId, and Oauth relate to each other?

All of them are used in simplifying granting and sharing access over the Web, but it is important to know the differences between them.

OAuth is different from OpenId and SAML. It is a framework that controls access to the resources, while OpenId and SAML are both standards for federated authentication.

In order to achieve single sign-on, organizations can use either SAML or OpenId to implement authentication. The use of OAuth, which is a framework, is different from SAML and OpenId and can be used together with either of them:

- OAuth provides delegated access in a secure manner. It allows an application or a website to access another website's resources on behalf of the user. As an example, you may grant a new application to source your Facebook contacts automatically; then, it was likely done via OAuth.

- SAML allows exchange of authentication and authorization information between service providers. As an example in the corporate intranet user can access different internal company services without the need to re-enter credentials.

- OpenId Connect allows users to sign in to a single web site (identity provider) and access other websites without the need to re-enter credentials. As an example usage of Google identity to log in to some online shop.

Enterprises to achieve the goals of securely authenticating users and granting the access to resources may use all three approaches together.

Multifactor Authentication

As it is in real life on the Web, there is always a threat for identity theft. If a third party in some way obtains a user's password, they can access the target website with a wide range of consequences starting from hacking for fun on social media and ending with stealing user's money from bank account or brokerage firms.

Clearly requiring only knowing the password to access resources creates the situation of a single point of failure from a security point of view. In order to make the access to important websites (like banks) more secure, the majority of enterprises implement one or another form of multifactor authorization in addition to passwords, which dramatically improves the security of the authentication process.

Multifactor authentication (MFA) is an electronic authentication method in which user's device is granted access to a website or application only after successfully validating two or more pieces of evidence (or factors) to an authentication mechanism: knowledge (something only the user knows), possession (something only the user has), and inherence (something only the user is). MFA protects the user from an unknown person trying to access their data such as personal ID details or financial assets.

How does multifactor authentication work?

When a user tries to log in to a website, MFA provides additional security guarantees by requiring a second validation step. This second step could be

- **Something the user has** – Some physical object in the possession of the user, such as a security token (USB stick), a bank card, a key, etc.

- **Something the user knows** – Certain knowledge only known to the user, such as a password, PIN, TAN, etc.

- **Something the user is** – Some physical characteristic of the user (biometrics), such as a fingerprint, eye iris, voice, typing speed, pattern in key press intervals, etc.

- **Somewhere the user is** – Some connection to a specific computing network or using a GPS signal to identify the location.[3]

---

[3] Seema, Sharma (2005). Location Based Authentication (Thesis). University of New Orleans

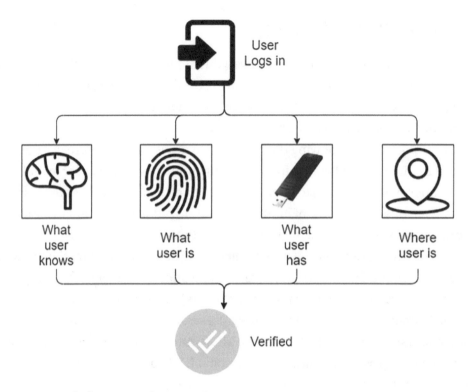

Figure 6-9. *Multifactor authentication types*

How to implement MFA?

When choosing the right MFA solution, it is important to have the key attributes: easy to use, easy to manage, and easy to deploy.

One of the most popular and easy to implement is onetime password (OTP). The approach uses something the user has, usually a smartphone, which receives a onetime password that can be used only for one session and expires relatively quickly, in the order of minutes, which is something the user knows. So OTP effectively combines two approaches of multifactor authorization. One of the most straightforward implementations is to send an SMS with the simple code to the registered user phone number after the successful enter of login/password information.

OTP generated typically as pseudorandom or random token, making a prediction of successor OTPs by an attacker difficult, and also cryptographic hash functions, which can be used to derive a value but are hard to reverse and therefore difficult for an attacker to obtain the data that was used for the hash. This is necessary because, otherwise, it would be easy to predict future OTPs by observing previous ones.

OTP can potentially replace the ordinary password in contrast to being supplemental to it in a form of second factor in the process of authentication. The most important advantage that is addressed by OTPs is that, in contrast to static passwords, they are not vulnerable to replay attacks. This means that a potential intruder who manages to record an OTP that was already used to log into a service or to conduct a transaction will not be able to abuse it, since it will no longer be valid[4]. On the downside, OTPs can be intercepted or rerouted, and hard tokens can get lost, damaged, or stolen.

Token-Based Authentication

Sometimes organizations need more flexibility and more control over authentication into the different servers or over accessing resources. Other additional goals may be to add an additional layer of security to critical resources. Often token-based authentication is the answer for such goals.

So what is token-based authentication?

It is a protocol which is used for identity verification. It lets users verify identity and gives in return a unique access token. Users can access service or websites the token was issued for during its lifetime, and they do not need to enter credentials again each time they visit the site or any other resource for which the token was issued. The user retains access as long as the token remains valid. Once the user logs out or quits an app, the token is invalidated. Token is also usually issued with limited time to live and gets invalidated when the timespan is reached,

Tokens offer a second layer of security to traditional password-based or server-based authentication techniques. And in such cases, administrators usually have expanded control over each operation.

Before the introduction of authentication tokens, logins and passwords were primarily used to ensure that the right people had access to the right things at the right time. Passwords are usually user generated and require users to keep that unique combination in their mind, and also involve a lot of repetition to enter passwords while accessing websites. Also passwords could be stolen, since users in order to remember passwords use different tricks such as writing them down, repeating across different sites, or slightly changing them.

---

[4] Paterson, Kenneth G.; Stebila, Douglas (2010). Steinfeld, Ron; Hawkes, Philip (eds.). "One-Time-Password-Authenticated Key Exchange". Information Security and Privacy. Lecture Notes in Computer Science. Berlin, Heidelberg: Springer. 6168: 264–281

Token authentication is different. A secondary service usually verifies a server request, and when verification is complete, the server issues a token and responds to the request. The user may still have one password to remember, but the token offers another form of access that's much harder to steal or overcome. And the session's record takes up no space on the server.

Tokens could be of three different types:

1. **Connected** – Some type of physical device (i.e., USB drive), which the user needs to plug in for access.

2. **Contactless** – A device that does not need to be plugged in but needs to be close enough to communicate in a contactless way.

3. **Disconnected** – A device that communicates over the long distance (like a phone in two-factor authentication).

In all these cases, users also need to perform some action to start authentication, like enter password, answer questions, or touch the device.

So how does token authentication work?

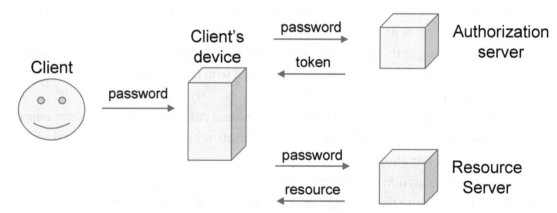

Figure 6-10. *Token-based authentication*

When using token-based authentication, the client will enter credentials only once, and then they will receive the token and will use it for subsequent access to resources. The process has the following steps:

1. **Request** – The user requesting access to a specific server or resource, which will require a login with a password, or it could involve some other authentication process.

2. **Verification** – The authorization server after checking the credentials decides to grant the access.

3. **Tokens** – The authorization server communicates with the authentication device, like a ring, key, phone, or similar, and after verification, the server issues a token and passes it to the user.

4. **Storage** – The token stays within the user's browser while work continues.

If the user attempts to get access to a different resource of the server, the token communicates with the server again. Access is granted or denied based on the token. Authorization server sets the time span of the token, which could be a one-use, and in such cases the token is immediately destroyed when the person logs out. Or the token can be set to self-destruct at the end of a specified time period.

What are the benefits of authorization tokens?

Authorization tokens provide benefits in the following scenarios:

- **When you often need to grant temporary access** – If the user base changes a lot based on time/date or related to some special events, then constantly granting and revoking access could be time-consuming. Token-based approach could help here by providing an easy way of giving temporary access.

- **When granular access is required** – For example, for an online journal, an owner wants everyone to read and comment on only one document, not on any others. Tokens could allow this.

- **Your system is a target for hacking** – The server contains sensitive documents and information which needs to be highly secured. A simple password doesn't offer enough protection. A piece of hardware helps here.

There are more scenarios where tokens enhance your security and keep your servers safe. But you need to follow best practices for tokens to work correctly. Your authentication tokens should be

- **Private** – Tokens should not be shared between users or authentication devices. The same guidance should be applied for tokens as for passwords, nobody should share any other part of your security system.

- **Secure** – Communication between the token and your server must be secure via HTTPS connections since encryption is essential here.

- **Tested** – Run periodic token tests to ensure that your system is secure and functioning properly. And spotted problems need to be quickly fixed.

- **Appropriate** – The right token type should be used for the corresponding use case. Ensure you're always picking the right tool for the job.

Identity Governance

When an organization implements a set of identity solutions either for users of the product or for its own employers, there are a group of questions that need to be answered beyond the technical implementations of selected protocols and frameworks, such as follows:

– Will the users of the system or companies employees have timely access to the resources they need?

– What risks do the organization have while managing identities?

– How can we manage identities and assess the risks?

– Are the right controls put in place?

– Are solutions compliant with the existing legal regulations in the countries and regions the company operates in?

All these questions and a lot of others need to be answered with the corresponding processes and solutions. The answer to such questions is identity governance, a policy-based orchestration which provides visibility to identities and better controls to detect and prevent inappropriate access or various intentional and unintentional security misuses.

So what does identity governance consist of?

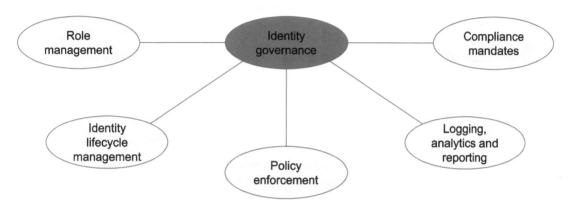

Figure 6-11. *Elements of identity governance*

- **Role management** – When your organization uses roles for managing identities and access, they frequently need to be created, updated, or deleted. Identity governance solutions typically can provide an easy way (user interface) for operations on roles, workflows for maintaining roles, keeping them up to date corresponding to users and resources.

- **Identity lifecycle management** – When a new employee joins the company, they need to have access to a certain set of resources (groups, files, data, etc.) in alignment with their specific role and team. Later when employees change the team, access to some of the resources needs to be revoked and to new resources granted. And finally when an employee leaves, all the access needs to be revoked and made sure that now an external person has no access to any of the company's internal resources. The right identity management solution would provide an automated and/or simplified way to manage such changes, which without it would be a manual nightmare.

- **Policy enforcement** – The approach to enforce the identity and access rules on users and employees preventing the single person to combine potentially dangerous combinations of permissions and roles, as an example to be creator of the payment plan and the

307

validator of it at the same time. It also includes an active discovery of violations of imposed rules to help find situations when a segregation of duties is not happening and conflict needs to be remediated.

- **Logging, analytics, and reporting** – The important aspect of security is to understand and keep track of what users are doing. Identity governance solutions often provide the ability to log the activities like when a user logs in, when users access particular resources, and when they are denied or granted access. Analytics provides valuable information on time of the day/week user activity, which resources are accessed the most, where do most of the access errors occur, etc.

- **Compliance mandates** – Organizations need to ensure that the proper security processes are in place to prevent security breaches, accounting malpractice, and user information privacy violations in accordance with regulatory requirements from different institutions like GDPR and CFAR. If an organization fails to comply with such mandates, it can face steep fines. Having right identity governance in place provides segregation of duties and tracking of user data that ensures compliance with these mandates.

Access Management

Access management is a security term used to refer to a set of policies for restricting access to information, tools, and physical locations. And you can separate access into physical and informational access.

Physical access control is a set of policies to control who is granted access to a physical location. Real-world examples of physical access control could be the following:

- Bar-room bouncers

- Subway turnstiles

- Airport customs agents

- Keycard or badge scanners in corporate offices

In the specified examples, for a person or device, a set of policies is applied. This helps to decide who gets access to a restricted physical location. For example, a hotel keycard scanner only grants access to authorized guests who have a hotel key.

Information access control restricts access to data and the software used to manipulate that data. Examples are the following:

- Signing into a laptop using a password

- Unlocking a smartphone with a thumbprint scan

- Remotely accessing an employer's internal network using a VPN

In these cases, software is used to authenticate and grant authorization to users who need to access digital information. Authorization, along with authentication, is an integral component of information access control. And while authentication is the security practice of confirming that someone is who they claim to be, authorization is the process of determining which level of access each user is granted.

User   **Access control**   **Data: files, object, etc.**

Figure 6-12. *Access control*

Once the user logs in to his work email account, he can access all the emails, attachment documents, and contact list he has. But he cannot see emails of other people working with him in the company.

So even with that user identity verified, he can only access certain resources or areas in the system or network. Access management is the process of controlling and tracking access. Each user within a system will have different privileges within that system based on their individual needs. An accountant does indeed need to access and edit payroll records, so once they verify their identity, they should be able to view and update those records as well as access their email account.

Access Control List (ACL)

The importance of managing access to resources was recognized with the first computer networks which had access by more than one user. While multiple users have access to the network resource, the situation dictated that not all of them should have equal access. The simplest example is to have a network administrator who can access everything and set up resources, and nonadmin users, who usually have simpler access as read. One of the first methods to manage granting access to users based on their identity was access control lists (ACLs). ACL represents a simple concept of records containing a resource and a user per row with the associated permission for it (read, write, create, etc.). For example, if a file object has an ACL that contains (Mark, read, write; John, read), this would give Mark permission to read and write the file and only give John permission to read it.

So access control list (ACL) is a list of permissions associated with a system resource (object). An ACL specifies which users or system processes are granted access to objects, as well as what operations are allowed on given objects[5]. Many kinds of operating systems implement ACLs, or have a historical implementation. The first of which was in the file system of Multics in 1965[6], where the access control lists were built into the file system and were maintained by the secondary storage system by the operating system.

There are different implementations and types of ACLs:

1. **File System ACLs** – Is a data structure, usually a table, which contains records of individual users or groups with rights to specific system objects such as programs, processes, or files. Such ACLs are widely used in operating systems like Microsoft Windows, OpenVMS, and Unix-like operating systems such as Linux and macOS. Each of these rights determines the type of access, such as the user's ability to read from, write to, or execute an object.

2. **POSIX ACL** – Portable Operating System Interface (POSIX) is a family of standards which among others attempted to draft the ACLs. Most of the Unix and Unix-like operating systems support POSIX ACLs.

---

[5] RFC 4949
[6] Elementary Information Security by Richard E. Smith, p. 150

3. **NFSv4 ACL** – More powerful than POSIX draft ACLs and defined by an actually published standard, as part of the network file system. NFSv4 ACLs are supported by many Unix and Unix-like operating systems as well.

4. **Active Directory ACLs** – Microsoft's Active Directory Service implements an LDAP (Lightweight Directory Access Protocol) server that stores and disseminates configuration information about users and computers in a domain[7]. Active Directory extends the LDAP specification by adding the same type of access control list mechanism as Windows uses for the NTFS file system.

5. **Networking ACLs** – On some types of proprietary computer-hardware (in particular routers and switches), an access control list provides rules that are applied to port numbers or IP addresses that are available on a host or other layer 3, each with a list of hosts and/or networks permitted to use the service. Both individual servers and routers can have network ACLs. Access control lists can generally be configured to control both inbound and outbound traffic.

6. **SQL ACLs** – ACL algorithms have been ported to SQL and to relational database systems. The same principle is used to control table/rows access.

Example of networking ACL:

```
access-list 110 permit host 192.168.4.18
access-list 110 deny host 192.168.4.7 log
access-list 110 permit tcp 92.128.12.0 0.0.0.255 any eq 80
access-list 110 deny any
```

ACLs checked in the order they appear on the list. In the preceding example, we allow access of the host with the IP 192.168.4.18, we explicitly deny the access for the host with the IP 192.168.4.7, and then we permit traffic that is coming from any address on the 92.128.12.0 network (source network) toward any destination IP on port 80. And at the end of the list we put explicit deny all to reject all other traffic even usually the ACL will have an implicit deny all if not specified.

---

[7] "[MS-ADTS]: Active Directory Technical Specification".

Role-Based Access Control (RBAC)

Often managing access to the resources becomes a tedious task using access control lists. In situations when hundreds of resources need to be managed for access by thousands of people (a situation often faced by big enterprise companies) with overlapping permissions, it is often not scalable to apply classic ACL approach.

The answer is role-based access control (RBAC). RBAC is a policy-neutral access control mechanism defined around roles and privileges. The components of RBAC such as role-permissions, user-role and role-role relationships make it simple to perform user assignments. It is used by the majority of enterprises.

Role-based access control (RBAC) is a method for controlling what users are able to do within a company's IT systems. RBAC accomplishes this by assigning one or more "roles" to each user, and giving each role different permissions. RBAC can be applied for a single software application or across multiple applications.

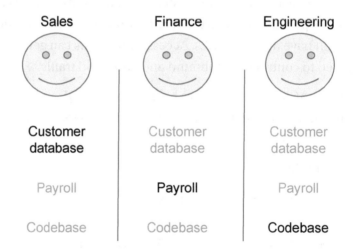

Figure 6-13. *RBAC, each user can access only relevant information*

Within an organization, roles are created for various job functions. The permissions to perform certain operations are assigned to specific roles. Members or staff (or other system users) are assigned particular roles, and through those role assignments acquire the permissions needed to perform particular system functions. Since users are not assigned permissions directly, but only acquire them through their role (or roles), management of individual user rights becomes a matter of simply assigning appropriate roles to the user's account; this simplifies common operations, such as adding a user or changing a user's department.

Most common entities of role-based access control:

- **Resources** – Entities in the system with which users interact in one or another way and which need to be managed to allow or deny access to. For example, in AWS:

  - arn:aws:s3:::bucket_name/key_name - unified resource name to identify an S3 bucket.

- **Permissions** – Usually represents the action a user can perform on a certain resource or system. Or represents the resource itself which the user can access in a certain way. For example, in AWS the resource is S3 bucket. The permission in such cases can represent a certain action which the user can perform, like listing objects in a bucket or creating/managing it:

  - **s3:GetObject** – The permission allows anyone to read the objects, for example, to give access to all users to objects as part of a static website hosted from a bucket.

- **Roles** – Is a job function or title which defines an authority level. It may or may not contain the list of permissions associated with the role (based on implementation). In case it does not contain, then policies specify attached permissions. In AWS the role represents an identity which is not associated with a single user, but a role is intended to be assumed by anyone who needs it. But in Google Cloud, the role also includes the list of permissions taking that part from the policy concept.

- **Policies** – Policies are objects that tight together identities (in a form of users, roles, and resources) with the corresponding permissions. A policy is usually a document which describes the list of identities which can perform a certain operation on a certain list of resources according to their roles. For example, a policy in AWS:

```
{
    "Version":"2012-10-17",
    "Statement":[
        {
```

```
            "Effect":"Allow",
            "Action":[
                "s3:PutObject",
                "s3:GetObject",
                "s3:GetObjectVersion",
                "s3:DeleteObject",
                "s3:DeleteObjectVersion"
            ],
            "Resource":"arn:aws:s3:::mycbucket/share/marketing/*"
        }
    ]
}
```

This policy then attached to a group of users which would have shared access to bucket identified by resource key: "arn:aws:s3:::mybucket/share/marketing/*".

The users will have the permission listed under the "Action" section: PutObject, GetObject, GetObjectVersion, DeleteObject, and DeleteObjectVersion.

Implementations of role-based access can differ between cloud solutions. For example, additional constraints may be applied such as roles can be combined in a hierarchy where higher-level roles subsume permissions owned by subroles. Or there could be hierarchies of resources (like in Google Cloud) where policies applied on container resources will propagate and apply for child resources as well.

RBAC differs from access control lists (ACLs), used in traditional discretionary access control systems, in that RBAC systems assign permissions to specific operations with meaning in the organization, rather than to low-level data objects. For example, an access control list could be used for granting or denying write access to a particular system file, but it would not dictate how that file could be changed. In an RBAC-based system, an operation might be to "create a credit account" transaction in a financial application or to "populate a blood sugar level test" record in a medical application. The assignment of permission to perform a particular operation is meaningful, because the operations are granular with meaning within the application. RBAC has been shown to be particularly well suited to separation of duties (SoD) requirements, which ensure that two or more people must be involved in authorizing critical operations. Necessary and sufficient conditions for safety of SoD in RBAC have been analyzed. An underlying principle of SoD is that no individual should be able to effect a breach of security through dual privilege. By extension, no person may hold a role that exercises audit, control, or review authority over another, concurrently held role.[8, 9] For example, for financial operations in an organization, we can have two roles: first with privileges to propose the supply vendor and second to approve vendor selection, SoD implies that the same person cannot have both these roles, effectively holding the audit and review authority (second role) over the operation granted by the first role.

The use of RBAC to manage user privileges (computer permissions) within a single system or application is widely accepted as a best practice. In an organization with heterogeneous IT infrastructure and requirements that span dozens or hundreds of systems and applications, using RBAC to manage sufficient roles and assign adequate role memberships becomes extremely complex without hierarchical creation of roles and privilege assignments.[10]

Attribute-Based Access Control (ABAC)

Attribute-based access control is an evolution of role-based access control. With this approach the important concepts of attributes and conditions are added to access management decisions. For example, the sales team distributed across the globe gets access to the folder with documents. With ABAC we can further customize access by requiring that location attribute for user match location attribute for document, thus implementing an additional condition for granting access.

Attribute-based access control defines an access control paradigm whereby access rights are granted to users through the use of policies which combine attributes together.[11] The policies can use any type of attributes (user attributes, resource attributes,

---

[8] D.R. Kuhn (1997). "Mutual Exclusion of Roles as a Means of Implementing Separation of Duty in Role-Based Access Control Systems" (PDF). 2nd ACM Workshop Role-Based Access Control: 23–30

[9] Ninghui Li, Ziad Bizri, and Mahesh V. Tripunitara (2004). "On mutually exclusive roles and separation-of-duty" (PDF). 11th ACM Conference on Computer and Communications Security. CCS '04: 42–51

[10] Systems, Hitachi ID. "Beyond Roles: A Practical Approach to Enterprise IAM". www.idsynch.com. Retrieved 15 August 2018

[11] Computer Security Division, Information Technology Laboratory (2016-05-24). "Attribute Based Access Control | CSRC | CSRC". CSRC | NIST. Retrieved 2020-11-22

object, environment attributes, etc.). This model supports Boolean logic, in which rules contain "IF, THEN" statements about who is making the request, the resource, and the action. For example, if the requester is a manager, then allow read/write access to sensitive data. The NIST framework introduces the main concepts of ABAC as its entities, i.e., PAP (Policy Administration Point), PEP (Policy Enforcement Point), PDP (Policy Decision Point), and PIP (Policy Information Point).[12,13]

So while role-based access control (RBAC) is based on predefined roles with a specific set of privileges associated with them and to which subjects are assigned, the key difference with ABAC is the concept of policies that express a complex Boolean rule set that can evaluate many different attributes. Attribute values can be atomic or contain more than one atomic value. Examples of multi-value attributes are role and project and examples of atomic attributes are clearance and sensitivity. Attributes can be compared to static values or to one another, thus enabling relation-based access control.

ABAC is considered a "next-generation" authorization model because it provides dynamic, context-aware, and risk-intelligent access control to resources allowing access control policies that include specific attributes from many different information systems to be defined to resolve an authorization and achieve an efficient regulatory compliance, allowing enterprises flexibility in their implementations based on their existing infrastructures. ABAC is also sometimes referred to as policy-based access control (PBAC).

An example flow for a user trying to access resource is shown in Figure 6-14.

---

[12] NIST, ABAC (2014). "Guide to Attribute Based Access Control (ABAC) Definition and Considerations"

[13] NIST (2016). "A Comparison of Attribute Based Access Control (ABAC) Standards for Data ServiceApplications"

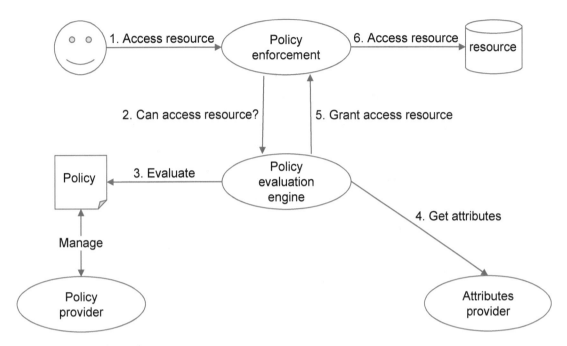

Figure 6-14. *Accessing resources via ABAC*

When a user requests access to resource, the system will perform a series of steps:

1. User's request gets to the policy enforcement system, which guards access to all the resources and either approves or denies access for every call.

2. Request got redirected to policy evaluation engine which contains logic for evaluation of access based on the policy associated with user and resource and corresponding attributes.

3. Policy evaluation engine gets Policy document from Policy provider system (which manage and stores policies)

4. Policy evaluation engine gets corresponding attributes for request from attributes provider system, which could be anything from resource prefix to user personal data.

5. Based on policy document and associated attributes, policy evaluation engine returns the result of evaluation, which is grant access in current example.

6. The user is granted access to the resource by the policy
    enforcement system.

So what are attributes in ABAC? Attributes can be about anything and anyone. We can break them into four different categories:

- **Subject attributes** – Attributes that describe the user attempting the access, e.g., age, clearance, department, role, job title, etc.

- **Action attributes** – Attributes that describe the action being attempted, e.g., read, delete, view, approve, etc.

- **Object attributes** – Attributes that describe the object (or resource) being accessed, e.g., the object type (medical record, bank account, etc.), the department, the classification or sensitivity, the location, etc.

- **Contextual (environment) attributes** – Attributes that deal with time, location, or dynamic aspects of the access control scenario

And policies are statements that bring together attributes to express what can happen and what is or is not allowed. Policies in ABAC can be granting or denying policies. Policies can also be local or global and can be written in a way that they override other policies. For example, a user can view a document if the document is in the same department as the user or deny access after 6 pm.

With ABAC you can have as many policies as you like that cater to many different scenarios and technologies.

One standard that implements attribute- and policy-based access control is XACML, the eXtensible Access Control Markup Language. XACML defines an architecture, a policy language, and a request/response scheme. It does not handle attribute management (user attribute assignment, object attribute assignment, environment attribute assignment) which is left to traditional IAM tools, databases, and directories.

The concept of ABAC can be applied at any level of the technology stack and an enterprise infrastructure. For example, ABAC can be used at the firewall, server, application, database, and data layer. The use of attributes brings additional context to evaluate the legitimacy of any request for access and inform the decision to grant or deny access.

An important consideration when evaluating ABAC solutions is to understand its potential overhead on performance and its impact on the user experience. It is expected that the more granular the controls, the higher the overhead.

Common ABAC applications include

1. **API and microservices security** – ABAC can be used to apply attribute-based, fine-grained authorization to the API methods or functions. For instance, a utility company service can expose a payBill API; ABAC can secure this endpoint. Policy authors can specify policy (e.g., managers can approve operations up to their approval limit) and attributes used: role, action ID, object type, amount, and approval limit.

2. **Application security** – With ABAC the authorization policies and attributes can be defined in a technology-neutral way. Common application examples are content management systems and web applications.

3. **Database security** – Security for databases are usually specific to the database vendors (like Oracle or Microsoft RLS) which means to achieve fine-grained ABAC-like security. For example, policy could be that managers can view transactions in their region:

   users with role == manager can do the action == SELECT on table == TRANSACTIONS if user.region == transaction.region

4. **Data and big data security** – Data security typically goes one step further than database security and applies control directly to the data element. This is often referred to as data-centric security. On traditional relational databases, ABAC policies can control access to data at the table, column, field, cell, and subcell using logical controls with filtering conditions and masking based on attributes. Attributes can be data, user, session, or tools based to deliver the greatest level of flexibility in dynamically granting/denying access to a specific data element. On big data, and distributed file systems such as Hadoop, ABAC applied at the data layer control access to folder, subfolder, file, subfile and other granular.

5. **File server security** – As of Windows Server 2012, Microsoft has implemented an ABAC approach to controlling access to files and folders.

An example of attribute based policy with conditions from AWS would be

```
{
    "Version": "2012-10-17",
    "Statement": {
        "Sid": "AllowRemoveMfaOnlyIfRecentMfa",
        "Effect": "Allow",
        "Action": [
            "iam:DeactivateMFADevice",
            "iam:DeleteVirtualMFADevice"
        ],
        "Resource": "arn:aws:iam::*:user/${aws:username}",
        "Condition": {
            "NumericLessThanEquals": {"aws:MultiFactorAuthAge": "3600"}
        }
    }
}
```

Use Cases
Use of Digital Signatures in DocuSign

Encryption serves multiple purposes across a lot of companies, but some of them used encryption as their core business. One of such companies is DocuSign which uses digital signatures to power electronic signing of documents. E-signing allows for much quicker agreements, arguably more secure and more environment friendly.

So how does digital signature work?

Digital signatures are like electronic "fingerprints" associated with the document. In a recorded transaction, a digital signature associates the signer with the document. Digital signatures are based on a technology standard called public key infrastructure (PKI). PKI is used to create a unique, tamper-evident "digital certificate" that associates a signer with a document and guarantees that the electronic document is authentic.

Digital certificates indicate that the signers have completed extra steps to confirm their identities.

When a signer electronically signs a document, the signature is created using the signer's private key, which is always securely kept by the signer. The mathematical algorithm acts like a cipher, creating data matching the signed document, called a hash, and encrypting that data. The resulting encrypted data is the digital signature. The signature is also marked with the time that the document was signed. If the document changes after signing, the digital signature is invalidated.

How is the signature being created?

DocuSign makes it easy to create signatures and sign documents. They provide an interface for sending and signing documents online and work with the appropriate certificate authorities to provide trusted digital certificates. DocuSign works with Trust Service providers from around the world to offer digital certificates and digital signatures through the DocuSign platform.

Depending upon the certificate authority you are using, you may be required to supply specific information. There also may be restrictions and limitations on whom you send documents to for signing and the order in which you send them. DocuSign's interface walks you through the process and ensures that you meet all of these requirements. When you receive a document for signing via email, you must authenticate as per the certificate authority's requirements and then "sign" the document by filling out a form online.

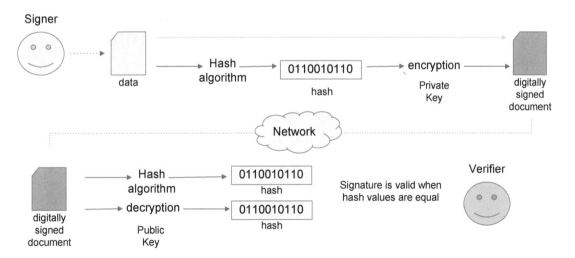

Figure 6-15. *Digital signature flow*

As an example, User 1 (seller) signs an agreement to sell a product using his private key. User 2 (buyer) receives the document. User 2 who receives the document also receives a copy of User 1's public key. If the public key can't decrypt the signature (via the cipher from which the keys were created), it means the signature isn't from User 1, or has been changed since it was signed. The signature is then considered invalid.

To protect the integrity of the signature, PKI requires that the keys be created, conducted, and saved in a secure manner, and often requires the services of a reliable certificate authority (CA). Digital signature providers, like DocuSign, meet PKI requirements for safe digital signing.

DocuSign managed to create a very successful business based on the digital signature concept with billions of documents being signed every year.

Use of JWT for Financial Transactions Through Stripe

Another technology from the information security space which is successfully used to power business is token-based authentication, which is actively used in secured communications. For example, Stripe implemented into their operations a special form of tokens called JSON Web Token (JWT).

JWT is a proposed Internet standard for creating data with optional signature and/or encryption whose payload holds JSON that contains some number of claims. The tokens are signed either using a private secret or a public/private key. JWT was developed as an answer for the increased need to authenticate users who access servers via mobile phones (apps) and web apps. JWT allows for safe, secure communication between two parties. Data is verified with a digital signature, and if it's sent via HTTP, encryption keeps the data secure.

The three main parts of JWT are

1. **Header** – Define token type and the signing algorithm involved in this space. For example:

```
{
  "alg": "HS256",
  "typ": "JWT"
}
```

2. **Payload** – Define the token issuer, the expiration of the token, and more in this section. For example:

```
{
  "loggedInAs": "admin",
  "iat": 1422779638
}
```

3. **Signature** – Verify that the message hasn't changed in transit with a secure signature. For example:

```
HMAC_SHA256(
  secret,
  base64urlEncoding(header) + '.' +
  base64urlEncoding(payload)
)
```

Let's look into which benefits can JWT bring in comparison to opaque access tokens (tokens in a proprietary format that you cannot access):

- **Performance** – JWT validation can be performed locally, without a remote call to the authentication service.

- **Accessible payload** – JWT may contain payload useful to the service such as user profile and permissions without a remote call to the authentication service.

- **Ease of use** – Tokens can be generated from almost anywhere and are easily understandable.

But there are also some disadvantages which come with it:

- **Visible payload** – Payload is not encrypted and visible can be a con too, since it is not suitable for encrypted data.

- **Slower to update token payload** – For example, permission updates are slower since the token is valid until expiration. Mitigation is to use shorter expiration.

- **Revoking access takes longer** – Mitigation is to add all revoked token into an exclusion list and do an additional check to disallow any unexpired token in the exclusion list.

- **Single key** – JWTs rely on a single key, and if that key is leaked, the entire system is at risk. Mitigation to this is a key rotation.

- **Limitations** – You can't push messages to all clients, and you can't manage clients from the server side.

- **Limited payload size** – Token is usually passed as a HTTP header and needs to be reasonable in size.

Currently, JWT implementations exist for many languages and frameworks and are widely used by companies across the globe.

Wrap-Up

In this chapter we learned about information security in modern applications and systems. We explored some of the most common threats to applications and users, as well as different digital assets. So to be prepared to deal with them, developers of the systems need to apply a wide range of solutions which makes systems robust and secure.

The usage of certificates, TLS, keys, and key management infrastructures are almost mandatory for a wide range of use cases and products. Companies widely utilize multifactor authentication to protect their clients, which brings an additional layer of security to a basic username and password login. Single sign-on is growing in popularity where companies "outsource" some of authentication details to several trusted providers (like Google).

Identity and access management instruments are required in the majority of cases as well. Role-based access control and attribute-based access control allow for complex use cases of managing users, resources, and access mapping between them. Usage of roles and attributes allows administrators to scale, apply automatic management, and support hundreds of thousands of users and resources.

In the next chapter, we would explore more specialized use cases which take the security theme of this chapter even further, such as blockchain and digital currencies.

CHAPTER 7

Blockchain: The Foundation of Web3

The various technologies and components that we have covered so far should cover most of the building blocks you would need to build any technical product. However, there is a growing interest in the development of decentralized applications (dApps) which run in Web3. If dApps and Web3 sound alien, what about smart contracts – nothing rings a bell yet?

Well, then I am sure you must have heard of cryptocurrencies, especially Bitcoin, the world first and most popular cryptocurrency with a market cap of over $500 billion as of June 8, 2022. Along with Bitcoin you must have also heard of nonfungible tokens, popularly called NFTs. They made global news when the founder of Twitter Inc., Jack Dorsey, sold his first tweet as an NFT for around $2.9 million. Figure 7-1 shows a screenshot of that tweet.

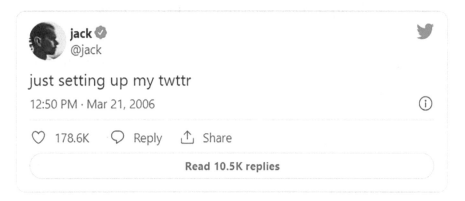

Figure 7-1. *Jack Dorsey's first tweet sold on the platform "Valuables"*

© Gaurav Sagar, Vitalii Syrovatskyi 2022
G. Sagar and V. Syrovatskyi, *Technical Building Blocks*, https://doi.org/10.1007/978-1-4842-8658-6_7

All these cryptocurrencies, NFT, and dApps run in a new iteration of the Internet called Web3 that is based on blockchain technology. Although things haven't gone mainstream with blockchain, it has growing interest among technology enthusiasts, investors, and developers. We feel blockchain is a building block that you should know about as for one you may work in a team that may use this technology for their technical product and, two, there is a lot of misinformation and hype around this technology, and we want you to be able to evaluate the real value this has when you make technology choices for your product.

Caution   You may find this chapter technically deeper that other chapters as here we will expose you to some code and some cryptography. You are not required to run any code, just get acquainted with it, so you are comfortable when you land in deep technical discussions around Web3.

Evolution of the Web
Web 1.0

Web as you know is the common name of the World Wide Web (www). English computer scientist Tim Berners-Lee invented the Web at the European research organization CERN and made it available to the general public in 1991. He developed the following to make the Web fully functional:

- Hypertext Transfer Protocol (HTTP) to transfer files over the Internet

- Hypertext markup language (HTML) to display documents in the web browser

- First web browser and web page editor, called "WorldWideWeb"

- First web server called CERN Hypertext Transfer Protocol daemon (HTTPd)

- First website that explained what web was, and how to create a website

This first form of Web is Web 1.0, also called "Read-only web." Here organizations would create websites which are a repository of organized static HTML pages that can be viewed over the Internet through a web browser. The HTML pages contain links to other HTML pages of the same or other websites, called "hyperlinks," which allow the user to click these links on the static HTML pages, which takes them to the HTML page of the link. I am sure you all know how this works.

The web pages (the content on the Web) were produced by a small set of companies owning the websites. There were online directories like those from Yahoo which categorized these web pages (and websites) into groups such as news, sports, entertainment, etc. to allow the Internet user to come to these directory websites and find the content they want from there. Display advertisements as banner advertisements on these websites and the directories were the popular form of revenue generation. It's critical to note that content was proprietary, and creation was in the hands of a few website owners and everyone else was doing mass consumption of information from these websites.

Web 2.0

This version of the Web began around 2004 and continues to this day. This started with the development of JavaScript, a programming language that could run code from the web pages in the browser of the user's machine, developed by Brendan Eich at Netscape, which was a popular browser at one time. JavaScript brought dynamic behavior to the web pages, controlled by the JavaScript code after the web page is loaded in the browser – a big move from the earlier static pages.

Cascading Style Sheets (CSS) were developed that improved the visual style and appearance of the web pages. Together HTML, JavaScript and CSS brought interactivity to the Web, where dynamic content on web pages is generated based on user's input. Finally, the Internet reached the masses through the mobile devices which became popular with iOS and Android phones.

These improvements led to more participation from the users, where instead of just viewing content produced by a select few organizations through their websites, users started to create their own content and publish it on the websites. It's important to note that although the users create the content, they still host it on websites, not owned by them. They can, however, add, change, and delete content. There was significant growth in Internet usage as web users started forming communities and interacting with each other.

Today, web users are creating content to the tune of whole encyclopedias like "Wikipedia," sharing content on video streaming sites like YouTube and TikTok, forming social networks on sites like Facebook and LinkedIn, and discussing ideas in web forums like Reddit. Two-sided marketplaces become common where buyers and sellers could come onto a platform for trade such as eBay, Airbnb, and Uber.

Content is searched on the Web not by means of a directory, but through search engines like Google that takes in a user's query to get the right content on the web pages. Revenue generation on the Web moved to tracking user engagement on the content with metrics like click-through rate (CTR) and views.

The most critical aspect to note here is that even though now the users are creating content and the content creating isn't in the hands of a select few organizations, there is still a powerful middleman – the platform – which acts as a trusted party between these users and has complete control over the content and the services provided to the end users, e.g., Twitter permanently suspended[1] the account of former U.S. president Donald Trump in early 2021 for violating Twitter rules.

Web 3.0

Popularly called Web3, this is an alternate version of the Web and still in its infancy. The term was coined by Ethereum (a cryptocurrency) cofounder Gavin Wood who says[2], "The internet today is broken by design," and it gained huge interest in 2021 where venture capital firms poured in more than $27 billion in crypto-related projects that year. The biggest shortcoming in the Web 2.0 as per the Web3 enthusiasts is the presence of middlemen. The Web today is owned by a few big tech companies primarily Meta (formerly Facebook), Amazon, and Google. This brings in some interesting attributes of Web 2.0:

- Users must live by the rules of these companies, essentially the platform owners on which the users add/update/delete content. These platforms choose who joins the platform and can suspend and revoke access of any user.

---

[1] https://blog.twitter.com/en_us/topics/company/2020/suspension
[2] https://gavofyork.medium.com/why-we-need-web-3-0-5da4f2bf95ab

- Users can't specify the monetization rate of their own content. The rate is decided by the platforms again, often which isn't fixed. The platforms usually take the lion share of the revenue generated from the user's content.

- The payment to users and from users must go through financial institutions like banks who take a cut in all business transactions. Also, these are governed by government tax laws, so the government takes a cut too.

Web3 proponents want to remove all these middlemen and give the ownership of the content and these platforms to the users – this idea is called "decentralization." Let's understand this with what hypothetically a social network like Twitter may look like in Web3:

- It would be close to impossible to fake anyone's identity as the identities will have cryptographic-based proof. This means the fake identity can't prove that the things done by the real identity are done by it or vice versa.

- There would be no guard-railing from the social network enterprise employees. This means users have complete freedom of speech in what to post. Also, users will own their content and can sell the rights of it (like paintings in an auction). However, in the app's interest, users may vote on decisions around content moderation.

- There wouldn't be an initial public offering (IPO). The platform will be owned by the users through some cryptocurrency token. The early adopters of the social network will get these tokens. All users would earn cryptocurrency tokens based on the engagement on their content.

- The value of the social network or we can say the value of the cryptocurrency tokens (if they are only used on the social network and nowhere else) will be based on Twitter's success, with the total revenue from advertising equating to the value of the tokens.

- The users will be able to exchange these cryptocurrency tokens directly with each other, without going through any financial institution.

All this vision around decentralization and token-based economy is based on a technology called blockchain. We can say that Web3 is the blockchain-integrated web. We will learn more about blockchain in the upcoming sections.

Before we move, I would like to bring your attention toward a term called "Semantic Web," a term coined again by Tim Berners-Lee in 1999, which is also called Web 3.0 by some; however, it has no relation to the Web3 version of Gavin Wood. The Semantic Web is a vision about an extension of the existing web, where the web pages have machine-interpretable metadata of the published information and data. This will enable machines (computers) to make meaningful relations between data called knowledge graphs and interpretations like the way humans do.

Did you know? Tim Berners-Lee sold the original source code for the World Wide Web, as an NFT titled "This Changed Everything" for $5.4[3] million in an auction that started at $1,000 in June 2021.

Blockchain

Blockchain is a distributed ledger that is maintained in a peer-to-peer network of nodes. The records of data to be stored in the ledger are verified and audited by the peer nodes before they are stored as blocks of records in the ledger. Decentralized blockchains are immutable; the data entered into them cannot be changed. We used quite some technical jargons in the definition above; let's understand them.

Peer-to-Peer network

In a peer-to-peer (P2P) network, multiple computers (also called nodes) are interconnected with each other to share resources and data (such as files). This is also called a decentralized network. Each node here acts both as a client and the server, which means it can request data from another node, as well as respond back with data to another node's request. Figure 7-2 shows the difference between a centralized and decentralized network.

---

[3] www.sothebys.com/en/buy/auction/2021/this-changed-everything-source-code-for-www-x-tim-berners-lee-an-nft/source-code-for-the-www

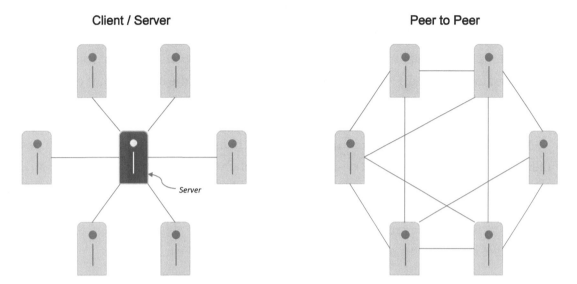

Figure 7-2. *Client server network is a centralized network and P2P is a decentralized network*

Since each node has the same rights regarding finding and using resources, validating other users (on nodes) and communication, they are called peers. An example of a P2P network is BitTorrent, which allows sharing of data and electronic files among peers over the Internet.

Distributed Ledger

In accounting, a ledger is a book in which all account transactions are recorded, i.e., the money spent and received. A distributed ledger can be thought of as a database (ledger) of transactions, which is consensually distributed (shared) and synchronized across the P2P network. Since each node has a copy of the ledger, they all can audit transactions. Any new transaction in the ledger is reflected and copied to all P2P nodes. Distributed ledgers are data storages and can store not just transactions but any form of data. Records entered into distributed ledgers cannot be changed by any other person once they are there. As a result, the records cannot be altered until the ledgers are disseminated. However, although a tamper-proof ledger of transactions is produced by blockchain technology, in modern day the blockchain networks are still vulnerable to fraud and cyberattacks.

Immutable Blocks

Transactions or any other form of data is stored in the distributed ledger (blockchain) in groups, and each group is called a block. The first block of the blockchain is called *genesis*. Once the blocks are added to the blockchain after they are verified by the nodes of the peer network, they can't be changed or deleted and become immutable.

The reason why blocks can't be updated (or it is near impossible) to update the block information is due to the use of cryptography, we touched briefly on it in Chapter 6, and we will revisit it once again here in more detail. The blocks contain the hash of the data in them and a reference to the hash of the previous block. Because of this, one can easily go from any block to the previous block and all the way to the genesis block, following this chain of reference. This is the reason why this is called blockchain.

Decentralized

Unlike the centralized ledger, where there is a central authority to authorize or validate transactions in the ledger, such as what financial institutions like banks do for our money stored in current and savings accounts, in the decentralized ledger (blockchain), no one in the distributed (P2P) network has to know or trust anyone. Each member in the network has a copy of the exact same copy of the ledger.

If a member's ledger has been manipulated wrongly or corrupted, it will be rejected by the majority of the members in the network. This means that when new data records are to be added to the network, the majority of the network should verify and form the consensus to add these records to the distributed ledger. There are algorithms to build consensus we will learn of shortly.

Blockchain Types

Based on who grants the permission to access the blockchain and how data records are validated, blockchains can be categorized into the following ways as shown in Figure 7-3.

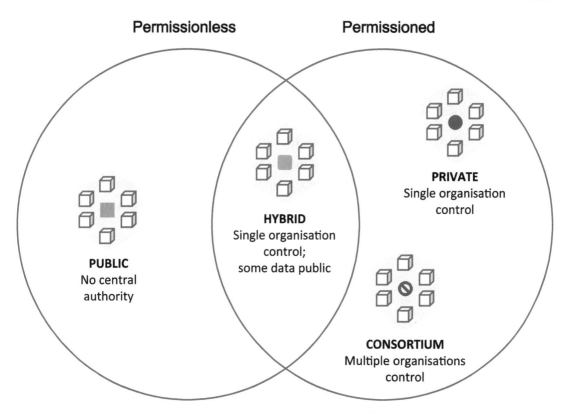

Figure 7-3. *Types of blockchain based on controlling authorities*

1. **Public blockchain** – This is a permission less blockchain, where anyone can join the distributed blockchain network. These are completely decentralized. Most cryptocurrencies such as Bitcoin and Ethereum are forms of public blockchains.

2. **Private blockchain** – This is a permissioned blockchain, where an organization sets control on who can access the blockchain. They are partially decentralized as there is a central authority to grant permission. Examples include most blockchain products offered by cloud vendors like AWS and Oracle Cloud Infrastructure (OCI).

3. **Consortium blockchain** – This is a permissioned blockchain, where a group of organizations (called a consortium) sets control on who can access the blockchain. However, these are more decentralized than private blockchains, but still less decentralized than public blockchain.

4. **Hybrid blockchain** – These blockchain are a mix of public and private blockchain features. Here, an organization controls granting permissions to access the blockchain; however, some or all data records (transactions) can be made public for verification purposes by the blockchain members.

The best way to understand what blockchain is and how it works is to learn of an application of it. Bitcoin is a digital currency, as we all know, but it is formed through the blockchain technology. Without blockchain technology, there'd be no secure way to trade in Bitcoin, making it useless. Let's understand blockchain by learning more of how Bitcoin uses blockchain.

Bitcoin

The roots of blockchain can be seen as far as 1982 in the dissertation of American cryptographer David Chaum, named "Computer Systems Established, Maintained, and Trusted by Mutually Suspicious Groups." However, it was popularized by a person with a pseudonym Satoshi Nakamoto, who published a white paper on a cryptography mailing list describing a digital cryptocurrency, titled "Bitcoin: A Peer-to-Peer Electronic Cash System" in 2008 and launched the Bitcoin software and the P2P network in 2009.

Bitcoin is not managed by any financial institution and is completely decentralized, and just like regular currency, users can exchange this with each other for purchase of goods and services, and it also has an exchange rate with other currencies such as USD.

Authentication

If blockchain (say Bitcoin) is decentralized, distributed, and anonymous, how are the people who are part of the network authenticated, i.e., how does the network verify the identity of the users in this anonymous network? Let's understand this with an example scenario that we will use throughout this chapter. John and Peter are roommates and live in an apartment in downtown Seattle. They settle their monthly expenses where they are both involved like ordering food, bills, etc. by transferring money to each other using a bank check. Both John and Peter have accounts in the same bank – Bank of America. So, Bank of America, the issuer of the check, acts as the central governing body here which also authenticates both John and Peter as it has the details of both.

Instead of setting their monthly expenses through check, John and Peter rather now want to settle in Bitcoins. To do that John and Peter first need to be able to identify themselves (authentication) on the Bitcoin network anonymously. This is where cryptography is used and hence comes the name "cryptocurrency," which is the use of cryptography for digital currency. Cryptography is the study of encryption and hashing techniques.

Bitcoin uses asymmetric encryption, also called public key cryptography that you read in Chapter 6, to solve for users to identify themselves on the network and claim ownership of bitcoins. In Bitcoin (and all blockchain-based assets), the user chooses a random number between 1 and from 2^{256} as his/her private key and thinks of this as the password for a traditional online bank account. The private key is then used to generate the public key, which is used to generate a Bitcoin address, which you can think of as the bank account name.

Crypto wallets are used to store these pairs of private-public keys of various cryptocurrencies and other digital tokens like NFTs. Private keys are used to spend cryptocurrency and public keys to receive the money; however, the keys are further modified. The private key is modified by mathematical functions to turn it into a *wallet import format (WIF)*, and the public key is modified to turn it into an *address*. If the private key is lost or stolen, all the cryptocurrency is lost too and can't be recovered. Let's see how these keys are generated and types of wallets to store them.

Generating WIF

Since a private key in decimal form will be a very large string, it is encoded in the wallet import format (WIF) which shortens the private key generated making it easier to copy and reduces chances of making mistakes while copying due to the presence of checksum for detecting errors. The following are the steps[4] to generate the *private key* and its WIF:

1. **Generate some random data** – Let's say John creates the following data:

```
6~q?yAb~}LY4PM8-!"q8X'ba4c}
Bf{XKM%G99y:~Kfe^Q~sj\2mLj]\.$`_YU:)y!}@Ee^kq>$SUR-
[!+C4x4))4P6!KXJ*/xJAWG8V$+\xGvbparMBS$}yJ
```

---

[4]http://gobittest.appspot.com/PrivateKey

2. **Create private key** – This is done by using the SHA256 hashing algorithm, which outputs a fixed 64-character hexadecimal string for any length of input data. The SHA256 hash of the random data is the following 64 characters. Since each character represents 4 bits, this is 64 x 4 = 256 bits:

268AA55FF9CD48DB50CAD4749EAD428DED35
CB32E572C9FA11B993687C0021BE

This hexadecimal number in decimal is as follows and lies between 1 and 2^{256}:

17432854516752903428243459902407005525465936272793
42612133405799305918074246

3. **Add version identifier** – Add "80" to the beginning of the hexadecimal string as every private key on Bitcoin's main network begins with "5," and this ensures that the final output has 5 in the start. Bitcoin also has a test network, where new features are supposedly tested:

80268AA55FF9CD48DB50CAD4749EAD428DED35CB32E572C9
FA11B993687C0021BE

4. **Add checksum** – Since the private key is large and prone to errors while manually entering it, we include a checksum which ensures that the key is valid. To do that:

   a. Take the SHA-256 hash of the hexadecimal string created in step 3:

   E22810B08FDD5AE1F2B8182C4F92500CBB09A6AB17C95F772D6920
   198D786029

   b. Take the SHA-256 hash of the hexadecimal string created in step 4a:

   DD464FE77BF302F4A3DC2D4314C7E25EF56865C8A9
   338BB397671F062FB69860

   c.   Take the first eight characters of string in 4b, and add it to the end of string in 3:

       80268AA55FF9CD48DB50CAD4749EAD428DED35CB32E57
       2C9FA11B993687C0021BE**DD464FE7**

5. **Get wallet import format** – This is the last step to encode the hexadecimal string from step 4c into base58. This is also the digital signature of a user:

       5J7G5HBhxLtFxeyqNMCe6s6mwX9wojEx1rJTng43WzVoEzsEcJS

As you can see, getting the private key from WIF is straightforward. Decode the WIF using base58. Then, remove the last eight characters and the first two characters, and your private key is there as it was in step 2 above. Private key is used to spend the cryptocurrency.

Generating Address

The next part is to create a public key for this private key, which will act as the username when compared to an online bank. Bitcoin uses an elliptic curve digital signature algorithm (ECDSA) for generation of public keys using a specific curve called *secp256k1*. We will not get into the details of the curve. The public key generated from this algorithm is 2x of the private key, and just like how we shorten the private key, we will shorten the public key, for easier sharing. This reduced form of public key is called the "address." The following are the steps[5] to generate a *public key* and the corresponding *address*:

1. **Create public key** – The private key from step 2 above is passed as input to the ECDSA algorithm to generate the hash. "04" is added to the start of the hash string resulting in the Bitcoin public key. This is an uncompressed public key, we could also create the compressed public key, which is shorter and saves disk space on nodes that store the bitcoin blockchain, but that needs one more step. For simplicity, we will stick with uncompressed:

       04B3F1AECA6179071342D6416821A4F6B0AE0CECF237D2FBB
       F7909EB43813074699A967F31953DAE6236C795799DA492AC
       D64F6DB3F1C9750826F088FC975A73B8

---

[5] https://darkvane.com/how-to-generate-bitcoin-address/

2. **Encrypt public key** – Here the public key generated is encrypted by two hash functions:

   a. Take the SHA-256 hash of the string created in step 1:

   3B36AB406FF5E3844D5C52C5A9E79EF92D88F1C3E61B949F
   6D2CD6A9E32CE223

   b. Take the RIPEMD-160 hash (another type of hashing algorithm) on the string in 2a step to convert it into a 160-bit integer, called the *encrypted public key*:

   81925E36F6CF4227CCB6445BE692E74EC74C43BE

3. **Add version identifier** – We must add "00" to the beginning of the encrypted public key to use it on the Bitcoin main network:

   0081925E36F6CF4227CCB6445BE692E74EC74C43BE

4. **Add checksum** – We include a checksum which ensures that the public key is valid. To do that:

   a. Take the SHA-256 hash of the hexadecimal string created in step 3:

   E180F71E787B1D560A8FAB5FF57695E43D96FDE23D958
   9CF9839553F1F40540A

   b. Take the SHA-256 hash of the hexadecimal string created in step 4a:

   6A5C717A9DCEA5BBD4395878F0B5BB71D1886DCE13193
   AC418D0428D81EA571C

   c. Take the first eight characters of string in 4b, and add it to the end of string in 3:

   0081925E36F6CF4227CCB6445BE692E74EC74C43BE**6A5C717A**

5. **Get the address** – This is the last step to encode the string from step 4c into base58:

   1Cp7WaLsYHqjs6qNG7BB4Fa92zunJV2bNh

Addresses are used to receive money, and these are publicly shared on the blockchain, whereas private keys (WIF) are kept secure and never shared. The address we generated here, starting with "1," is a legacy address, and these addresses were in common use until 2017. However, it is advised not to use them as they are case sensitive and may cause unwanted errors, incur the most expensive transaction fees while sending payments, and limit the Bitcoin's network's ability to scale[6]. Addresses that start with 3 or bc1 are more modern and recommended.

It's important to remember that the crypto wallet doesn't hold the cryptocurrency or any tokens (digital assets), it only stores the keys. The cryptocurrency never leaves the blockchain and can only be accessed through these keys. You may be wondering that if generating these keys require all these steps and the knowledge of cryptography, how do people not so well versed in these use cryptocurrency and other digital assets, the answer is that crypto wallets not just store the tokens and keys but can also generate these keys, and that is the most common form of how these keys are generated and used by regular people.

By now we have solved for authentication. Users like John and Peter will use addresses the same way they use bank accounts to store currency and key pairs the same way they use username-password pairs to log into their bank accounts. The anonymity and security come from the fact that it is impossible to generate the public key from an address or generate the private key from the public key. This means that no one will ever know who (person or organization) the bitcoin address belongs to, but the owner of the private keys associated with that address.

Wallet Types

You realize how important these keys are to store and manage securely, and that is where the types of wallets come into the picture. Based on the storage medium of the keys, the crypto wallets can be categorized into two types:

1. **Hot wallets** – These are software wallets that need to connect to the Internet for them to work, and they have the risk of being hacked; however, they have more user-friendly features. There are hot wallets available as desktop applications, mobile apps, and web apps. The web wallets are most popular as they only

---

[6]https://bitcoinbriefly.com/practical-guide-bitcoin-addresses-explained/

need a browser to access them; however, the website hosting the wallet has the ownership of the keys to the user's crypto wallet. Figure 7-4 shows an image of a hot wallet where it is storing multiple cryptocurrencies.

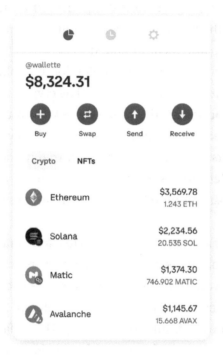

Figure 7-4. *Coinbase wallet – a form of hot wallet. Source: Coinbase*

2. **Cold wallets** – These are hardware or physical medium-based wallets that don't need the Internet and are considered more secure than hot wallets. These can be password-protected USB drives, keys printed on paper – called paper wallets – or built through special hardware devices from companies like Ledger. Figure 7-5 shows a Bitcoin paper wallet which has the address and the private key. Please don't send any bitcoin to this address.

Figure 7-5. *A sample paper wallet created at bitaddress.org*

Bitcoin Transactions

John and Peter are determined to settle their monthly expenses in bitcoins, and by now they have already got crypto wallets and have generated and saved the keys in them. Say John needs to pay Peter $1,500 to settle expenses from last month. To do that John needs to have bitcoins worth $1,500, so he decides to trade $2,000 USD for 0.1 BTC, with a floating exchange rate of 1 BTC = $20,000 USD through a cryptocurrency exchange, such as Coinbase. Bitcoin exchange rates are floating exchange rates as they fluctuate in response to the demand and supply.

But then he wonders that the debit card he will use to buy the bitcoins on the exchange can be mapped to his bitcoin address by the exchange, and since the debit card is issued to him by a bank, there will be traceability to his bitcoins on the blockchain. John wants more privacy and doesn't want to associate in any way his personal identity with the Bitcoins, so he buys 0.1 Bitcoin from another friend Olivia, who has been using bitcoin for a couple of years. The process was simple:

1. Oliva took $2,000 from John in cash and opened her crypto wallet on her phone and saw that she had 10 BTC in her crypto wallet.

2. She scanned the QR code of the Bitcoin address created by John and entered 100 mBTC (read as 100 millibits) in the amount.

3. She saw a transaction fee of 0.00001 BTC but didn't ask John for an additional $0.20 and pressed confirm to initiate the transaction.

4. An *unconfirmed* label against the transaction showed up in Olivia's app initially which turned to *confirmed* in a few minutes.

5. John's balance in his crypto wallet got updated to 100 mBTC (0.1 BTC), and Oliva's balance in her crypto wallet got updated to 9.8999 BTC.

Next, John scans the QR code of Peter's address and sends him 75 mBTC or 0.075 BTC which is equivalent to $1,500 to settle the monthly expenses. This brings the balance of John's wallet to 0.024 BTC (he paid the transaction fees too), and Peter has 0.025 BTC as his balance in the crypto wallet. You might notice that the transaction fees in BTC have a lot of decimals which makes it a small value but also that Bitcoin can be broken down into very small units. Just like how 1 USD can be broken down in 100 cents, 1 BTC is equal to 100 million satoshis. This means the smallest amount one can transfer through Bitcoin is 0.00000001 BTC or 1 *satoshi*. To John, Peter, and Olivia, this is as simple as transferring money through an app like Venmo and Zelle, but behind the scenes is where the blockchain is used. Let's go over the processing of these transactions in detail.

Structure of a Transaction

A transaction on the blockchain is like the entry in a regular ledger. Transaction contains the following main elements:

- **Inputs** – There can be one or more inputs which are like debits. Each input shows the bitcoin address and the amount in BTC that is transferred from in the transaction.

- **Outputs** – There can be one or more outputs which are like credits. Each output shows the bitcoin address and the amount in BTC that is transferred to in the transaction. Technically these are called Unspent Transactions Outputs (UTXO).

- **Transaction Id (TXID)** – This is an identifier for the transaction created by hashing (SHA256) the transaction data twice.

- **Size** – This is the size of the transaction in bytes.

- **Transaction fees** – This is the amount paid to Bitcoin miners for adding the transaction on the Bitcoin blockchain. The fee is calculated based on the size of the transaction in bytes, different from how banks charge fees by amount.

The sum of outputs and the transaction fee equals the sum of inputs. Since transactions contain both inputs and outputs and one of the outputs (UTXO) of one transaction becomes one of the inputs for another transaction, the transactions can be referenced from one another. This chain is called the *transaction chain*. Figure 7-6 shows the transaction chain where Oliva first transfers some Bitcoins to John and then John transfers some bitcoins to Peter.

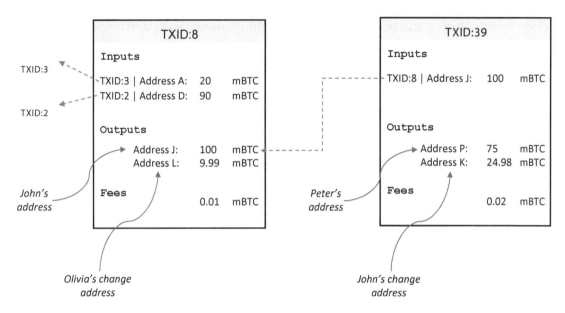

Figure 7-6. *Transaction chain of the transactions between Oliva and John and John and Peter*

You may notice in the figure above that there are two inputs to the transaction Id 8, made by Oliva to John. This means that Oliva has the private key of multiple addresses, and she chooses the two addresses whose total bitcoin value is over 100 mBTC. Crypto wallet automatically chooses the addresses, and Oliva wouldn't have to manually do it. Generally, the wallets keep track of all the addresses that the wallet owner has and show the owner sum of BTC of them as wallet value. In our example, Olivia saw 10 bitcoins in her wallet before she made the transfer to John.

The other noticeable thing is that there is a *change address* in both transactions. A change address is owned by the owner of the input address, where the left-over change from the transaction is stored. You may question why Oliva put all the 90 mBTC from address D. Can't she just put 80.01 mBTC from address D? The answer is that Bitcoin protocol treats the BTC stored at an address as a single currency bill, so the whole bill is required for the transaction, and the change is then returned to the address specified by the one initiating the transaction. For added privacy, a new change address is generated by the wallet, instead of storing the change at any of the input addresses.

Transaction Creation

The transaction structure shared earlier was a simplified version to make you understand some concepts as transaction chaining. Now, let's get into more details and see how transactions are created[7] and signed[8]. Let's see what happened behind the scenes when John used his crypto wallet to scan the QR code of Peter's address and pressed the confirm button to send him 75 mBTC.

Create Draft Transaction

The crypto wallet of John first creates an unsigned transaction, i.e., without the value of scriptSig, which may look like the one in Listing 7-1.

Listing 7-1. Transaction without signature

```
version: 01000000
inputs:   01
  txid: b7994a0db2f373a29227e1d90da883c6ce1cb0dd2d6812e4558041ebbbcfa54b
  vout: 00000000
  scriptsigsize: 00
  scriptsig:
  sequence: ffffffff
outputs: 01
  amount: 983a000000000000
  scriptpubkeysize: 19
  scriptpubkey: 76a914b3e2819b6262e0b1f19fc7229d75677f347c91ac88ac
locktime: 00000000
```

---

[7] https://developer.bitcoin.org/devguide/transactions.html
[8] https://learnmeabitcoin.com/technical/ecdsa#signing-a-transaction

Version tells Bitcoin peers and miners the format to follow to identify the various fields in a serialized transaction based on field length. Each transaction has at least one input and one output. The transaction id in the input refers to the previous transaction where John received bitcoins from Olivia and the *vout* of 0 refers to the first output specified in that transaction. If you refer to Figure 7-5, you may be able to visualize this. Locktime is the earliest time the transaction can be included in a block. Setting it to 0 means the transaction can be included at any time in any block. Sequence is a deprecated field. The amount is the number of satoshis to be transferred to the address (here address of Peter).

Fields in a transaction are in hexadecimal format. The fields version, txid, vout, sequence, amount, and locktime are in reverse byte order, also called little-endian. To interpret these fields manually, you would have to reverse the bytes of the hexadecimal string. Since each byte is two characters in the string, you would reverse the string two characters at a time. For example, "ab12cd90" will be reversed as "90cd12ab." The hex amount would translate to 3a98 in Big-endian, which would be 1,500 satoshis, or 0.015 mBTC. Yes, this isn't equal to the 75 mBTC John has to give Peter – this is just an example transaction to show the working behind the scenes. By the way, did you notice some fields starting with the word "script"?

Script Overview

Script[9] is an assembly language, a low-level programming language created by Satoshi which uses opcodes (abbreviated from operation code), also called machine code to lock and unlock transactions in the Bitcoin network. The opcodes are executed in a stack which means it follows last-in first-out (LIFO) which means the last opcode is processed first, then the second last opcode, and so on. It is Turing incomplete, which means that it lacks logical functions, including loops. This limits the capability of the language and ensures that no harm can be done to the network nodes deliberately – improving security and keeping Bitcoin simple.

The presence of a programming language is the reason why Bitcoin and other cryptocurrencies are called programmable money. Programmable money can have built-in logic, allowing for the programming of complicated situations. Programmable

---

[9] https://river.com/learn/terms/s/script-bitcoin/

payments are automatic transactions that are initiated by smart contracts or other cryptocurrencies technologies – we will learn of them in more detail later. For now, just know that Bitcoin was the first known programmable money.

All Bitcoin transactions use Script to program (read: define) how outputs (UTXO) can be spent. In the preceding transaction, we can see the following two scripts:

- **scriptSig** – This is present in inputs of the transaction and is called the "Unlocking Script" as it contains the digital signature and the public key to unlock the UTXO in the input to be spent. This is how it is coded in Script:

```
<Sig> <PubKey>
```

- **scriptPubKey** – This is present in the outputs of the transaction and is called the "locking script" as it locks the bitcoins on the UTXO until someone can provide the correct scriptSig, which has what it needs to satisfy the condition defined in this script. Most of the bitcoin transactions use this script, and it is also called pay-to-public-key-hash (P2PKH), which means pay to the one that can prove she/he has the private key to the hash of this public key. There are other locking scripts for bitcoin too, such as pay-to-Pubkey (P2PK), pay to script hash (P2SH), etc. The following is how P2PKH is coded in Script:

```
OP_DUP OP_HASH160 <PubkeyHash> OP_EQUALVERIFY OP_CHECKSIG
```

The meaning of these opcodes is

- **OP_DUP** – This pushes onto the execution stack a copy of the data currently on top of it. The hex code is "0x76."

- **OP_HASH160** – This pushes onto the execution stack a hash of the data currently on top of it. The hex code is "0xa9."

- **OP_EQUALVERIFY** – This checks the two values on top of the stack are the same. This returns a true or false. If they are different, the program terminates, else it continues. The hex code is "0x88."

- **OP_CHECKSIG** – This takes in the two values on top of the stack, that is, the digital signature and the public key, and checks if the signature matches the public key and was generated using all the data required to be signed. It returns true or false. The hex value is "0xac."

The value of scriptPubKey in a transaction is simply the hexadecimal value for the opcodes and the public key hash arranged in the form of P2PK script. Figure 7-1 shows the representation of the scriptpubkey for the transaction created in Listing 7-1 in the form of opcodes and pubkeyhash. The public key hash is the bitcoin *address* of the recipient. In Listing 7-1 it's the address of Peter, to whom John wants to transfer the bitcoins.

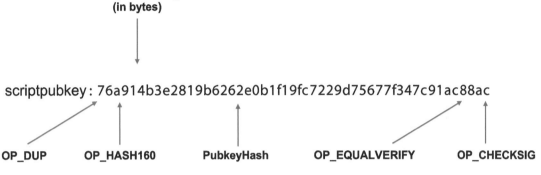

Figure 7-7. *Representing scriptpubkey in a transaction into opcodes and public key hash*

Prepare Transaction for Hashing

This is again a series of steps, and the resultant transaction looks like the one shown in Listing 7-2:

1. **Add the value of scriptSig:**

   This is added from the previous transaction that has the UTXO which is now used as the input into this transaction. This would be the scriptPubKey from the transaction made by Olivia where she put a specific scriptPubKey for the UTXO meant for John. The crypto wallet does this automatically with the help of transaction chaining.

2. **Add the value of scriptSigSize:**

   This is the size of the scriptSig.

3. **Add sighash field:**

It is a field called sighash to the transaction, which has predefined values, which one can choose to sign some combination of inputs and outputs. The value of "01" means to sign all inputs and outputs in the transaction.

Listing 7-2. Updated transaction with script signature and signature hash for unlocking

```
version: 01000000
inputs:   01
  txid: b7994a0db2f373a29227e1d90da883c6ce1cb0dd2d6812e4558041ebbbcfa54b
  vout: 00000000
  scriptsigsize: 19
  scriptsig: 76a9144299ff317fcd12ef19047df66d72454691797bfc88ac
  sequence: ffffffff
outputs: 01
  amount: 983a000000000000
  scriptpubkeysize: 19
  scriptpubkey: 76a914b3e2819b6262e0b1f19fc7229d75677f347c91ac88ac
locktime: 00000000
sighash: 01000000
```

Create and Encode Signature

There are a series of steps to create the signature for the transaction that needs to be replaced with the one we created earlier before broadcasting. The encoded signature will look like the one shown in Listing 7-3.

1. **Serialize raw transaction**

   The raw transaction created above is serialized, into a bitcoin prescribed format. Serialization[10] is the process of converting an object into a stream of bytes to store the object or transmit it over the network. The serialized form of the transaction looks like the following:

   ```
   0100000001b7994a0db2f373a29227e1d90da883c6ce1cb0
   dd2d6812e4558041ebbbcfa54b000000001976a9144299ff
   317fcd12ef19047df66d72454691797bfc88acffffffff01
   983a0000000000001976a914b3e2819b6262e0b1f19fc722
   9d75677f347c91ac88ac0000000001000000
   ```

2. **Double hash serialized transaction**

   This is where the above serialized transaction is hashed twice using SHA256. The resultant looks something like the following:
   a6b4103f527dfe43dfbadf530c247bac8a98b7463c7c6a
   d38eed97021d18ffcb

3. **Convert hash from HexDec to decimal**

   The resultant looks like the following:
   75402077471587956851360588120356244127735644
   00694297387734091081473079384 4683

4. **Sign the decimal hash**

   The same ECDSA algorithm is used to sign the hash, which we used to generate the private and public key pairs. The inputs to create the signature are a random number, message hash, and private key. Let's say the signature looks like the following:

   {40512939985856747849916395927822149728201583913 7178
   59810043523594654503 69227, 141359899688364205157 0982
   977181162886577595316379656285109228783923022274 4152}

---

[10] https://docs.microsoft.com/en-us/dotnet/csharp/programming-guide/concepts/
serialization/

5. **Encode the signature in DER format**

The signature is encoded in the DER format, and the sighash created earlier is added.

Listing 7-3. Encoded signature in DER format

```
type: 30
  length: 44
  type:    02
    length: 20
    r:       08f4f37e2d8f74e18c1b8fde2374d5f28402fb8ab7fd1cc5b786aa40851
             a70cb
  type:    02
    length: 20
    s:       1f40afd1627798ee8529095ca4b205498032315240ac322c9d8ff0f205
             a93a58
sighash: 01
```

6. **Serialize the encoded signature**

This converts the signature into a byte stream as follows:

```
3044022008f4f37e2d8f74e18c1b8fde2374d5f28402fb8ab7f
d1cc5b786aa40851a70cb02201f40afd1627798ee8529095ca4
b205498032315240ac322c9d8ff0f205a93a5801
```

Sign Transaction

The following is done to create the transaction that is ready to be sent to be broadcasted to the bitcoin network:

1. **Create scriptSig**

Scriptsig is just <sign><publickey> put together. The length of these values is added before each of the values to turn it into assembly <sign length><sign><public key length><public key>. Since both the serialized encoded signature and the public key are known, the signature for the transaction – the value of scriptSig – becomes

```
473044022008f4f37e2d8f74e18c1b8fde2374d5f28402fb8ab7fd1
cc5b786aa40851a70cb02201f40afd1627798ee8529095ca4b20549
8032315240ac322c9d8ff0f205a93a580121024aeaf55040fa16de3
7303d13ca1dde85f4ca9baa36e2963a27a1c0c1165fe2b1
```

2. **Update scriptSig in transaction**

   This is where the scriptSig created above is updated as the value
   in the transaction and sighash field removed. The scriptsigsize
   value is updated to reflect the size (in bytes) of scriptSig as seen in
   Listing 7-4.

Listing 7-4. Transaction with the updated signature

```
version: 01000000
inputs:  01
  txid: b7994a0db2f373a29227e1d90da883c6ce1cb0dd2d6812e4558041ebbbcfa54b
  vout: 00000000
  scriptsigsize: 6a
  scriptsig: 473044022008f4f37e2d8f74e18c1b8fde2374d5f28402fb8ab7fd1cc5b78
             6aa40851a70cb02201f40afd1627798ee8529095ca4b205498032315240ac
             322c9d8ff0f205a93a580121024aeaf55040fa16de37303d13ca1dde85f4c
             a9baa36e2963a27a1c0c1165fe2b1
  sequence: ffffffff
outputs: 01
  amount: 983a000000000000
  scriptpubkeysize: 19
  scriptpubkey: 76a914b3e2819b6262e0b1f19fc7229d75677f347c91ac88ac
locktime: 00000000
```

3. **Serialize the transaction**

   This is where all the values of the fields in the transaction are put
   together to form the serialized transaction. The version is what
   tells the structure of the transaction and the size of fields, etc., to
   the peers and nodes in the bitcoin network.

0100000001b7994a0db2f373a29227e1d90da883c6ce1cb0dd2d6812e4558041eb
bbcfa54b000000006a473044022008f4f37e2d8f74e18c1b8fde2374d5f28402fb
8ab7fd1cc5b786aa40851a70cb02201f40afd1627798ee8529095ca4b205498032
315240ac32c9d8ff0f205a93a580121024aeaf55040fa16de37303d13ca1dde85f
4ca9baa36e2963a27a1c0c1165fe2b1ffffffff01983a0000000000001976a914b
3e2819b6262e0bf19fc7229d5677f347c91ac88ac00000000

Transaction Broadcasting

John's crypto wallet has created and signed the transaction, and it is ready to be broadcasted to the Bitcoin network for validation and processing. Since the wallet is not yet part of the Bitcoin network, it needs to connect to it. The wallet does the following to join the Bitcoin network and then broadcasts the signed transaction for further processing:

1. Hit the domain name servers (DNS) hardcoded in the Bitcoin core code called seeds[11]. These seeds are maintained by Bitcoin community members. This is like how our browser hits the DNS when we need to reach a website whose IP address isn't known to the browser.

2. The seeds give the wallet the IP address of the nodes that may accept incoming connections, i.e., allow the wallet node to join them.

3. The wallet node makes connections to some of these nodes. The wallet node is now a node connected to the bitcoin network.

4. The wallet node broadcasts the transaction created earlier to the nodes it's connected to. These nodes validate the transaction (more on this later) and further broadcast the transaction to their connected nodes, and so on. This method of broadcasting is called *flooding*.

---

[11] https://developer.bitcoin.org/devguide/p2p_network.html

Authorization

Once the network has the transaction broadcasted by John's wallet, the next part in the journey of this transaction is authorization, which is how does the bitcoin network authorize John to spend the bitcoins mentioned in the inputs of the transaction, so that he can send them to Peter.

Transaction Validation

The validation step takes place right when the node receives a broadcasted transaction. Just like how a bank validates a check for correctness such as it has the details filled in the right fields, the signature of the payee is correct, the amount in the check is available in the bank account, etc., the node also validates the transaction against a set of rules, for example, transaction contains the right format, it has at least one input and output, the total amount in the output is more than the total amount in the UTXO in the inputs, etc. However, the key validation is that the one who asked for confirming this transaction (in our example John):

- Is indeed the one who created this transaction

- Can prove that he has the right to spend the bitcoins in the inputs

Nodes solve for both things by executing the scriptSign (unlocking script) present in each of the inputs of the transaction being validated and the scriptPubKey (locking script) for each of the UTXO of the inputs in order. As you may remember, the scriptPubkey is not taken from the output of the transaction being validated; it is taken from the previous transaction that generated the UTXO (output) that the current transaction is using as input.

In simple words, if John wants to spend the bitcoins sent to an output address by Olivia, he must prove that he is the owner of that address, and for that he must satisfy the conditions present in the scriptPubKey of the transaction signed by Olivia by presenting his signature and public key, which are present in scriptSign of the transaction to be validated. The following are the data and opcodes of the script executed by the node. Parts highlighted in yellow are the scriptSign (unlocking script), and the nonhighlighted part is the scriptPubKey (locking script). The order of execution is shown in Figure 7-8.

`<Sig> <PubKey>` `OP_DUP OP_HASH160 <PubkeyHash> OP_EQUALVERIFY OP_CHECKSIG`

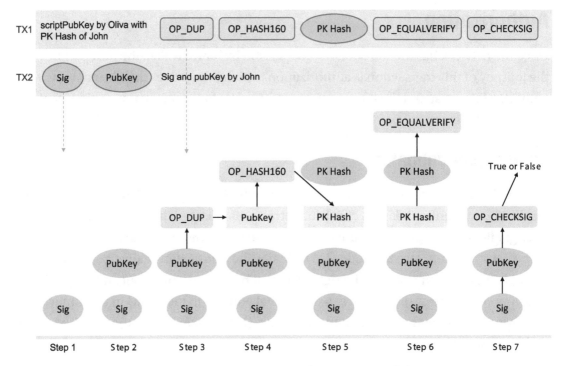

Figure 7-8. *Validation of transaction through execution of the script. Source: Bitcoin developer guide*

If the script's output is "True" (a nonzero integer value), the transaction is valid, and the node adds it to a pool of transactions called "mempool" or "memory pool." If the script's output is "False" (zero is the output), the transaction is discarded and not broadcasted further by the node. All transactions in the memory pool are valid but unconfirmed.

Mining

Even if a transaction is valid, it is not confirmed right away. The primary reason is to prevent double spending. Double spending is when someone tries to spend the same bitcoins in two or more transactions at the same time. Say John sends 75 bitcoins to Peter and 75 bitcoins to Olivia from the same input address (UTXO) in two separate transactions broadcasted at the same time. The input address only has 100 bitcoins, and he shouldn't be able to spend more than what he has in an address (UTXO), but there is nothing stopping him from doing that. Once broadcasted and received by the nodes, both these transactions will turn out as valid transactions as they will return "True" when the combination of unlocking script and locking script will be executed by the node. To prevent double spending, mining is done. Bitcoin network is composed of two types of nodes:

- **Full nodes** – These nodes are powerful dedicated machines that store locally the whole blockchain (ledger) with all the transactions. As of June 2022, the blockchain is a little over 400 Gb[12]. Their main function is to autonomously verify the state of the blockchain, by downloading every block and checking them against Bitcoin's consensus rules. It removes any transaction or block that violates any rules.

- **Lightweight nodes** – These nodes run on machines with low resources such as smartphones, tablets, etc. and are mostly used as crypto wallets. They don't hold the whole blockchain ledger but only a small part of the blocks and can verify transactions, however, may need to fetch data from a peer full node.

Mining can be done by either full node or lightweight node. However, if it's a lightweight node, it is connected to a full node to quickly get the validated transactions from its memory pool as only full nodes can validate transactions. To confirm a transaction, the transaction needs to be a part of a valid block that is the part of the blockchain. This process of confirming a transaction is done by miners and is called mining. Let's get into some details of it.

Miners pull in valid transactions from the memory pool, and aggregate them into a *candidate block*, while at the same time it also keeps receiving, validating, and saving new transactions broadcasted to it into its memory pool. The block size is fixed at 1 MB, so sometimes miners can't fit all the transactions from the memory poll in the block. In those cases, miners prioritize transactions with the higher fees to be added to the block. Over the last one year, the average number of transactions per block has been around 1,800[13].

---

[12] www.blockchain.com/charts/blocks-size
[13] www.blockchain.com/charts/n-transactions-per-block

Note   Only if the candidate block is proved valid and accepted by the majority of the bitcoin network, it is added as a part of the blockchain. A block is mined by the nodes on an average every 10 minutes.

Coinbase Transaction

Along with the transactions from the memory pool, the miner adds a special kind of transaction as the first transaction in the block called *Coinbase transaction*. Coinbase transaction contains the number of bitcoins that the miner will get if the block is added to the blockchain. The amount comes from two means, the first is the fees of each transaction in the block, and the second is called block reward, which is the amount of bitcoin awarded to the miner for the work done to confirm the transactions.

The block reward started at 50 bitcoins for the first valid block added to the blockchain and is halved every 210,000 blockers (which is every 4 years). At present each miner earns 6.25 bitcoins per block, and this will reduce to zero rewards by the year 2130 with the total supply of 21 million bitcoins. Since miners mint (crypto) money through these Coinbase transactions – if they are able to add a valid block to the blockchain – this process is called mining.

The most interesting role of Coinbase transactions is the generation of new bitcoins in the blockchain, as it doesn't have any inputs and only has the outputs with the address of the miner to collect block reward. Block reward is the only way new bitcoins are generated in the blockchain.

Block

A block is composed of valid transactions pulled from the memory pool and a block header. The first block in the blockchain is called the genesis block. The genesis block of Bitcoin was mined by Satoshi in 2009. The block header[14] contains metadata and summary of the block. Its key constituents are

- **Version** – The version of the block structure.

- **Previous block hash** – Reference to the hash of the previous block in the blockchain.

---

[14] www.datadriveninvestor.com/2019/11/21/a-decomposition-of-the-bitcoin-block-header/

- **Merkle root** – Hash of the root of the Merkle tree of the transactions in this block.

- **Timestamp** – Datetime of when the miner started the mining of the block.

- **Difficulty** – It's a measure of the effort the miner had to put to mine the block.

- **Nonce** – Short for number once, is a number used in the algorithm to validate the block.

Merkle Tree

The Merkle tree is a binary hash tree and used in Bitcoin and other cryptocurrencies to secure and validate the data in a block. The leaf nodes of the tree are labeled with the hash of the transactions in the block, and the parent nodes are created by hashing the concatenated hash string of their children. This hashing continues for the parent's parents, until a single parent is left which is tree root, also called *Merkle root*, which is a constituent of the block headers.

Note   All hashes in Bitcoin are a double hash of the data with the SHA256 algorithm.

Hash = SHA256(SHA256(data))

The Merkle root can be used to identify if the data in the block has been tampered with, by allowing anyone to recompute the Merkle root from the transaction data in the block and matching it with the Merkle root in the header of that block taken from a trusted source in the network. You may wonder that could have also been done by taking the hash of all the transactions in a batch, why go in pairs and make a tree. The main benefit of creating the Merkle tree is that it becomes very efficient to verify that a transaction is a part of the block by just the information in the block headers, i.e., without the need to download all the block transactions. This is very helpful for lightweight nodes that don't have resources to download the whole blocks, and only download the block headers of the block chain.

If any node (say a lightweight node) wants to verify if a transaction is a part of the valid block, all it must do is fetch the *authentication path* of the transaction to the root of the tree and be able to compute the hashes to derive the Merkle root and then match it with the Merkle root present in the block header. The size of the authentication path is significantly smaller than the actual transaction data or the hashes of the transaction data, which makes this a very efficient way to summarize and verify transactions for blockchains.

To understand this, let's take Figure 7-9 which shows a bitcoin block. Let's say the transaction of John sending bitcoins to Peter is TX3 and Peter wants to check through his wallet (light node) if this is a part of the valid block. Peter's wallet only has the block header which has the Merkle root and the transaction Id, which is the hash of the transaction which is "H3" in the figure. Now, all Peter's wallet has to do is ask the full node for the authentication path of H3 to the root of the tree. This request will be returned H4 and H12 by the full node. So, now Peter's wallet has H3, H4, H12, and Merkle root. The following is what will be next by the wallet node for verification:

1. Compute the hash of H3 + H4, to get hash 34. "+" sign here refers to concatenation of strings of the hashes H3 and H4.

2. Compute the hash of H34 and H12, to get hash 1234.

3. If hash 1234 is the same as the Merkle root, H3 part of the block else not.

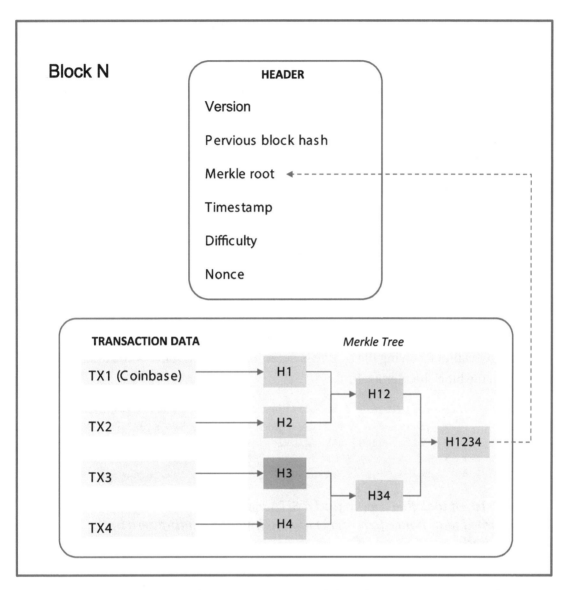

Figure 7-9. *Composition of a bitcoin block with header, transactions, and Merkel tree*

As you may realize this is a very efficient[15] way for finding if a transaction is a part of the block. Instead of downloading the whole transaction data containing thousands of transactions from the block, which will take time and put strain on the limited resources

---

[15] https://brilliant.org/wiki/merkle-tree/

of the lightweight node, the lightweight node can identify if the transaction of interest was part of the block by just requesting a few hashes which form the authenticated path. To give you a reference on how efficient this is, to verify a transaction in a block containing 1,000 transactions, the verifying node needs less than 10 hashes as a part of the authentication path for verification.

Proof of Work

The miner can only get the standard block reward and the transaction fees if he can show proof of work. *Proof of work* (PoW) is a simple task but computationally very heavy on the node as is also called the *mining puzzle*. If you didn't notice already, miner has value for everything in the block header but the nonce. The puzzle is to find a number that when put as a nonce value in the block header makes the hash of the block header with the leading number of zeros to solve the puzzle. We can see in Figure 7-10 that nonce value of "5" results in a hash with one leading zero for the string "I <3 Seattle". The leading number of zeros required in the hash of the block header for the miner to be able to have claimed solving the puzzle is determined by the value of the difficulty field present in the block header itself:

```
I <3 Seattle0 -> 9c09e87a5b28704ec5ad074e45794012ff7610b6eaba9814e469da289764933b
I <3 Seattle1 -> 673979cdd56f9818c6158038356b672e030bc55e47c102c8c49505570faafc82
I <3 Seattle2 -> 46e1fd790cee246eb5c27b12c14e786f6e7808037fc3f8ea62f5579bd151e7d4
I <3 Seattle3 -> b0888938d9a2465b9bd9459a73e6bf1170f3432d79d6af7cf0ca69027e4d1cae
I <3 Seattle4 -> 08b40519f40c2733434ad9fb177968fb965ba61aa42e1c443e0e484e7c2abbf3
```

Figure 7-10. *It took five tries to find a SHA256 hash of the string "I <3 Seattle" concatenated with nonce (counter) value to find one leading zero in the resulting hash*

Mining difficulty isn't a fixed value and keeps getting adjusted based on the simple ratio of the time it took to add the last 2,016 blocks to the blockchain, and the time it should take 2,016 blocks to be added to the blockchain. The number of leading zeros in the hash of the block header is increased if this ratio is less than 1 and decreased if the ratio is greater than 1. Since the Bitcoin blockchain expects each block to take 10 mins to be accepted in the blockchain, 2016 blocks should take 20,160 minutes or 14 days. So, the difficulty is adjusted automatically by the blockchain every 2 weeks. If more computational power has been added to the blockchain, say more miners are added or miners have upgraded their nodes with more processing power and are able to find nonces to solve the puzzles faster than 10 mins, the difficulty is increased to maintain the average of 10 mins per block. It is also reduced if the computational power reduces, simply by increasing or decreasing the leading zeros based on the ratio.

```
Hash: 08b40519f40c2733434ad9fb177968fb965ba61aa42e1c443e0e484e7c2abbf3  Nonce: 4
Hash: 0073c86031b349696b47c48e9bbbbaa62acae3e75c44aeb8447b0aaa66b85f69  Nonce: 324
Hash: 0006df0a1da1ca938468c7885b9ab40b5aee31c59552a74946ff2401e4064492  Nonce: 8163
Hash: 00006a9d1846a1c88771c1d052d387169cbbd9d39776efac0c03478bffad4729  Nonce: 27485
Hash: 00000256c906b6733c10c055d1d30b9badbb366fb8c406d9a6daead24a9a5ecf  Nonce: 1513830
```

Figure 7-11. *Nonce values to get the hashes with 1–5 leading zeros*

Figure 7-11 illustrates how nonce value increases as we try to find the hash of the string "I <3 Seattle" with 1 leading zero all the way up to 5 leading zeros, indicating more attempts required by miners to find the solution to the puzzle (PoW) as the number of zeros (difficulty) increases. If you are interested in how we computed the hashes of the string "I <3 Seattle" with various values of nonces for the various requirements for leading zero, you may refer to the Python code in Listing 7-5.

Note   Bitcoin isn't the only cryptocurrency that uses proof-of-work (PoW) consensus; many other cryptocurrencies such as Litecoin, Ethereum, and Dogecoin also use PoW.

Listing 7-5. Python script that finds the nonce that meets the trailing number of zeros for the hash

```python
import hashlib
import re

blockHeader = "I <3 Seattle" # blockheader content

# First 5 hashes created by incrementing nonce value
# Hash with nonce 4 has one leading zero
for nonce in range(5):
    trans = blockHeader + str(nonce)
    result = str(hashlib.sha256(trans.encode()).hexdigest())
    print(trans, "->", result )

print("\n")
```

```python
# Creating a function to find the hash with a given number of leading zeros
def findNonce(blockHeader, zeros):
    """ Function to find the hash for a blockheader with the defined
        leading number of zeros.

    Parameters
    ----------
    blockheader: str
        The string representation of a blockheader
    zeros: str
        The leading zeros required in the hash
    """

    nonce = 0
    while True:
        nonce  = str(nonce)

        # adding the nonce to the blockheader
        trans  = blockHeader + nonce

        # Encoding transaction into bytes and then taking a hash, then
        # turning it into hexadecimal value, and finally into a string
        result = str(hashlib.sha256(trans.encode()).hexdigest())

        # Finding if the hash contains the required leading zeros
        if re.match(zeros, result) is not None:
            print("Hash: " + result + "  Nonce: " + nonce)
            break
        nonce = int(nonce) + 1

# Finding the nonce that meets the trailing zeros with increasing
difficulty
zero_array  = ["0", "00", "000", "0000", "00000"] # array of strings of
leading zeros

for difficulty in zero_array:
    findNonce(blockHeader, difficulty)
```

Consensus

As soon as a miner has the proof of work which is this block header that has the leading zeros equal to the difficulty set by the network, the miner broadcasts this new minted block in the network. The other miners verify this by computing themselves the hash of this newly minted block's header and comparing it with the leading zeros. If 51% or more of the miners reach the consensus that the block solves the puzzle, then the block is added to the blockchain, and the height of the blockchain is increased by 1. All other miners then stop finding the solution to their block as a winner has already been identified and move all the transactions from the block back to their memory pool. Then, they remove all the transactions from the memory pool that are present in the newly minted block, and from the other remaining transactions, including the ones they received in the last 10 minutes, then create the next candidate block and start competing again among one another to find the proof of work the fastest.

Since the speed of finding the solution to this puzzle is so important to get rewards, miners initially started with using CPU for computation, but when that started to become slow, they moved to graphical processing units (GPUs) as they could do multiple computations in parallel with GPUs and increase their chances to win, which shot up the stock price of GPU manufacturing companies like Nvidia and AMD, however, even that is turning out to be slow and nowadays the miners use application-specific integrated circuits (ASIC), which are custom built for mining to increase their odds. Also, more and more miners are joining mining pools, where they pool their mining compute resources increasing their chances of winning. They later distribute the bitcoin rewards among themselves in the same ratio they added the computational power.

The miner who minted this new block is awarded the bitcoins from the block reward and the transaction fees as specified in the Coinbase transaction. All other transactions in the transaction data are marked confirmed from just being valid earlier – this means that all these transactions are now authorized. It's important to understand that when we say the block is added to the blockchain, we simply mean that the block is now considered valid. Since the blocks have the timestamp, we can find the most recent block and find the previous block to it, from the hash of the previous block stored in the block's header, and we can continue doing that until we reach the first block of the blockchain, i.e., the genesis block. This linking of blocks to one another through the presence of previous block hash results in virtual chaining of the blocks and hence the name *blockchain*.

With respect to our example, this is when Peter receives the bitcoins sent to his address by John in TX3. However, what about double spending, how is that prevented? The set of all existing UXTOs at a given point in time is called the UTXO set[16]. The sum of the number of bitcoins on these UXTOs is the total supply of Bitcoin at that point in time. Bitcoin nodes keep track of the UTXO set to determine how much cryptocurrency exists. When a new block is added to the blockchain, the UTXO set is updated, as some UTXOs are created, and some spent based on the transactions in that block. Since blocks are timestamped, and chained to the previous blocks, only the first confirmed transaction on an UTXO is allowed. All other transactions that try to use the same UTXOs are automatically rejected as the UXTOs are marked spent in the earlier transaction and not available anymore in the UTXO set. All nodes have an identical copy of the UTXO set. Hence, Olivia will never receive the 75 bitcoins as that transaction will be rejected.

Caution   Proof of work (PoW) isn't the only consensus algorithm. There are multiple others like proof of stake (PoS), proof of burn, proof of capacity, etc. Ethereum is planning to switch from PoW to PoS by the end of 2022.

Blockchain Forks

A blockchain isn't always a single series of connected blocks; sometimes a blockchain splits into branches, called *forks*, which could be accidental or intentional. Figure 7-12 shows the different kinds of forks which we will learn of in the next sections.

---

[16] https://river.com/learn/terms/u/utxo-set/

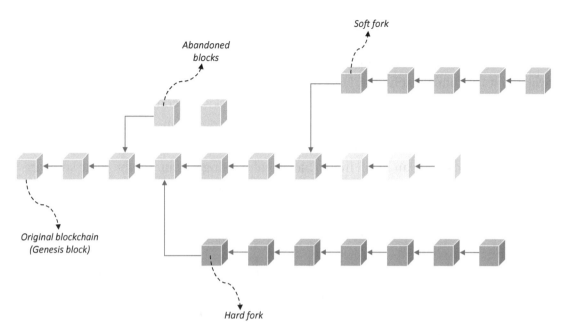

Figure 7-12. *Hard fork creates a new blockchain not compatible with original blockchain, soft fork updates the original blockchain with new forward compatible rules, and accidental chains are abandoned automatically in favor of the longest chain*

Accidental Forks

Accidental forks are created when two or more mining nodes mine a new block at the same time. This is automatically resolved as overtime new blocks from miners are added to one of the chains and the shorter chain is abandoned as the chain with more blocks has more proof of work added to it and hence is more trustworthy. The abandoned blocks are called orphaned blocks.

Intentional Forks

Intentional forks are created to add or change existing functionality to the software protocol of the blockchain. They are of two types, namely, hard forks and soft forks.

Hard Fork

Let's say the developers want to increase the block size from 1 MB to 4 MB, so they will update the bitcoin software. Only the nodes that upgrade their software to the one that can manage 4 MB blocks, so this change is not backward compatible and hence is called a hard fork. When a hard fork occurs, the community members (owners of nodes) decide if they want to update their node and switch to the fork or continue with the old software – this can result in two blockchains using variants of the same software. When a hard fork happens, all the transaction history and addresses are copied to the new blockchain. This means that owners of cryptocurrency or the NFTs on the main blockchain automatically get the equivalent of these cryptocurrency and the same NFTs on the new blockchain.

Hard forks are more common than you may think; Bitcoin Cash is a hard fork of Bitcoin and had a block size of 8 MB when it forked and now has a block size of 32 MB which allows for more transactions to be confirmed. It forked from Bitcoin in August 2017, when all nodes that updated to Bitcoin cash started rejecting bitcoin transactions and blocks. For another popular blockchain called Ethereum (we will learn more it shortly), hackers stole $50 million[17] worth of the Ether (ETH) cryptocurrency that runs on its network. To reverse the hack, the developers forked the blockchain, and most of the nodes voted to join it, so the forked chain started to be called Ethereum. The nodes that choose not to upgrade their software still run the original Ethereum which is now called Ethereum classic.

Soft Fork

Soft forks are when there is forward compatibility, which means that blocks created by the new software are also valid under the old rules of the old software. This means that the nodes on the old blockchain will continue to accept blocks from the nodes running the forked version of the software, as well as participate in the upgraded fork for validating transactions.

An example of soft fork is the segregated witness (SegWit) update in the Bitcoin protocol in 2015. This allowed nodes to be able to accept both 4MB[18] blocks along with the 1MB block, reducing the fees of transactions.

---

[17] www.sofi.com/learn/content/ethereum-classic-etc-vs-eth/

[18] https://freemanlaw.com/hard-and-soft-forks-a-detailed-and-simplified-explanation-of-how-blockchains-evolve/

Blockchain Explorers

Blockchain explorers are online tools that enable anyone to get real-time and historical information about a particular blockchain, such as data related to blocks, transactions, addresses, etc. These days websites host explorers of multiple blockchain to provide a single platform for users to track and monitor all things cryptocurrency. Individuals and businesses can check transactions they have interest in, and miners can check if they have successfully mined a block.

An activity a lot of people do is to monitor any activity of whales. A crypto whale[19] is a high-net-worth individual (HNWI) – or organization – that holds a large amount of a specific cryptocurrency. While there is no exact monetary threshold, a whale's asset holdings (when converted to USD) typically exceed $10,000,000. The number of coins (or tokens) necessary to be considered a whale varies by project. For example (in 2021 prices), an Ethereum whale might have over 10,000 ether (ETH), and a Bitcoin whale might have more than 1,000 bitcoins (BTC). Notable Bitcoin whales include Satoshi Nakamoto, Tim Draper, Barry Silbert, and the Winklevoss twins.

If you are interested in cryptocurrency, I would encourage you to go to a blockchain explorer and see how the transactions, blocks, signatures, fees, etc. look like. You can start with some popular blockchain explorers like blockstream.info and blockchain.com/explorer. Figure 7-13 shows the value of bitcoins on an address in USD.

---

[19] www.gemini.com/cryptopedia/glossary#whale

Address ⓘ

This address has transacted 420 times on the Bitcoin blockchain. It has received a total of 79,957.21806726 BTC ($1,699,908,046.70) and has sent a total of 0.00000000 BTC ($0.00). The current value of this address is 79,957.21806726 BTC ($1,699,908,046.70).

Address	1FeexV6bAHb8ybZjqQMjJrcCrHGW9sb6uF 📋
Format	BASE58 (P2PKH)
Transactions	420
Total Received	$1,699,908,046.70
Total Sent	$0.00
Final Balance	$1,699,908,046.70

Figure 7-13. *A bitcoin address having $1.7 billion USD worth of bitcoins (80K BTC)*

Smart Contracts

We already saw that for anyone to spend bitcoins, the condition in the scriptPubKey of the input UTXO transaction needs to be met – this essentially is a contract, which defines who can spend the money. But there are other forms of contracts that one may need; let's say John wants to buy an expensive cuckoo clock in bitcoins from this person named Paul who lives in Germany. Paul will ship the clock to John in the United States. John doesn't want to pay Paul upfront as he is worried what if Paul takes the money and never ships the clock. Paul doesn't want to ship the clock without payment as he is worried what if John never pays once he receives the clock. To handle these situations, there are escrows in the real world. Bitcoin provides this kind of capability through multisig (multiple signature) contracts, which simply is to add another person, say Eva, as an arbitrator into this transaction who both John and Paul trust. The contract with multisig can be defined with a condition that two of the three people need to sign it for Paul to receive the money. This solves the issue now:

- John creates a multisig transaction using his, Paul's, and Eva's public key that needs two of the three signs to transfer the money to Paul.

- Paul sends the clock to John, and then upon receiving the clock, both John and Paul sign and Paul gets the money. If John cheats and doesn't send the bitcoins, Eva who knows that John has received the clock can sign along with Paul to get the bitcoins from John to Paul.

- If the clock is never received (say Paul only claims to have shipped the clock), then Eva and John wouldn't sign, and Paul will never receive the bitcoins from John.

This seems foolproof, but what if Paul gives Eva some money to sign and gets the money without sending the clock to John? So, there is still a problem. How can we solve this?

You may know already that Bitcoin isn't the only cryptocurrency or the blockchain; there are numerous cryptocurrencies such as Ether, Shiba Inu coin, etc. and blockchains such as Ethereum, Solana, Hyperledger, etc.; however, the most popular blockchain among developers is Ethereum. Ethereum is a decentralized, open source blockchain with Ether (ETH) as its native cryptocurrency. It was conceived in 2013 by Vitalik Buterin and has the following three big benefits over Bitcoin blockchain:

1. **Smart contracts** – Ethereum has support for sophisticated contracts. We will discuss its various applications throughout the remaining part of this chapter.

2. **NFT** – Ethereum can not only have fungible tokens but also nonfungible tokens. We will discuss this more in detail.

3. **Speed** – Ethereum takes less than 20 seconds to create a block vs. 10 mins taken by Bitcoin. Ethereum can handle 30[20] transactions per second (TPS) vs. less than 10 TPS of Bitcoin.

Coming back to the problem of John and Paul, what if John can write a contract in the transaction where only if the delivery status of the package from the FedEx API shows "Delivered" can Paul unlock the transaction to spend it? This is a smart contract which is completely programmatic and doesn't need Eva.

---

[20] https://cointelegraph.com/ethereum-for-beginners/bitcoin-vs-ethereum-key-differences-between-btc-and-eth

Unlike Bitcoin whose programming language "script" is turning incomplete, Ethereum commonly uses a high-level programming language called "Solidity" that is Turing complete, which means it can do any computation. Smart contracts are written in Solidity and are like classes in an object-oriented programming language (as Java) consisting of variables to store the state of the contract, functions to retrieve and update the state, errors to define failure situations, etc. The contracts are then compiled into a bytecode (assembly level like how we saw in Bitcoin) and application binary interface (ABI) – these are used to interface with the contract. The bytecode is then deployed on an address in the blockchain. Finally, it is executed in the Ethereum stack (like Bitcoin's) called Ethereum virtual machine (EVM) which is present in the nodes of the Ethereum blockchain. Figure 7-14 shows how a smart contract is deployed on the blockchain.

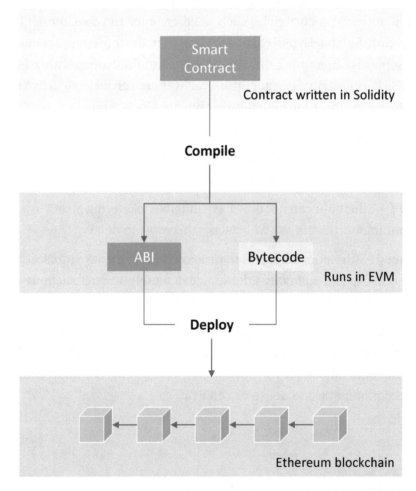

Figure 7-14. *Contracts get compiled first and the output of it is deployed on the blockchain*

The state of the smart contract (values in the variables) is updated through transactions, which are recorded in the blocks on the blockchain by miners. In simple words, to execute the functions listed in the smart contract program, transactions are created which are validated and recorded in the blocks on the blockchain through the process of mining, like Bitcoin's which you already now know in detail.

Ethereum has two types of accounts, i.e., entities that have some ether balance and can send transactions on the Ethereum blockchain. The first type is called Externally Owned Accounts (EOAs), which are derived from a private key (just like Bitcoin's address) and can generate transactions. The second type are for (smart) contracts, called contract accounts, which store and execute code when prompted by a transaction from an EOA. There are three[21] different types of transactions between these accounts, and mining of each transaction costs transaction fees in Ethers, called gas fees. The three transaction types are

1. An EOA sending Ether to another EOA (just like all Bitcoin's transactions). Figure 7-15 illustrates this type of transaction.

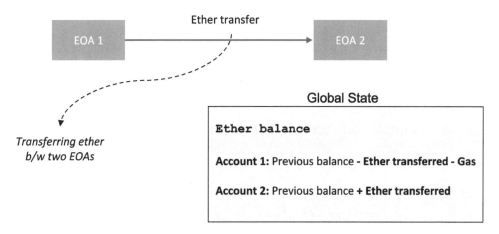

Figure 7-15. *Transfer of ether between two EOAs where the global state of Ethereum is updated*

2. An EOA creating (deploying) a contract. The *To* field here in the transaction contains the address of the contract created.

---

[21] https://docs.ethhub.io/guides/deciphering-a-transaction-on-etherscan/

3. An EOA sending a transaction to a contract. The *To* field here in the transaction contains the address of the contract invoked. Figure 7-16 illustrates this type of transaction.

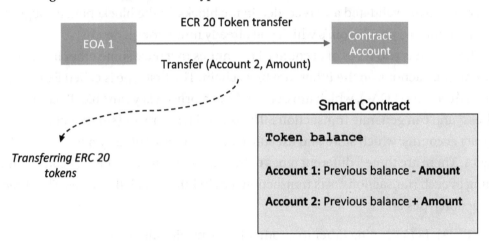

Figure 7-16. *Transfer of ERC-20 tokens where the balance in the smart contract is updated*

You can see in Listing 7-6 a sample (smart) contract written in Solidity. This contract when deployed on the blockchain initiates with the value of "Hello World" for the state of the greeting.

Listing 7-6. A sample contract written in solidity

```
pragma solidity ^0.4.0;

contract HelloWorld {
    string public greeting; // state variable

    // Executed upon contract's creation to initialize contract's data
    constructor() public {
        greeting = "Hello World";
    }

    // Get Function to retrieve value of greeting
    function read_greeting() public view returns(string) {
        return greeting;
    }
```

```
    // Set Function to update value of greeting
    function update_greeting(string value) public {
        greeting = value;
    }
}
```

Ethereum Token Standards

One of the most widespread uses of smart contracts today on the Ethereum blockchain is to create tokens. To understand what a token is, let's recap what a cryptocurrency is – a cryptocurrency coin is a native digital asset used for exchange of goods and services on a blockchain, such as BTC for Bitcoin and ETH (ether) for Ethereum. A token doesn't have its own blockchain and therefore uses an existing blockchain. A token is created through a smart contract and may be used for payments (like cryptocurrency) or something else like the NFTs, stable coins, security tokens, etc.

Stable coins   These are tokens like cryptocurrencies but have a one-to-one mapping to the traditional currency (called fiat currency) such as USD or Euro. Tether is a popular stable coin with 1 Tether (USDT) = 1 USD.

Ethereum has multiple token standards that define the smart contract's code operations and how the code works. Let's learn more of its two most popular standards.

ERC-20

This standard is used for the development of tokens that are fungible in nature and used mostly for payments like native cryptocurrencies as they have value. Fungible tokens are nonunique and can be divided. For instance, just like a $5 bill with John as the same value as the five $1 bills with Peter and they can exchange their bills and still have the same value of the money, similarly ERC-20 tokens as well as cryptocurrencies are fungible; 10 BTC with John is equal to 10 BTC with Peter. Shiba Inu (SHIB), Tether (USDT), and Chainlink (LINK) are some popular ERC-20 tokens.

We wouldn't go into the details of the smart contract of ERC-20 as it will be outside the scope of this book, but let's cover the ERC-20[22] smart contract in brief:

- **Balances** – This is a state variable and is the main part of the ERC-20 token. It has a maplike data structure that stores who has how many units of the token. For example, if John has 10 units of an ERC-20 token and Olivia 5 units, this variable will have a value of 10 against John's address (on the blockchain) and 5 against Olivia's.

- **Transfer** – This is a function that allows sending the units of the token from one address to another by updating the values in the balances variable. For example, if Olivia executes the function transfer (John's public address, 2), it will send 2 units from Oliva to John, and now the balances will show Oliva with 3 units and John with 12 units of the token.

- **transferFrom** – This function allows a third-party address to send the units on behalf of another address, say John wants Peter to send 2 units of the token to Olivia on behalf of him. To do this John will first execute another function approve(Peter's address, 2) which will update the allowed variable with information an address has been authorized to spend 2 units of another address. After this Peter can execute transferFrom(John's address, Olivia's address, 2), which will first update the allowed variable and then make the transfer which will reflect in the balance variable.

ERC-721

This standard is used for the development of tokens that are nonfungible in nature and used for representing unique and indivisible items both tangible (physical) and intangible (digital). The biggest use case of this is to easily prove ownership of the token (asset) such as digital art, intellectual property, music, etc. Say John has a nonfungible

---

[22] https://blog.finxter.com/how-does-the-erc-20-token-work/

token of a digital art he purchased for 100 ETH and Peter has NFT of some music audio he also purchased for 100 ETH, their NFTs are not the same. Let's cover the key parts of the ERC-721[23] smart contract.

- **_owners** – This is a state variable that stores a map of token ID and its owner's address. The nonfungibility is achieved for an ERC-721 token as the owner's information of each token is stored in this variable. If John owns an NFT of some digital art, it just means that John's address is saved in this variable against the token Id of that art. Given a `tokenId`, the `ownerOf` function returns the address of the owner by looking up the `_owners`.

- **_balances** – This keeps track of the number of tokens owned by the various addresses. The function `balanceOf` takes in the address of an owner and returns the number of tokens owned by it.

- **_mint** – This function creates (or mints) a new token based on the smart contract. It updates the _owners variable with the address of the owner and the `tokenId` corresponding to the minted token and updates the _balances variable with increment in token for owner address.

- **transfer** – Like in ERC-20, the ERC-721 tokens can be transferred, but they also have the tokenId in the function parameter as they are nonfungible. So, John can transfer his NFT art to Peter by executing this: `transfer(John's address, Peter's address, tokenId)` which updates the _owners variable with the new ownership.

- **transferFrom** – Like ERC-20, this allows a third party to transfer ownership of a NFT on behalf of someone to another. This is done by first approving the third party to make the transfer through the `approve` function executed by the owner which updates the _tokenApprovals variable which contains information on the approvals.

---

[23] `https://blog.finxter.com/how-do-erc-721-tokens-work/`

- **tokenURI** – This is an optional metadata extension to give each token a unique URI (uniform resource identifier) such as an HTTP address. This function can be called to get more information about the token such as the description of the token like something about the digital art, URL of the image, etc.

There is some overlap in some technical parts of ERC-20 and ERC-721 tokens, but they have completely different applications. To see the comparison between ERC-20 and ERC-721 tokens, refer to Table 7-1.

Table 7-1. *Comparison of the ERC-20 and ERC-721 tokens*

ERC-20 tokens	ERC-721 tokens
1. These are fungible.	1. These are nonfungible.
2. Value of a token remains the same.	2. Value fluctuates based on uniqueness.
3. Each token does not have a specific identity to be able to distinguish one from another.	3. Each token has a specific identity to be able to distinguish one token from another.
4. These don't have any ownership attribute built within them.	4. These have the concept of ownership built in them.
5. These are commonly used to create cryptocurrencies.	5. These are commonly used for collectibles.

Minting an NFT

Minting NFT means converting digital files (includes digital twin of physical assets) into crypto tokens that are stored on the blockchain that enables proving the ownership of these digital items. NFTs are minted (created) using the ERC-721 standard smart contract which we learned of above. Minting NFTs has been greatly simplified on NFT marketplaces like OpenSea.io through intuitive web-based GUIs. If you want to do it manually, the process is still very easy. It consists of three steps[24], and let's go over them by creating an NFT of an image.

---

[24] https://blog.postman.com/tatum-api-build-full-blockchain-apps/

Upload Metadata

Let's say there is the image of a cat which we want to mint an NFT of. The first step is to upload this image to a decentralized storage. If we keep the image on Web2 storage mediums like Google Drive, Dropbox, etc., then the owners of these mediums can delete or remove the image, which will break our NFT. InterPlanetary File System (IPFS) is a protocol and peer-to-peer network for storing and sharing data and is widely used for storing the NFT asset data such as image, audio, video, etc. as well as the metadata of the asset. One of the biggest benefits of IPFS is content hashing, where when the data file is uploaded on the IPFS, IPFS returns the hash of the data file called a content identifier (CID). CIDs are unique identifiers (or addresses) of the file in the IPFS network.

This is so much better than HTTP links where the same link can store one image on one day and another some other day or the HTTP link may just break. However, the biggest benefit is that since IPFS is a decentralized P2P network, the image will be there till the network exits. If you are wondering, why are images stored off chain and not on the blockchain itself? It is because storing data on the blockchain is very expensive. As a reference, storing just 500KB of data on the Ethereum blockchain costs $20,000[25].

So, first upload the image file to IPFS. Save the URI (address) of the image file on the IPFS. Then, create a metadata JSON file that has at least three fields, the name of the image, a short description of the image, and the URI of the image, which is the URI saved earlier. Now, upload the metadata file to IPFS, and save the URI of the metadata JSON file. Listing 7-7 shows how the metadata looks like. The value after /ipfs in the image field is the hash of the image, the CID.

Listing 7-7. Metadata of an image NFT

```
{
    "name": "NFT White Cat",
    "description": "This image shows a white cat that is enjoying.",
    "image": "https://ipfs.io/ipfs/bafybeigdyrzt5sfp7udm7hu76uh7y26n
    f3efuylqabf3oclgtqy55fbzdi",
}
```

---

[25]www.techtimes.com/articles/271313/20220202/study-shows-costs-20k-store-500kb-ethereum-blockchain-nfts-risk.htm

Create, Compile, and Deploy Contract

Now create a contract say "NFTCat.sol" in Solidity that is of type ERC-721. Listing 7-8 shows a NFT contract[26]. See that the NFT token has been given a ***name*** and a ***symbol*** in the constructor function. Compile the .sol file using Solidity compiler to generate the contract bytecode (a .bin file) and ABI. Next, deploy the bytecode in Ethereum by a transaction.

Listing 7-8. An NFT contract based on ERC-721

```
// SPDX-License-Identifier: MIT
pragma solidity 0.8.0;

import "https://github.com/0xcert/ethereum-erc721/src/contracts/tokens/
nf-token-metadata.sol";
import "https://github.com/0xcert/ethereum-erc721/src/contracts/ownership/
ownable.sol";

contract newNFT is NFTokenMetadata, Ownable {

  constructor() {
    nftName = "WhiteCat NFT";
    nftSymbol = "WCN";
  }

  function mint(address _to, uint256 _tokenId, string calldata _uri)
  external onlyOwner {
    super._mint(_to, _tokenId);
    super._setTokenUri(_tokenId, _uri);
  }
}
```

---

[26] www.quicknode.com/guides/solidity/how-to-create-and-deploy-an-erc-721-nft

Mint the NFT

Minting the NFT is creating an instance of the NFT token and assigning ownership of that token (instance) to someone on the Ethereum blockchain, through the *mint* function defined in our contract. The key fields are

- **_to** – Recipient's blockchain address to which the token is being sent (would be owner of NFT token)

- **_tokenId** – Token Id which is the unique identifier for the token instance and usually put in numerical order starting at 1

- **_uri** – URI of the metadata

Invoking this function will create a transaction on the blockchain and once the transaction is successfully mined and added to a block. Now the NFT is minted and assigned to the owner of that NFT.

Uniqueness of NFT

The uniqueness of the NFT comes from the fact that the token is on a blockchain and that the token can't be copied and can only be transferred from one owner to another. One may argue that they can download the media content (image, audio, etc.) from the metadata of the token, so how is the NFT unique? The short answer is that the token is still unique on the blockchain, and this activity of downloading is analogous to photocopying a physical book.

The artwork (media) contained in the NFT and not the NFT itself comes under copyright[27] protection laws as the copyright for the media of the NFT remains with the original artist. Now if someone after downloading the media creates another NFT, it will be a different NFT (even with the same media file in the metadata), and since the whole history of the NFT can be tracked, there wouldn't be any buyers for the copied NFT as people want to collect NFTs only from the authors of the artwork or media. Think of it like that only the original Mona Lisa painting has the real value, copies of the painting don't have value remotely close to that of the original Mona Lisa painting.

This scarceness and limited availability are what make NFT so high in value in the eyes of the collectors. Bored Ape Yacht Club (BAYC) is a collection of 10,000 Bored Ape NFTs. This collection as of March 2022 had an overall trading volume amounting to

---

[27] www.rennoco.com/post/nfts-minting-and-copyright-what-you-should-know-as-an-artist

almost $1.4[28] billion showcasing the popularity of NFTs as collectibles. It's important to keep in mind that although NFTs get a lot of limelight due to artwork, they have applicability in multiple industries such as gaming, real estate, finance, etc. Figure 7-17 shows the top NFT collections over the last 30 days on the NFT marketplace OpenSea as of July 27, 2022.

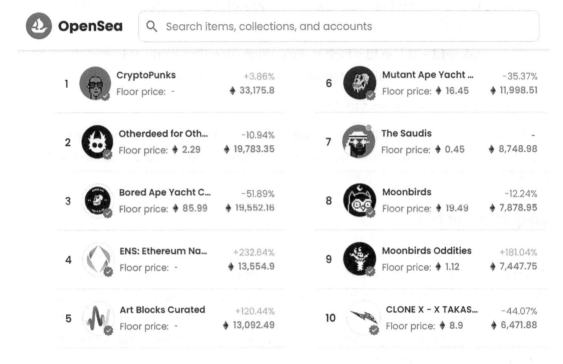

Figure 7-17. *A screenshot of the NFT marketplace OpenSea.io showing the top NFT collections over the last 30 days*

dApps

Decentralized applications popularly called "dApps" are applications that look and operate like normal apps that we interact with daily, but they operate independently using smart contracts on a blockchain, which makes them decentralized as they aren't controlled by an organization or person. There are several benefits of a dApp that make them attractive for some:

---

[28] https://101blockchains.com/top-nft-collections/

- dApps are decentralized; there is no way to do censorship which means an organization or government can't take them down.

- There is no server downtime as the dApp runs on a blockchain which is a P2P network. For a dApp to go down, all the nodes of the network must go down.

- Other benefits like data transparency due to it being on blockchain and open source code of the dApp.

- Complete privacy for users of the dApp as there is no concept of real-world identity to interact with the dApp.

dApps form the Web3, which we started with in this chapter, and everything you read until now was to prepare you to understand how dApps are built. It's easier to understand the dApp's architecture if we compare it to Web 2.0 application architecture. At a high level, an application has following key components:

- **User interface** – This is the front end that the user interacts with. This is usually in modern JS frameworks like Angular and React, along with HTML and CSS. This is the same for both Web 2.0 and Web3 applications. dApps may host the front end in a decentralized storage like IPFS.

- **Identify management** – Unlike in Web 2.0 where the usual form of authentication and authorization of users of the applications are usernames and passwords, in a dApp, the authentication and authorization is done through private and public keys stored in a crypto wallet.

- **Application logic** – This is where the business logic of the application is present. This is where the execution of code happens and is a web server in Web 2.0. However, in Web3 this business logic is present as smart contract(s) written in a high-level language like Solidity and Viper on a blockchain like Ethereum. The execution happens on the nodes of the blockchain.

- **Media and data** – The media and data such as images, audio, video, and data files are stored in CDNs and object stores in Web 2.0 applications, whereas in dApp these are stored in the decentralized P2P networks like IPFS and Swarm.

dApps may look like the holy grail for solving all the issues with Web 2.0 applications, but they are not free of any issues[29]. First, dApps are harder to maintain as the protocols running them are complex and maintaining, debugging, and updating applications on a distributed network isn't easy. Second, dApps run on blockchains, and as we learned the authentication and authorization on blockchains is done using private and public keys, which isn't something people are comfortable with. Third, as blockchains can't process way too many transactions per second for instance Ethereum can only process 15 transactions per second, there is a scaling problem. The users of the dApp see a notifiable lag in using the application when the blockchain network is congested with too many transactions in the memory pool of the nodes. In a nutshell, even with all the promising features, there is a long way for dApps to become mainstream.

Web3: Hype or Hope

Web3 sounds very exciting and promising. The surge in valuation of popular cryptocurrencies like Bitcoin and Ether over the last few years, and the price at which some NFTs got sold, keeps bringing Web3 in the news almost every other month. To add to it, the growing excitement about the metaverse, essentially a virtual world where real people can have digital twins of themselves, and physical assets has brought in newfound interest and love for Web3 technologies. Payments in the metaverse can happen through cryptocurrency to streamline transactions, and NFTs can be used to own digital goods there.

With all this buzz going around Web3, it is very important for us to be able to identify the utility of it and separate it from all the hype before making decisions to build dApps, develop new cryptocurrency, or invest in crypto assets. We already know that blockchains have slow transaction processing rate which should be accounted for in your decision if you want your dApp to be highly performant for a huge active user base. This also applies if you are planning to use cryptocurrencies as the mode of payments. There is also huge volatility in cryptocurrency value with respect to stable fiat currencies like USD. In May 2022 a stablecoin called TerraUSD and the cryptocurrency associated

---

[29] https://ethereum.org/en/developers/docs/dApps/

with it called "Luna" plunged[30] to near $0 per coin bringing massive losses to people who owned it. The biggest cryptocurrency by market cap – Bitcoin – was down 61% in June 2022 from the $48K for a bitcoin 3 months ago in March[31] 2022.

Then, there is the issue around losing crypto. If one loses the private key, one loses all the crypto assets. To give you a reference on how common this is, around 3 million of the 19 million[32] bitcoins circulating today have been lost. There is also the aspect of hacking, since the code of the smart contracts is usually open sourced, and hackers can exploit bugs in code. In March 2022, hackers stole $540[33] million worth of cryptocurrency from Ronin Network, which owns the NFT-based online video game Axie Infinity, where customers can exchange the digital coins they earn in the game with other cryptocurrencies like Ethereum.

The biggest of all I would urge you to think of is the environmental impact which most corporations today want to be mindful of. Climate change is real and mining with using proof of work as the consensus algorithm consumes a lot of energy. The University of Cambridge[34] estimates that Bitcoin alone generates 132.48 terawatt-hours (TWh) annually, which easily surpasses the annual energy usage of Norway at 123 TWh in 2020. The amount of carbon dioxide emitted by this energy usage will vary depending on how that energy was created. In the United States, nearly 40 billion pounds of carbon dioxide was produced from Bitcoin mining alone in 2020. The United States accounts for 35.4% of Bitcoin mining since China banned cryptocurrency mining in 2021.

Wrap-Up

In this chapter, we learned about the evolution of the Web and the foundation of Web3 blockchain, which is a distributed P2P network. We learned of the motivations of Bitcoin, why it is called the first programmable money, and learned through it how blockchains

---

[30] www.bloomberg.com/graphics/2022-crypto-luna-terra-stablecoin-explainer/

[31] www.reuters.com/markets/us/bitcoin-falls-below-19000-further-shaking-crypto-markets-2022-06-30/

[32] www.bankrate.com/investing/how-to-recover-lost-bitcoins-and-other-crypto/

[33] www.bbc.com/news/technology-60933174

[34] www.businessinsider.com/personal-finance/cryptocurrency-environmental-impact

function. We extended the programmability aspect to learn of smart contracts, a concept made popular by Ethereum. We learned about the two most common forms of standard smart contracts, namely, ERC-20 which is used to create fungible crypto tokens and ERC-721 which is used to make nonfungible tokens (NFTs) on the Ethereum blockchain. We finally learned how applications in Web3 called dApps are architected using blockchains, smart contracts, off-chain storages like IPFS, crypto wallets, and regular front ends.

Index

A

C

Made in United States
Troutdale, OR
05/22/2024

20048550R00237